THE PROBATION HANDBOOK

Alison Jones, Brynna Kroll, John Pitts,
Philip Smith and Jacqueline L. Weise

LONGMAN

Published by Longman Industry and Public Service Management, Longman Group UK Limited, 6th Floor, Westgate House, The High, Harlow, Essex CM20 1YR, England and Associated Companies throughout the world.
Telephone: Harlow(0279) 442601
Fax: Harlow(0279) 444501
Telex: 81491 Padlog

© Longman Group UK Limited, 1992

All rights reserved. No part of this publication may be reproduced, stored in a retrieval system, or transmitted in any form or by any means, electronics, mechanical, photocopying, recording or otherwise, without either the prior written permission of the Publishers or a licence permitting restricted copying issued by the Copyright Licensing Agency Ltd, 90 Tottenham Court Rd, London WP1 9HE

A catalogue record for this book is available from The British Library

ISBN 0-582-09143-8

Typeset by Expo Holdings
Printed and bound in Great Britain by
Biddles Ltd, Guildford and King's Lynn

Contents

Acknowledgements iv
Introduction v

1. Some days in the life 1
   I   Kay's cases – Claudette, Ron and Terry 2
   II Seymour's cases – Francis, Dawn and Dave 19
2. Organisation and structure of the probation service 33
3. Offenders and the courts 47
4. Sentencing 60
5. Working in court 74
6. Writing pre-sentence reports 82
7. Working with offenders I: the probation order 102
8. Working with offenders II: pre- and post-release supervision 123
9. Child protection and the probation service 139
10. Keeping records 150
11. Survival 166
12. The origins of crime – criminological theories 174
13. Responding to crime – practice theories 190
14. The 'What kind of probation officer are you?' Quiz 212
15. Postscript: The correctional crossword 217

Index 221

Acknowledgements

The idea for this book arose from discussions in the West London Institute of Higher Education [WLIHE] 'Probation Liason Group' in 1990. John Cordon of the Middlesex Probation Service, Angela Slaven of the Inner London Probation Service and Cathy Aymer, Andrew Cooper and David Whitehouse of WLIHE encouraged us then and have continued to do so. Ron Millett at the Central Council for Education and Training in Social Work [CCETSW] also offered advice and encouragement and CCETSW awarded us a 'probation improvement' grant for the larger project of which the present book is a part. Without the enthusiasm and active support of Alan Dearling, our commissioning editor, this book may not have seen the light of the day. To all of them, many thanks.

Alison Jones, Brynna Kroll, John Pitts, Philip Smith and Jacqueline L. Weise
1992

Introduction

This book is designed to be used in different ways by different people.

Those who are considering a career in, but know very little about, social work or the probation service will find that Chapter 1 offers an authentic account of some days in the lives of two probation officers in training. It will tell them about the roles and tasks performed by probation officers, some of the dilemmas they face, and the satisfaction they get from their work. In subsequent chapters they will learn more about the legal, social and professional issues encountered in the first chapter.

Social work students who are new to the probation service will find all of this plus an account of the structure of the probation service and the courts, and an examination of when and where the skills, knowledge and values of mainstream social work can be utilised in probation work. They will also be able to test their knowledge and explore their values and attitudes by using the **exercises** and **knowledge checks** they will find throughout the book.

Students following a **Probation Option** will, in addition, find an introduction to the ways in which probation officers use the law and the complexities of court work, the supervision of probation orders and throughcare. Beyond this, we imagine that all students, **Probation Option** or not, will refer frequently to the chapters which show them how to produce pre-sentence reports and keep their records up-to-date.

New entrants to the probation service who have worked in other social work settings, can use the book to find how their existing skills and knowledge may be applied to work with offenders in the courts, the community, and the prison.

Probation **practice teachers** or **student unit supervisors**, whether supervising beginners or more experienced students, individually or in groups, will find that the book complements their ***practice curricula***. The ***exercises*** and ***knowledge checks*** can be used to promote either group or individual learning.

Tutors on social work courses will find that the book brings together, in one volume, material which is usually dispersed and often inaccessible. The ***exercises*** and ***knowledge checks*** can form a basis for seminars and workshops and the references will enable students to use the book as an informative introduction to probation-related topics they wish to study in greater depth.

Senior, Assistant Chief and Chief probation officers probably won't admit to owning *The Probation Handbook*, but if they want to know what everybody else is reading, they'd better buy a copy.

1 Some days in the life

Prologue

Midnight, somewhere in Little Acop-in-the-Wold ... a social work student throws off the duvet, tossing and turning, unable to drop off to sleep, thinking of tomorrow, the first day of placement ...

> What on earth am I going to wear ... what happens if I go to court tomorrow ... I know they can be a bit funny about how you look in the Probation Service ... I wonder if this was such a good choice ... maybe I would be happier in a voluntary organisation ... Still, it's too late now and the practice teacher seemed OK ... very bright, though ... wonder if I'll be able to keep up ... seemed ever so together and organised ... will probably expect me to know all that theory ... criminology, interviewing skills ... and there's all the stuff about equal opps, anti-racism etc. , etc ... what will they expect of me? What can I expect of them? I do know something about something, at least I thought I did, but my mind's gone a blank and I can't remember anything ... sentencing tariffs, juvenile justice, changes in legislation ... all those court reports, too ... I've never written one before ... I hope I don't make a mess of this ... I wonder what the Probation Officers there are like ... I hope they don't expect me to be wildly dynamic, just because I'm a student ... I think I'll get up and have a hot drink or I'll never get to sleep ...

It was 9.15 am on a grey and drizzly morning as a black woman and a white man, both smartly dressed and carrying suspiciously new looking brief cases sprang purposefully off the bus. Kay and Seymour looked across the road and saw the tall, imposing and somewhat dilapidated building, which they recognised to be Little Acop-in-the-Wold Probation Office. It was the first day of their final placement and they were about to join four students from various other courses in the Home Office Student Training Unit. They were both a bit nervous but at least they knew one another from college, where they were both doing the Probation Option of the Diploma in Social Work Course.

Kay rang the bell to attract the attention of the receptionist, while Seymour yawned and straightened his tie – he hadn't slept very well ... It was a relief to find they were expected ...

Let us follow them through their placement, listening in to their personal thoughts and reflections about three of their clients. Let's eavesdrop on them at three separate stages – within the first few days, at the interim stage, and right at the end of their placement – to find out how they are getting on. Put yourself in their shoes – would you have approached things in the same way? Would your theoretical perspective have been different? Would you have known what to do? What methods would you have favoured? What would your assessment of the clients needs have been? You can explore these issues further in later chapters. Don't expect all the answers ... we don't have them either, but there will be plenty of food for thought ...

Part 1: Kay's cases

Kay had been allocated three clients – Claudette, Ron and Terry. We will introduce them to you one by one, and at the three stages of her placement, Kay will be faced with different issues in each case, including:

- in Claudette's case, the position of black women in the criminal justice system, and the role of the probation officer in relation to through care;
- in Ron's case, the dilemmas generated in working with sex offenders;
- in Terry's case, working in the magistrates court, and with vulnerable young offenders.

Introducing Claudette

'The practice teacher had prepared a pre-sentence report (PSR) for Claudette's appearance at the Crown Court that week. The recommendation was for a probation order with a condition to reside at a local drug resettlement project. Claudette is black, aged 29 years, lives in her own flat with two children aged 6 months and 10 years. The practice teacher described her as a victim of the designer drug scene. Until fairly recently, when her increased use of cocaine began to seriously affect her functioning, she was holding down a high-powered job. She is well supported by her family but they despair of her drug abuse.

Claudette has been charged with deception – a credit card fraud, amounting to £3500. Prior to that, she had appeared in court for a range of offences, beginning five years ago with possession of cocaine for which she had been fined £100. She was then convicted of dishonestly handling stolen property – expensive clothes to finance her habit – and had several similar convictions, until 9 months ago when she was made subject to a 12 month prison sentence suspended for two years.

I said to my practice teacher that I just couldn't see Claudette getting off with this one – a credit card fraud of £3500. What Judge is going to let her off? Yes, I had heard all the arguments in her so called 'favour' – 29 years old, bright, intelligent, two young children, good supportive family etc. , etc ... . BUT only 9 months ago a suspended sentence! 'What Judge', I said to my practice teacher, 'is going to let her off again? Yes, you've argued that point well in your report,' I said to her, I mean the one about Claudette having an impeccable record until she started to dabble in drugs when her marriage began to crumble.

I felt my practice teacher was getting a bit annoyed with my negativity, so I decided to shut up for a while, sit back in my seat and listen to the gentle chug, chug, chug of the train in motion. I'd had to get up really early to meet my practice teacher, at the station to get this train to the court. It was now only 8.15 am and some time before the court would make its final decision about Claudette's fate. Why was I feeling so negative, I wonder ...

The fact is, that Claudette, no matter how educated and how intelligent, and no matter what high powered job she'd had in the past, is still a black woman. Now, as a black woman myself, even though a student, I know the plight of black women in the criminal justice system, and what's more, so does my practice teacher, (who incidentally is white) and it annoys me that she seems to be ignoring this as being a potentially crucial factor in what happens to Claudette today. I wonder who she's trying to kid with all this rubbish about 'justice and equality' before the law. She can get away from me with all that nonsense. Statistics show that black women constitute over a quarter of the British female prison population, when we are only about 4–5 per cent of the general population. Why, only the other day, she and I were looking at a NACRO briefing paper (NACRO 1991) which highlighted that black people, and black women in particular, received prison sentences with fewer previous convictions than their white counterparts. So who is she, my white practice teacher, to imply that I should not be so cynical?

We were 10 minutes from our stop, when I asked her what her views were about working with people with drug addictions. I was quite interested in the possibility of Claudette going into a drug project. I mean, how many black women were in places like that? I must admit, I was a bit curious about Claudette, as being one of those 'new emerging groups' of black people who were addicted to drugs like cocaine. There was something for me about having to work through the quite strongly held prejudice that this kind of offence was more of a problem for white than black people. I felt that I needed to be upfront about this and said as much to my practice teacher.

She didn't say a great deal in response to this, but started to tell me about the current debates regarding work with drug offenders. The Little Acop-in-the-Wold Probation Service has adopted a policy of working to a 'harm reduction' rather than a 'total abstinence' model. Quite revolutionary for the Probation Service, it seems. Of course it makes a lot of sense to work with clients towards cutting down and reducing the risk to themselves, rather than asking them to give up completely, which at times must feel like an impossible task. I only have to think for a minute about trying to give things up myself – chocolate for example!

When I asked about this shift, my practice teacher said something about this being based in present realities – that it was aimed at giving drug offenders the same opportunities to take responsibility for reducing their offending as is given to other offenders, and of course there are all the issues to do with needle sharing and the increased dangers of passing on or contracting the AIDS virus HIV.

I'd always thought that probation officers were professionally autonomous in the way they worked but clearly there are times when pressures from outside lead to policy decisions that affect this quite dramatically. The significance of this example, I thought, was the way in which good probation practice was endorsed by a clear policy statement – always the ideal, my practice teacher said.

I hung around the court, while everything was being arranged for the pronouncement of the verdict on Claudette. She looked very nervous and frightened. Her mother and sister were with her, and I was surprised to see that her husband had turned up, looking very concerned, even though I knew from the court report that the marriage was in trouble. Her father was at home with the baby and her 10 year old was at school.

'So what, in your view, is the likelihood of the defendant adhering to the terms of a probation order with a condition that she resides at the drug project?' the Judge was asking my practice teacher, who was confidently standing in the witness box answering his questions. 'Your Honour, I think there is every likelihood that she will ... ' she responded with such authority, as would inspire confidence in even the hardest of sceptics. 'But £3500 is a lot of money' he said to my practice teacher 'and, furthermore, only 9 months ago she was given a suspended sentence, which she has now breached. What do you say to that? That society should give her another chance to do it again?' he asked.

I could see the anger in the eyes of my practice teacher, who nevertheless struggled to keep her composure. I was glad I wasn't in her shoes – public speaking is certainly not one of my strong points. It was almost as if everyone in the courtroom knew what the sentence was going to be from this moment on. 'Yes, thank you. I've heard what the barrister has said in mitigation. I've read the probation officer's report and listened very carefully to your arguments for the defendant to be placed on Probation with a condition to reside at a drug project. I have taken into account everything that has been said by the Probation Officer about prison and the potentially negative effects it has on individuals dispatched thereto for whatever period. However,' (and here came the inevitable) '£3500 is a lot of money and the defendant has been given a number of chances in the past to do something about her problems. Instead of taking advantage of the leniency of the court, she seems to have flouted the law, and for that reason, together with the seriousness of the offences and the breach of suspended sentence, I sentence her to a total of 15 months imprisonment.'

Claudette was extremely dignified. She didn't utter a word, just looked a little beseechingly at her mother, before she was led away by the woman goaler.

Although I had been expecting it, I still felt quite stunned, especially by the length of the sentence. The way they led her down without even the chance to talk to her mother was awful. I accompanied my practice teacher down to the cells to do the post-sentence interview. Claudette looked numb as she listened to her barrister telling her that there were no grounds for appeal and that under the circumstances it was a reasonable sentence. After she'd gone, my practice teacher started to commiserate with

Claudette, and formally introduced me, reminding her that I would be taking over. I offered to visit her soon and she looked grateful. She didn't seem up to talking about the possibilities for throughcare today, so I briefly explained what she might expect when she got to the prison. She asked if she could see her mother before she went off and I told her this would be possible. I added that during her sentence she would be entitled to regular visits from her family, and there would be no problem with the children going too. I asked her whether there were any practical things I could do for her, but she said her parents would be taking care of everything. Afterwards my practice teacher warned that this question was a tricky one to ask, as we were not really allowed to do practical things, and that if she had asked me to look after her cat during her sentence, I would have been rather stuck. Practical help tends to be confined to writing letters or telephoning people, but that's about it – it's a question of resources, and best use of an officer's time.

With a bit of help from my practice teacher, I completed the standard pro forma for post-sentence interviews, which gives details of special needs, suicide risks, contact person in the Probation Service etc. One copy is given to the goaler to take to the institution, and the other copy, together with a PSR would be sent to the Prison Probation Department.

Three months later I took on Claudette's throughcare and managed to visit her just a couple of days after she'd been sentenced. She was still totally numb then and hardly seemed able to take in what had happened to her. She is now three months into her sentence and more or less coping. Claudette initially refused point blank to have her children brought to the prison to see her. However, she has since changed her mind about this, largely I think, due to persuasion from her older sister. The children were absolutely delighted to see their mother, to know that she was OK and she was equally pleased, if the truth be known, to see them.

The main focus of my work with Claudette has been to help her settle into, and cope with, her environment, giving her space to talk about the experience of custody which was and still is very painful for her. At first I felt pretty inadequate, as though I wasn't really 'doing' anything when I visited, but talking it through subsequently, in supervision, I was able to see that helping somebody to make sense of what they're feeling and trying to minimise the negative effects of the institution is a valid role. We've also focused quite a bit on how Claudette can fill her time as constructively as possible while she is inside. Because of the relatively short length of her sentence she'll be released on licence at the halfway stage which is just four and a half months away. Her sights have been set on this from the outset which is perhaps why she has found settling in so difficult.

Recently, we've been spending more time talking about the future and how she wants things to be. She told me that her floundering marriage was at the bottom of her drug misuse but that this wasn't the whole story. By dint of sheer hard work she'd been promoted above a male rival for the post of director of a large electrical company, and she's been telling me how life 'on stage', as she calls it, started to take its toll. She began to worry that she might not be up to the job and she recalled the subtle racism and sexism that she was constantly faced with. Claudette was first introduced to drugs at a rather smart party – she said she just took a little at first and felt strong enough to take on the world, but she had no idea how quickly she'd get addicted, and come to feel as though she couldn't do without it, but that it seemed to happen in no time at all.

She now feels very ashamed of herself and talks about the 'weakness of character' she showed in succumbing to drugs. She even said that she is glad to have been sent to prison as it has really served to 'shake her up' and she vehemently proclaimed that there is no way she is going to succumb again.

We've talked quite a bit about what's going to take the place of drugs and she's been spending some time in the last few weeks reading stress management books, which she'd found interesting. I thought she would when I first suggested them – she's been able to relate to lots of the points they make.

Three months later Claudette has less than 6 weeks to go now before her release. The ***pre-discharge plan*** – basically a 'tick box' pro forma – was easy to complete in her case as she has a settled home and family to return to. She's been very well supported by her family, which is great, given the position of many women, particularly black women who have no one to visit them. Once when I visited Claudette she spoke about the contact she'd had with the many black women doing 7 or 8 years for drugs importation on what's popularly referred to as the 'Lagos Run'. She was quite keen to join or even set up an organisation to publicise their plight.

Claudette will be on ***licence*** up to the three quarter point in her sentence – that works out at about two and a half months.

The PO who will be supervising her came along on my last visit. We looked at the sort of adjustments Claudette would need to make, particularly easing her way back into the lives of her children who'll have become used to responding to the 'rules' of her parents for the last 7 and a half months – that won't be easy for any of them. Her youngest is going to be a year old in a few days time and I know that she is hurting because she can't spend the day with him on the outside – her sister bringing the children to the prison will hardly be the same. Whether or not Claudette gets back with her husband remains to be seen – he's been to visit her once and she's not ruling it out although she's determined that things would have to be a bit different from before, and I'm sure she won't rush into anything ....

I doubt that Claudette will be before the courts again. It seems ironic, but the trauma of being sent to prison does seem to have brought about some changes. As my practice teacher pointed out, it's likely that the same outcome could have been achieved through a less damaging disposal. Had Claudette been given the opportunity of a probation order earlier, possibly at the point at which she was given a suspended sentence, there might have been a similar result without all the pain and disruption that she and her family have suffered.'

Introducing Ron

Ron is nearing the end of the first year of a ten year prison sentence for indecent assault and buggery. The offences had taken place over a period of two years and the victims (a total of six) were all children. He has previous convictions for indecent exposure and indecent assault.

Ron is white, aged 55 years and prior to his imprisonment, he was living with his 80 year old mother and had been working for many years as a caretaker.

'I gobbled down lunch, then rushed off to my first prison visit to see Ron. Wasn't that an experience and a half!! The prison officer on the gate, who asked to see my ID, looked at me as if I'd either forgotten to remove my third eye from the middle of my head, or else had provocatively hitched up the back of my skirt in my knickers! I unwaveringly held and returned his stare, to show that I wasn't to be intimidated by his behaviour. His level of overt racism did not surprise me – I'd expected worse.

What did surprise me however, was the extreme thoroughness of the search made of my briefcase and bag and also the inordinate amount of time we had to wait for the

Some days in the life

electronically operated doors to open and close behind us. Both aspects immediately made me think about the invasion of privacy and loss of liberty, which I was prepared for Ron to want to talk about. The prison officer took the dictaphone I had in my briefcase. I didn't even realise I had it in there. He said something about it not being allowed in the interview room – security reasons.

In the rather nondescript waiting room, I tried to remember what I knew about throughcare and, more specifically, the purpose of my meeting with Ron today. My mind was a blank, and I was aware of feeling rather nervous – I'd never been inside a prison before, let alone to see someone like Ron. I forced myself to concentrate ... I remembered something about **throughcare** being divided into three distinct parts – a beginning, middle and end – and that, in each phase, there was a difference in the focus of work to be done. As far as I could understand, the process starts with an initial heavy concentration on the offence/offending behaviour, and helping the inmate to cope with life in an institution, and to maintain links and contacts with outside supports such as family and friends. The ultimate aim is to work towards rehabilitation back into the community and of course there's the issue of parole. That won't apply to Ron for a good while, as he got 10 years.

Fortunately I had some notes with me about Ron's case and some photocopied papers from his file (my practice teacher told me that it was the agency's policy not to allow original papers to be removed from the office). I was therefore able to refresh my memory for the hundredth time about Ron before being beckoned by a prison officer to follow him to the interviewing room.

I wasn't sure what I'd expected Ron to look like. He certainly didn't appear to have any horns or a tail and was actually quite ordinary looking. He seemed very deferential – was there the air of a victim about him? I know that the perpetrators of sexual offences have often been victims of abuse themselves.

Anyway, before I had time to collect my thoughts together on this issue, Ron, looking concerned, asked why they had sent me and whether I would be OK dealing with his case – wasn't I too young and wouldn't a man be more appropriate? I firmly asserted myself and my ability to work with him as I suspected that his anxieties would have been the same, whoever had come to see him, due to the nature of his offences.

I tried to explore this with him and immediately he went onto the defensive, hotly denying that he had hurt any of the children. He said that in fact he was the only person in their lives who had given them what they wanted – that it was love and not abuse. He added that if I had come to make his life hell, as had a number of inmates and prison officers alike, then I could go. He told me he was on **Rule 43**, kept himself to himself, and that if he was to rot away on his own, as he had more or less been doing for the last 12 months, then he was quite prepared to do so. He was really angry by now, and he went on to say that on top of everything else, his mother had died on the day of his conviction, so he had literally no one outside who cared for him.

I felt caught and temporarily confused about what do do with all of this. On the one hand, I knew that as a professional worker, I had to challenge him about his attitude to his offences, which were, after all, pretty abhorrent, and his attitude towards them was making me very angry. On the other hand, I felt there was also something about me as a professional social worker which needed to respond to the pain he was feeling about the loss of his mother and his subsequent total isolation in the world. But which was to come first? Immediate confrontation about his denial of his responsibility for his offences or empathic response to his bereavement?

I decided that I had to start *where the client was*, and that my initial aim was to build up a necessary rapport with him. This was vital if I was to be anywhere near the position to achieve the overall objective of supervision, this being to work towards the reduction of offending behaviour and hence the rehabilitation of the offender back into the community as a law abiding individual.

I made a simple statement to Ron that I did not and could not accept the position he took about his offences and that at some point I would be wanting to talk to him about that in some detail. However, in the meantime, I was very sorry to hear about his mother's death (there was no reference to it on file) and that I was sure it must have been awful for him to hear about it in the way that he had ... not what I'd planned to do at all. I wonder what my practice teacher will say about this when I tell her in supervision? Will she think I was too soft, and that I should have spent the time more wisely confronting Ron about his attitude to his offending? HELP!!!... I want to pass my placement ...

Three months later This was my sixth visit to Ron since our first meeting, three months ago. I've been visiting him on a regular fortnightly basis, and he is now quite used to my coming – in fact on the last occasion, he mentioned that he looks forward to our discussions, despite the fact that they are not always easy or comfortable for him. Although I said I was pleased he found our meetings useful, I felt that I had to remind him once again that I would be leaving in three months and someone else would be taking over. I'd begun to feel quite anxious about the degree of dependency I might have inadvertently encouraged in Ron, particularly as I was aware how alone and vulnerable he was. I spent a supervision session discussing this issue with my practice teacher, wondering about the wisdom of giving a long term throughcare client to a short term student. My practice teacher pointed out that a short, good experience could only be beneficial to Ron, and learning to work with another officer would give him confidence in building new relationships with adults – something he will need to conquer if he is to avoid re-offending on release. Each time I have raised the subject of my departure, Ron acknowledges what I have said but that he doesn't want to think about it yet – he'd cross that bridge when he got to it. I feel that I must just go on raising it from time to time – at college they made quite an issue of the importance of endings for clients, emphasising that it was important that we consciously work towards a positive experience of one.

Far from shooting me down for counselling Ron, my practice teacher actually praised me! She said it was only by working on the immediate issue for the client that we would ever be likely to get anywhere towards working on their offending behaviour. I've been doing a lot of **confrontative work** with Ron, based on a technique of deliberately making assumptions about his offending behaviour.

Our discussions in recent weeks have been a good illustration of what I mean. I've learned a lot about confrontation on this placement – most importantly that it's not about aggressively challenging but, more about bringing people 'face to face' with what they have done or are doing. Anyhow, today I went in and explored with Ron the gap between his previous and current offences. His **609** says his last offence for indecent exposure and indecent assault occurred ten years ago. I said I found it hard to believe that he had not offended for all those years. Ron was initially taken aback and started to become quite defensive. Quivering like a leaf inside, but quite calm (I hoped) on the outside, I gently challenged him again. I pointed out that his last series of offences had taken place over a period of two years. I said I was sure that if it hadn't been for one of the children telling a friend who told her mother, who in turn told the police, his offending would still be going on.

Ron looked uncomfortable, then angry, then thoughtful. I too was feeling uncomfortable and a bit scared – had I gone too far? Ron was silent for what seemed like ages. Although I was tempted to say something, to ease my own tension as much as anything else, I was aware that silences could be both useful and necessary and I tried to relax into this one until Ron was ready to respond. I struggled to remain calm, but Ron looked so distressed that I felt I had to convey that I was not trying to judge him or put him down but help him face the truth about what had happened and the reality of the situation. My main concern was that we could address his offending, in the hope that he would not reoffend in the future.

Eventually Ron looked up and admitted that I was right – that he'd been having sex with young boys for some years and had simply not been caught. This was the start of some quite intensive work with Ron, who said he would try not to keep any secrets from me. I said I accepted this but that I was sure there would be times when he might struggle with this because of a real fear that I might reject him, like all his friends had done, if he told me anything he thought was too awful.

Ron seemed to ponder on this for ages and eventually said nothing. I thought that perhaps I might have gone over the top so asked him gently if he was alright. He suddenly started to tell me how his father used to 'fondle him' as a boy. His father, he felt sure, really loved him – he always gave him money for sweets and never bullied him as he had his younger brother. He recalled that his father had described all sorts of sexual fantasies before ultimately abusing him, and that he found he had similar fantasies just before 'caressing' a child. (Ron still, at this time, found it hard to refer to his actions as 'abuse' and tended to use words like 'caress', and 'love' – this remained a constant issue in our work together.) Listening to Ron's story, I felt, as I so often did, a mixture of revulsion and pity but what he'd told me helped me to understand more clearly the 'world' he inhabits, and we will be able to continue to explore this whole area of his childhood and what he learned about relationships, power and abuse.

Three months later Today I visited Ron in prison for the last time and it was quite a mixed experience. On the one hand there was a degree of real sadness and loss – Ron and I had done a lot of work together, although it is evident that there is still a long way to go ... On the other hand, there is a real sense of relief in me – there is something draining about working with this type of offender, who physically seems so weak and powerless, but who is able to use, misuse and abuse power himself. It was the very dissonance of these elements that seemed to wear me out in my work with Ron. On top of that, the details of the offences were very hard to take and in spite of what I said to Ron, and however hard I tried to convince myself otherwise, I did feel an abhorrence of him – not just him and his offences either, but of men generally. This was all pretty difficult but I felt very supported by my practice teacher, who helped me to sort out my mixed feelings, and praised me for being able to be so open about them.

Ron acknowledged that if it hadn't been for the confidence with which I challenged him about his offending behaviour, without making judgements, he might not have revealed all sorts of things to me. In fact, he said that, apart from his parents, I was the only person who knew about his relationship with his father. It made me realise the links that so often appear between victims and victimisers.

In working with Ron, I found I was using a ***psychodynamic*** perspective to make links between his childhood experiences and his adult offending, as well as bringing him face to face with what he had been doing. This only goes to prove what my practice teacher has said more than once – you often have to mix and experiment until you find a way of looking at a client's life that makes sense. I certainly think the confrontational model helped to break down Ron's defences, and that enabled him to tell me about the elements of his childhood – after 40 years of secrecy – which were so relevant to his offending.

A few weeks ago, I had introduced Ron to his new PO, who came with me to visit and he seemed to cope with the introduction quite well. He was happy for me to fill her in about where we'd got to and although I think he was sad to see me go, I think there was also anticipation of new beginnings.'

Introducing Terry

Terry is 19 years old, and white. Kay meets him for the first time when he appears in court charged with several burglaries and with taking a vehicle without consent.

'I arrived at Little Acop-in-the-Wold Magistrates Court at precisely 9.15 am, as I'd been told it was essential to be on time when you are on ***court duty***. I felt rather strange but at the same time quite smart and professional in the formal get up I'd been advised to wear. I made my way round to the side entrance of the court building, conscious that the main doors did not open to the public until 10 am and followed the instructions I'd been given to get in and across to the probation office in the court.

Ned, my allocated court supervisor, and duty officer for the day, was already there. We'd met briefly before and had spoken on the telephone the previous day to confirm today's arrangements. I haven't quite got the measure of him yet. Everything here is still quite new and different to what I had expected. He seems tough but hopefully he'll be fair. I get a feeling he is also trying to 'size me up' – as if he's already attempting to make an assessment about whether I'll make the grade or not. I worked as a ***probation service assistant (PSA)*** for almost a year before starting the Dip SW course and believe I'm here to 'demonstrate competence'. Although I feel confident, I think I may need to act a little more cautiously at this stage of the game. Like those black officers said, there is a danger that my eagerness to prove myself might be misinterpreted as undue arrogance. They had been telling me about the ***Association of Black Probation Officers (ABPO)*** meetings which are held monthly.

On this occasion there were two courts sitting; the court duty officer and I sat in one, and the PSA went into the other. Ned began my induction by explaining the court procedures to me – where relevant forms, files, papers, keys and so on were kept, and about the different ***diaries*** that need to be filled in when the court is over. There was one for recording details of remands for reports, and another used to record any incidents of a discriminatory nature, experienced personally or witnessed during court duty. Ned said something about this diary enabling the court senior to take up any instances of discrimination with the relevant personnel in the court... interesting ... we certainly didn't have this system at the court I used to work in as a PSA ... .

Before we went into court, we spent some time reading through the PSRs which were to be presented that day. Ned described this as essentially a ***checking exercise,*** where it was our responsibility to ensure that there were no issues which could reflect negatively on the credibility of the probation service, like an unlawful proposal or discriminatory remarks and ambiguous statements ...

By 10.30 am we were sitting in court. Although it was not usual to sit through 'applications', such as requests by the police for warrants, people requesting more time to pay fines, and publicans asking for licensing extensions for pubs in order to hold parties ... that sort of thing ... I thought I would just stay out of interest.

At about 11.30 am Terry was led up from the cells into the dock – what a defiant look he had on his face! He was represented by a duty solicitor and two charges of attempted burglary were put to him, along with taking a vehicle without consent, and failing to appear at court. There were also five similar offences being taken into consideration (TICs). Terry pleaded guilty to all of them. The Chair of the Bench said that this was the sort of case in which a PSR might be helpful before sentence was passed, so adjourned the case for four weeks. The **Crown Prosecution Service (CPS)** was objecting to **bail** on the grounds that Terry might commit further offences and may abscond. Terry's solicitor requested that the case be 'put back' to enable the probation service to investigate the possibility of a bail hostel place for him ... I didn't think the magistrates would buy it but strangely enough they did! Just goes to show ... .

I went down to the cells with Ned to interview Terry ... the gaolers were courteous, which made a change ... I'd forgotten how grim cells are ... so bleak, and the smell ... We weren't allowed into Terry's cell but had to talk to him through a hatch in the door – hardly conducive to effective one to one communication, but still ... Initially Terry refused to say anything to us but Ned was really good, didn't give up, and somehow managed to get him to come to the hatch and talk. Ned asked him about his offending, going through his list of previous convictions, known as a **609**, which he had brought with him. He asked if he'd stayed in a hostel of any kind before and told him about the general rules and regulations of hostels, taking care to explain that these tended to vary slightly from one place to another. He also spoke to him about his relationships and attitudes towards black people and gay people, explaining that many hostels now had policies against hostel residents using discriminatory language or displaying offensive behaviour towards one another. Ned asked him if he felt he could abide by the conditions of a bail hostel, highlighting that failure on his part to do so, once he had agreed he would, could lead to re-arrest and a remand in custody.

After Terry had indicated that he would go to a **bail hostel**, should one be available and willing to accept him, Ned and I went off to telephone a number of hostels to see if they had a space and whether they would take Terry. Terry had a bad record for someone his age, but there were no convictions for violence or, arson which, Ned said, would certainly have lessened his chances of being accepted at a hostel. He did however admit to 'drinking too much at times' but strenuously denied having a drink problem ... Hmmm ... was he protesting just a little too much? I wasn't sure what to make of this ... .

We found a hostel prepared to accept Terry, and the court remanded him on conditional bail, ordering him to reside at the address given for a period of four weeks. During this time, the court asked for a PSR to be prepared, and that Terry also be assessed for community service. They emphasised however that they were 'making no promises', that 'all options were open'.

When Terry emerged, having been released from the cells after reclaiming his property, I sat down with him in the court concourse to obtain the information needed for the ***PSR referral form***. Ned told me these forms have a number of names and numbers depending on where you work – SPR 20 (Surrey); M1 (Greater Manchester); Court Process Form (Devon); FR8 (Inner London). I was surprised as it would make much more sense to standardise them, I would have thought ... Still, no time to think about this – it was pretty hard work getting the info from Terry, as he didn't seem that keen to talk to me, but this did not deter me. As he had no money, Ned told me he could be given bus tickets to get him to the hostel, and advised him to go straight there.

Three months later Writing Terry's PSR had proved to be really hard work. Whilst he was very polite and kept both appointments offered him, Terry seemed determined that the barrier between us stayed in place. After the first interview I decided to adopt a different tack. I stopped frantically taking notes while he was talking, and just listened, making more eye contact and practising the skills of reflection and conveying empathy (at least I thought that was what I was doing ...) This seemed to work better – he relaxed slightly and I felt I got a clearer sense of what he was all about. Since then we have been able to reduce the 'distance', and Terry has been honest with me. He's now admitted to a drug problem – he got into heroin in a big way and that had been the reason for his spate of burglaries. Then his parents found out and had tried to help him come off, which he said he finally managed to do. About three months ago, though, just before he went to court, and we first met, they found out he was gay. He was instantly rejected.

Desperate, he attempted to burgle his own home. His parents had not gone to the police on the first occasion, but did so on the second – hence the two charges. The five TICs related to the earlier period when he was on heroin. Terry told me that he did not want to get back into drugs, and, so far, had resisted the temptation, largely because he hadn't got any money.

After discussing the situation with my practice teacher, although Terry was acceptable for ***community service,*** we decided that a probation order with a condition to reside at a probation hostel would be the most appropriate disposal at this stage. This would hopefully give him some stability, as there were no other real options in terms of accommodation.

Unfortunately, the court refused to follow my recommendation and sentenced Terry to consecutive six month sentences at a young offender institution (YOI) – 'as an example to other young men who might be tempted to follow your path' said the

Chair. Terry had been devastated by this sentence and has twice since attempted suicide. As a result he has been kept under close supervision in the hospital wing of the YOI. Initial attempts that he made to contact his parents were unsuccessful, and concern about his general well being and mental state led me to agreeing to write to them on his behalf.

I wrote two letters. I received no response at all to the first and it was only at seeing the disappointment in Terry's face that I plucked up courage to write again. My second letter drew forth a kind of curt 'thank you for the interest and concern you show for our son but please do not trouble us again' kind of reply, that had really taken me aback. I marvelled at the strength of a prejudice which enabled them to totally turn away from their son in this manner, although I guess that this could also be their way of dealing with the 'where did we go wrong? we gave him everything – it must be his fault' conundrum.

It was at this point that I could well have reached a crisis in terms of my work with Terry. I had become so caught up in his pain that I was hardly able to function professionally. I'd worried so much about my 'failure' as a social worker to win over his parents that I had become quite depressed and actually cancelled a visit to Terry – I made up all sorts of excuses about being unwell ... I had also become quite concerned about failing my placement and it was this which inspired me to take advantage of the 'support slot' in the ABPO meeting – essentially I wanted advice about what I should do.

The advice I got was that I could not right the wrongs of the world, that I needed to be upfront about the situation with my client, and that he needed to be counselled so that he could learn to cope and manage what was happening in terms of his rejection by his parents. They said he wouldn't be able to do this if he was picking up my feelings about the rejection being wholly 'unnatural' and 'unfeeling'. I needed to be helped to handle this matter, and they told me I needed to put away my fears about failing the placement and raise the whole thing more openly with my practice teacher.

This I did in my very next supervision session. My practice teacher was very supportive. She helped me to regain confidence in my capacity to work effectively with clients, by getting me to go through and identify my own good practice in a number of my cases. We then looked at my work with Terry, helping him to accept his sentence, and then we looked at why it was that I so readily began to doubt my ability at the first sign of 'trouble'. She accepted that in part this might have had as much to do with herself as with me, since she recognised that she had not been very good at commenting on things I had been doing well. We realised that supervision had concentrated on 'things that needed improving' which was appropriate but it also needed to highlight the areas of work which were being done well. It was only after coming back from the ABPO meeting that I began to think that my temporary confusion could possibly have been related to issues to do with 'internalised racism' – particularly the fear of confirming that black people are 'second rate' ... I am not sure that my white practice teacher could have got me to see it in a way which I could have accepted, at that stage, but the discussion at ABPO gave me the confidence to raise this issue in supervision ...

Three months later I was amazed at Terry's reaction when I told him about the letter I'd got from his parents. It was almost as though a great weight had fallen from his shoulders, and he was freed to stop hoping and to start living in a far more realistic way. 'This is my life, Kay,' he'd said. 'As you say, I can sit here wasting away and I'll hurt no one but myself ....' He was hurt and angry, of course, but then he began to talk to me about growing up in his family, and all kinds of things came out ... Terry told me he was the younger of two boys, and always felt overshadowed by his brother whom he described as 'extremely intelligent and very clever'. He never felt he got on with his father, whom he said was a rather aloof man 'especially with members of his own family'.

Terry told me about how he was first introduced to gay sex while he was at boarding school. He had hated school, and felt very abandoned and lonely – physical contact had been very comforting. He was 14 when he had his first real sexual encounter with a boy a couple of years older than himself. He'd felt elated at the time – it had all felt so natural – but ashamed at the same time. He'd been brought up, he said, to abhor homosexuals – his father had very strong prejudices against gay people, and Terry had always been scared that his father would find out about his sexuality. 'Well, now he knows, there you go – he'll survive,' said Terry ... at least he could be himself a bit more now and could stop pretending, making up stories about non-existent girlfriends ... He was sadder about his mother's rejection – he was closer to her.

Terry's mother relented a little after a while, and came in to see me at the office, although she refused to visit her son in 'that place'. She wrote to him in the end though and sent him one or two personal and luxury items. She's told him that she'll help him find a flat on his release which will be a couple of days after my placement ends – I'm sorry that I'll miss that but I've explained the licence procedure to him and he knows the name of his new PO. After our difficult beginning, we seem to have got somewhere and I feel I've learned a lot. He seems quite prepared for my going and has been talking much more positively about his future.'

Part 2: Seymour's cases

Like Kay, Seymour had been allocated three cases, Francis, Dawn and Dave. We'll introduce them, as we did Kay's, and follow their progress as the placement proceeds. Seymour, too, will be faced with a range of issues including:

- in Francis' case, report preparation and liaison with a day centre ;
- in Dawn's case, child protection issues and attendance at a case conference;
- in Dave's case, probation supervision and breach.

Introducing Francis

Francis has just been remanded for a PSR, having been charged with burglary of private houses, together with a codefendant a little younger than himself. He has a string of previous offences and is currently subject to a YOI licence, having been released six months ago.

Francis is black, 20 years old and currently unemployed. He lives at home with his parents.

'I got into the office half an hour before Francis was due to arrive, so I could get out his file and reread the information I had about him. All I had was a referral form from the court and a list of his previous convictions. I felt a bit daunted by this – he's obviously been through the system lots of times, and probably knows more about PSRs than I do ... or would he? What was that discussion we were having at college about black people often being sentenced without the benefit of reports...? I will need to check this ... there must be a file on him somewhere. I wasn't sure whether to dig it out and read it before I met him, or leave it till afterwards. Then I decided I'd rather try and make my own assessment, before looking at what others had to say about him.

Burglary of private houses ... hmmmm ... it's very likely he'll go down, but it's my task to suggest a community alternative especially since imprisonment didn't seem to put him off last time ... he's only been out six months ... wonder what the options are? Let me think ... they say we should consider probation orders for **high tariff** offenders like Francis, but would a court actually accept that without quite stringent conditions ... unlikely. Mind you, should I be trying to focus on what's most constructive for him, rather than try and second guess what might be going on in the court's mind? Then of course there's community service ... he's never had that before ... depends what he's given to do ...

I was still deliberating when the receptionist phoned me to tell me Francis had arrived ... I panicked and my mind went blank. Fortunately I'd made a list of things I needed to tell him at the start of the interview and basic questions I would need to ask him ...

I went along to reception to meet Francis, who was sitting with his feet up, reading the paper. Before I had a chance to speak, Francis told me he could only spare me 20 minutes, as he had to go and sign on. My heart sank ... I knew I shouldn't let him get away with that, but I couldn't work out what to do about it, so I said nothing and showed him into the interview room.

Francis immediately launched into his account of the offence, before I had a chance to explain that I'd need to see him a couple of times, may want to meet his family, may need to take some notes etc .... but at least my worst fears of complete silence, with me not being able to think of a thing to say, were not realised. Rather than stop him, I tried to write down what he was telling me, although I realised afterwards that this probably hadn't been a very good idea because I missed all sorts of opportunities of exploring bits of the story which, as I realised later, did not hang together. What did seem clear, however, was that Francis was held in high esteem by his codefendant and that his offending – at least these current matters – was related to this, plus his desire to maintain his 'tough, don't care' image. He certainly had a lot of energy, but what was I supposed to do with it?

Francis eventually got to the end of his story which gave me a chance to ask him about his home and his family. He said he didn't know what that had to do with anything, although he was fed up with living at home and could the probation service get him a flat? I asked him what the problems were and he said his dad was always on at him to get a job, and his mum complained he was always coming in late, not eating, wasting the food she'd left for him and she didn't like his friends either.

I'd just started to talk to him about his experience of school and in the employment market (most of which seems to be negative) when there was a knock on the door – it was a friend of his who'd been seeing a PO upstairs. Francis jumped up, ready to go and it was all I could do to get him to sit down for a further five minutes, during which time he got quite angry. In a burst of temper which took me by surprise, he told me what was really getting to him was the way people – his parents, the court, me – were always trying to control him, telling him what to do, threatening him. On top of that, the police were constantly harassing him, pulling him up in the street for no reason, especially since he'd been released six months ago. I didn't know what to say. I was completely stunned, so ended up mumbling that I'd be round to see him at home with his mum and dad next week. He seemed reluctant about this – both parents, he said, worked during the day. I made an early evening appointment ...

After Francis had gone, I felt a mixture of things – relief that it was over, 'mind boggled' by all the information he'd given me, cross with myself for not having picked up on the experiences he's been having, particularly with white authority and, if I'm honest, a bit cross with Francis for having got the better of me. Next time I'll really have to be more structured. I'll need to get more specific details about his 'previous', about his friends, about his experiences at school and finding work ... It does seem as though he gets quite a buzz from breaking into houses – I wonder about *'peer group pressure'* – would he be able to retain such high status if he didn't commit offences? And what on earth am I going to propose – he said his friend who is on probation was playing in a band – I wonder if he's talking about that day centre?

Three months later Francis was put on probation for two years with a condition that he attend a **schedule 11 day centre** for 60 days. I'd recommended this when he first went back to court and then he had to be remanded further for **assessment** there, before the final order was made.

I still haven't managed a very long interview with Francis, as he's usually got something much more important to dash off and do, but at least he keeps most appointments, and he's managed to turn up regularly to the day centre. I was reminding him today that the 60 days will be over in a couple of weeks, and then we're on our own. Although he'd never admit it, I think he'll be quite sorry to leave. He thinks some of the things they do in the group sessions are stupid – self perception exercises, and role play in particular, but he's really got enthusiastic about the computer down there. We've talked about the possibility of him doing a course, but he's very sceptical at the moment – I guess he sees it a bit like going to school (we'll have to focus more on what might be in it for him). He's talked quite a lot about school in the last couple of sessions, when he wasn't quite so determined to come across as the cool guy without a care in the world – he said he was quite put out by the way the white kids seemed to get everything so easy, and about the low expectation teachers seemed to have of him and the other black pupils in the school. I thought it was a shame that the only positive experiences he spoke about having there were when he was in a position to challenge white authority, telling the teachers where to get off, and pinching things from the local shops. I remember him being quite animated about this at one point and it was obvious that he got a real kick from all that. I thought it was vital to confront him over this, if only because of its close relationship to his offending. We needed to find more constructive ways for him to feel better about himself. So far we've spent two sessions on some of these issues although it's been tough going! From listening to Francis talking about his experiences at school, I could see how racism may have been a factor in prompting him to seek some esteem in the eyes of this peers – and in his own eyes, for that matter. What I couldn't quite get to grips with, though, was whether this was a sufficient explanation for all that had happened to Francis. After all, he wasn't simply a passive agent being acted upon by the system – at some point Francis must have made his own choices. All in all, though, Francis seems to be doing quite well, but it's early days, and with a record like his, I clearly need to take this one step at a time ... he's still not speaking to his dad, but he hasn't been on at me to get him a flat for a while now.

Three months later I felt quite sad when I introduced Francis to his new probation officer today. He was my very first client – seems years ago now and I've really enjoyed working with him although he's driven me mad at times. He hasn't reoffended and he's actually applied to do the computing course in September.

We had spent our last couple of interviews preparing for the handover, and reviewing our time together and what had been achieved. The more I've got to know Francis and to think about him, the more I have realised just how complex getting into trouble is – so many things seem to have contributed – it's been a bit difficult to know where to draw the line. It's obvious he gets a bit of a buzz from his offending, but there's a lot more to it than that and once we started looking at what he'd lose if he gave up committing offences, it wasn't just excitement and money, but his self esteem and the image he presents would be affected too. As time went on, I guess he began to trust me a bit more, and we did a lot of work on the impact of racism on his current attitude and behaviour and in turn how these were having a significant influence on his life chances and opportunities. There were some difficult sessions for me, as a white person, while I fumbled around the realities of anti-racist practice, as opposed to anti-racist practice theory, as taught at college ... I did not always achieve my goal but Francis did not hesitate to let me know when I was going right off key! We learned a lot from one another through learning to listen to each other's perspective, to confront and challenge when we felt necessary or able. Overall, I think we began to develop a healthy respect for one another. Certainly working with Francis made me very conscious of our different situations – about the authority and hence power I had over him, which although I initially felt uncomfortable about and perhaps even tried to deny, I ultimately had to acknowledge.

This came to a head when I had been struggling to work out my role in relation to the day centre. Francis couldn't see why he had to see me while he was going there, but finally we reached a mutual agreement – that I would liaise weekly with the day centre staff to see how he was getting on, and meet up with him or one of my colleagues at the centre at specifically arranged points for a general review of how things were going.'

Introducing Dawn

Dawn has just been made the subject of a one year probation order for an offence of actual bodily harm (she attacked a neighbour whom she believed had stolen her giro). She has four previous convictions – one for a similar offence, one for possession of an offensive weapon, and two for shop-lifting.

Dawn is white, aged 18 years, and has spent most of her life in and out of care. She now lives with her partner, Clive, and her two children, aged 3 yrs and 18 months. She is three months pregnant. Her relationship with Clive is rather stormy and there are financial problems; she is dependent on income support.

'I was a bit anxious about whether or not Dawn got my letter telling her I was coming ... she didn't confirm the appointment, so I hoped for the best. Her offence sounded pretty serious to me – actual bodily harm on a neighbour (how does that differ from grievous bodily harm, I wonder?). She's also been convicted for violent offences before, as well as shop-lifting and she's still only 18. I found it quite hard to think about the idea of an adolescent girl behaving in this kind of way, although it's totally normal, in a way, for an adolescent boy ... I've only got to think about what I was like at school and my own friends – but I can't remember any of the girls behaving in that way ... strange that, after all that anti-sexism training at college, I still found myself thinking that way ... I must be careful not to allow this to get in the way. I need to grapple with some of my stereotypical ideas in supervision, I think ...

I managed to read Dawn's record before I went, in particular the PSR that had been prepared about her. She's obviously had a very tough time, one way and another ... I wondered how she was managing with two small children and another on the way, particularly if Clive isn't much help or support to her ... What can she really know about parenting, given her own experiences of being brought up in care, and having such a dodgy relationship with her own mum ... I vaguely remember a lecture that talked about girls having babies to compensate for their own lack of love and affection ...

When I got to the gate, a huge Alsatian bounded up to me, barking furiously ... I hoped he's already had breakfast ... Fortunately Dawn appeared and grabbed it. I told her who I was, she looked a bit cross, said she had forgotten I was coming and it really wasn't very convenient, but she supposed I could come in for a few minutes if I really had to. We went into the sitting room, where I discovered she had a visitor. Dawn said to her friend 'He's from the council about the drains'. I was completely staggered by this, and didn't know what to do. I sat there feeling really uncomfortable and keeping one eye on the dog, while the three year old, Anna, tried to climb on my lap and look in my briefcase, while clutching a rather grubby bottle (should she still have a bottle at her age? I couldn't remember) ... she seemed amazingly friendly, too, considering she'd never seen me before ... meanwhile, Kim, the baby, was whining in the corner with a very full nappy on that looked as though it was going to fall down at any second. She also had a rather nasty bruise on the top of her leg, and both children looked quite pale with dark circles under their eyes. From time to time Kim would go up to her mum, but Dawn seemed very irritated by her and kept pushing her away. Neither Dawn nor her friend seemed to take much notice of the children and fortunately the friend left quite soon.

By this time I had forgotten what I was supposed to be talking to her about ... but I managed to get my thoughts together eventually and reminded her of the issues which her PSR had indicated she'd wanted to focus on – her relationship with Clive, financial problems, and of course her offending behaviour – learning to control her temper. Dawn was not particularly forthcoming – in fact she seemed quite aggressive and hostile – and said that everything was alright now, she didn't really have any problems and she wasn't going to get into trouble again. She said she'd let me know if she wanted any help, but anyway what was this in the letter about me being an assistant probation officer? Why hadn't they given her a proper one? I'd anticipated this – we'd role played this in college – so I explained that I'd have very close supervision and much more time to devote to her, as I wasn't as busy. I had to tell her, of course, that I was only going to be at the office for six months, and then her order would be transferred to someone else, or possibly discharged early for good progress. Dawn got very angry at this stage, saying what's the point of telling me all her problems, if she'd then have to start again with someone else, and that she was sick of social workers coming and going – she had to put up with all that when she was in care and they were all useless anyway. I said I could understand how she felt but this seemed to make things worse, especially when I said I'd have to see her every week for at least the first three months, either at home or at the office, if she could get somebody to look after the children. I gave her an appointment at the office for the following week, and she said she'd try and make it, but didn't sound very convincing – I think she just wanted to get rid of me. I really didn't know whether an office appointment had been a good idea or not because on the one hand I wanted to talk to Dawn without interruption and give her time for herself, but on the other I was concerned about the children, and felt I ought to have another opportunity of seeing them.

When I got back to the office, I went straight to see my practice teacher, because I felt increasingly unhappy about the children. She helped me to identify the *'predictive factors'*, as she called them, in child abuse, many of which applied to Dawn – becoming a parent very young, having several children close together in age, parents who had had difficult childhood experiences and/or unsatisfactory relationship with own parents, parents who have a stormy relationship and financial pressures.

My practice teacher also reminded me that there was some question of Clive being disappointed that Kim was a girl, as he'd desperately wanted a son, and in such instances bonding could be problematic – she felt some of the rejecting behaviour seemed to bear that out. We looked at the **agency guidelines** for **child protection,** and decided that this fell into the *'early concern'* category, which would involve checking with social services records about the family, and rigorous recording and monitoring. We also decided to write a letter to the Director of Social Services, outlining our concerns, both as a formal record and in case anything else was reported by anyone else subsequently.

I was a bit worried about doing this behind Dawn's back, and we looked at the effect of telling her at this early stage, while at the same time recognising her right to know what was going on, and the fact that the ***welfare of children*** always takes precedence over any other considerations. When my practice teacher asked me to process record the next interview, I felt like going home and not coming back ... especially when I realised it was 3.30 pm and I hadn't had any lunch ...

Three months later This was my first visit to Dawn, since the ***case conference***. That was quite an experience in itself, although of course my practice teacher was there with me, as she had to take over responsibility for the case, as soon as our concerns became more serious and we decided we had to ask social services to convene a case conference. It was a bit like appearing in court, really – I had to do a chronological account of the events leading to the request for the case conference, and I actually had to present the case as I was the main person working with it. It was quite anxiety provoking, as there were lots of people there – police, health visitor, GP, social workers, nursery staff – and I was asked a lot of questions. Fortunately my practice teacher fielded quite a few of them, particularly the ones which implied that probation officers are only concerned with crime, and don't know much about the welfare of children.

At the end of the meeting the major concerns were felt to be the poor relationship between Kim and her mother, and the neglect of both children, and it was decided to put them on the Child Protection Register, particularly as a third child would be born imminently which would increase stress levels. A social worker was appointed as ***key worker*** ... fortunately for me, probation officers are not allowed to be key workers in abuse cases ... but this did involve clarifying our agencies respective roles in relation to this family. My practice teacher and I therefore confirmed that as the order had nine months to go, we would continue to work with Dawn, focusing on her offending behaviour and budgeting. There will be another case conference in six months time.

When the case conference reached its decision, Dawn and Clive, who had been waiting outside, were invited in, and the principal social worker, who was chairing the meeting, informed them of the decision that had been made and asked them if they had anything they wanted to say. Dawn reacted forcefully, accusing the social workers of wanting to take her children away –

she'd been in care, she knew what it was like, and they weren't going to do that to her children. Clive was a bit calmer, and said things weren't half so bad as they'd been painted, but it was very difficult living in a small, damp flat with two little ones and no money.

When my practice teacher and I arrived at the flat today, Clive was in too. He and Dawn were still pretty unhappy about the case conference, but they didn't really want to talk much more about it. This was a relief to me, because we had spent a long time, over the last few weeks, working through their anger with me for setting this process in motion in the first place. It then emerged that Dawn and Clive had just had a major row. From what they told us, it seemed to start about money, but then the real issues came to the fore – Dawn suspects Clive of having an affair, he's often out late, spending too much money that they haven't got, and he never takes her anywhere. Clive says that he has to get out of the flat because she's always going on at him about something, and once she hit him. They told us that they had been having rows like this recently, and had just about had enough of it.

I was a bit thrown, because I was all ready with my budgeting exercise, but realised this wouldn't be at all appropriate. Fortunately I was able to sit back and gather my thoughts, because my practice teacher started asking some very detailed questions about the circumstances surrounding the rows, and how each thought the other felt about what was happening between them. What emerged was that neither had really tried to understand the other's position, and they weren't listening to one another either. My practice teacher then suggested that we spend the next four sessions with them together, looking at what sort of changes they would like to see in their relationship and how these might be achieved. Clive and Dawn seemed quite keen and actually offered us a cup of tea!!!

I'm quite excited about the prospect of some joint work, as, although we had a lecture about working with partners at college, I've never done any. I'm a bit apprehensive, though, about coworking – particularly with my practice teacher.

Three months later Today was my last visit to Dawn, although my practice teacher will be keeping the case. Dawn's been home from hospital for a couple of weeks now, and the baby, who they've called Gary (aka Gazza) seems to be fine. The health visitor and social worker are both very much involved. Clive was delighted to finally get a son, and he and Dawn seem to be getting on a bit better.

For the last few weeks we've been preparing Dawn for my

departure – despite the ups and downs, we have developed quite a good relationship, and because I was conscious of the losses she has experienced in the past, I knew it was essential to deal with **endings** properly. She refused to acknowledge that it was going to happen at all for a while, and denied that I'd told her I'd only be around for six months. Then she asked if she could have my home phone number, as she'd like to invite me to the baby's christening! She went through a variety of different reactions this time, which reminded me quite a bit of the stages of mourning that I'd read for an essay I had written about loss. We got through all this somehow, and today Dawn was actually able to admit that she'd be sorry to see me go, and told me not to forget that it was she who had taught me everything I know! I told her that I had enjoyed working with her and was sure that things would work out.

    I really learnt a lot from the four sessions we had jointly with Dawn and Clive. My practice teacher and I felt that, given all the circumstances, it was important not to be too ambitious in our aims, and that if we could just improve their communication, we would be doing well. My PT suggested what was basically a **behavioural approach** – helping them to get a sense of what it was like to be the other person, using role play, empty chair techniques, listening exercises, and giving them things to try as homework, between sessions. It really brought it home to me that, although one theoretical framework might be the most appropriate for making sense of somebody's predicament (in this case, a psychodynamic perspective, given the significance of Dawn's early experiences) when it comes to doing something about the problems, a totally different approach might be the most effective.'

Introducing Dave

Dave is the subject of a two year **probation order**, made the previous week for an offence of affray which took place at a local takeaway. He has previous convictions for assault on police, criminal damage, drunk and disorderly and threatening behaviour.

    'Dave is white, single, aged 30 and lives alone, supporting himself doing casual work, mainly as a carpet fitter. He spends most of his free time with a younger group, either in pubs or at football matches – his passion in life.

    Most of the probation officers seemed to have quite a few people coming in to see them tonight and it was the Young Offender Team's drop in, so there were clients everywhere, but fortunately I only had one appointment – I was shattered and really ready to go home.

This was Dave's first appointment – he'd only been put on probation last week as recommended in the PSR, which said he needed to do some work on controlling his temper and on his heavy drinking. I knew I had to **serve the probation order**, talk about my expectations and get to know him a bit, but I didn't intend to do much more than that till next week.

I didn't like Dave much – he seemed too good to be true, extremely charming, plausible and anxious to please – not at all like the person I'd read about in the PSR. I gave him a copy of the probation order and explained about keeping appointments and being taken back to court if he didn't. Dave asked if he could come in monthly, as he said he didn't have any problems and didn't want to take up my valuable time, as I probably had far more difficult cases than him to deal with. When I said that everybody had to come in weekly to start off with, he asked what would happen if he got a job working away during the week. That threw me and I said I'd have to ask my supervisor and tell him next time. I hope he moves out of the area pretty quick!

I decided to end the interview by establishing a suitable time for regular appointments, and fixed one for next week. Oddly, though, Dave seemed reluctant to leave. Half of me thought that he was just messing around, trying to ingratiate himself, and the other half of me thought 'well I'd better stick around in case he really has got something important to say'. He started asking what football team I supported and whether I lived locally, and then went on to say that the probation officer he'd seen in court was 'a bit of alright' and guessed I enjoyed working late with her! I felt it was essential to let him know that it wasn't on to say that sort of thing, but I wasn't quite sure how to handle it and probably over reacted and sounded very pompous. Dave just smiled a rather knowing smile that seemed to imply that I'd confirmed his fantasies, then said 'Sorry I embarrassed you'. I was furious at that stage, both with Dave, and with myself, for not knowing how to handle it. I said, fairly abruptly, that I'd see him next week and very pointedly opened the door for him.

Three months later The power struggle with Dave has continued, and through exploring this in supervision, I have come to realise that he probably feels powerless himself and tries to wrest some power for himself at every opportunity. This has taken various forms over the last three months – he regularly tried to alter appointment times, or asked me to ring up and remind him when his appointment was. It has seemed that every plan I've made for work with him – from asking him to fill in a drink diary, to exploring with him what triggers his temper – has been met with resistance, constant argument and questioning of the reasons for everything. I have made him well aware of his right to go back to court and ask for the order to be terminated, but he has no objection whatever to coming in to see me – why can't we just chat about things, he says, instead of me droning on about his drink problem, which he says is all in my mind!

Dave's racism has become increasingly apparent, and I am beginning to suspect that he might be a member of some right wing group or other, although he strenuously denies this, and my assertion that some of this offending behaviour is racially motivated. He has made the odd racist remark about particular footballers but has not persisted since I challenged this, pointing out the agency's policy with regard to equal opportunity issues and what will and will not be tolerated in the office.

Just before Dave came in today, I had a phone call from court telling me that Dave had appeared this morning charged with drunk and disorderly and had been fined. This gave me a certain degree of malicious satisfaction, and I wondered how he was going to talk his way out of this one – a case of mistaken identity perhaps? I debated whether to raise it as soon as he came in or to wait and see if he mentioned it himself. I was conscious of the fact that this second option seemed a bit like playing games, but it seemed very appealing, and a way of getting my own back. I don't think my practice teacher would have approved!

Dave arrived, charming as ever, and started talking about a programme that was on telly last night. Eventually, after giving him several opportunities to bring up the offence, I had no choice but to tell him that I knew. He looked a bit shamefaced and said he had hoped I wouldn't find out – it was a one off, someone's birthday, he'd had too much to drink, but that doesn't happen often. I knew that this was my opportunity to confront this once and for all. I told him that ever since he'd been on probation, he'd had an excuse for everything, all his offences were nothing to do with him, never his fault, and even if he didn't see himself as having a drink problem, I told him that I thought that alcohol was certainly contributing to his court appearances. I remembered my **counselling principles**, and said I knew these things were sometimes difficult and frightening to face, especially if it means admitting something about yourself that you don't particularly like or it has painful associations. (I think this might have been verging on an advanced empathic response!!)

Dave didn't say anything for a while. I always find silence difficult, but I was determined to stick it out this time. Eventually Dave grudgingly admitted that he had been drinking a lot more than usual lately – he didn't really know why. I asked whether, now he'd got over the difficult part and acknowledged it, he'd be prepared to take things a bit further ... Dave looked very subdued and said he'd think about it.

After Dave had left, I felt quite pleased with myself – it felt as though we might have turned a corner and perhaps would stand a chance of getting down to some work.

Three months later What a way to finish the placement and my work with Dave – an application to the court this morning for a **warrant** in respect of breach of his probation order. He's disappeared – left his bedsit a few weeks ago and hasn't been in touch with me since. Despite a role play session in college on applying for a warrant and my practice teacher talking me through it the week before, I still got into a bit of a muddle but nothing too disastrous. I'd forgotten that the magistrate would ask me about **bail**, so I had to think quickly on my feet and I said that as far as I knew, he'd always turned up for court before. I knew I had no choice but to breach him, but I felt bad about it, and couldn't help wondering if I could have handled things differently over the last few months.

After that court appearance for drunk and disorderly, Dave and I had a few really good sessions. He started admitting to some of his problems, and his behaviour started making a lot more sense to me. He was bullied at school, and a bit of a loner, always had difficulty making friends, and so tended to hang about with younger people, because he felt they looked up to him and he became a bit of a leader. It seemed to be the thing to do to drink a lot, and he said it stopped him feeling so depressed. The last time I saw him, he told me that his father, whom he hated, and who was quite violent to him, had been an alcoholic. Dave got quite upset and tearful during this discussion, and I thought I had tried to deal with this as sensitively as I could, but he never came back, after that.

I was convinced I must have done something wrong, but my practice teacher pointed out that, sometimes, especially with someone like Dave, who has very highly developed defences, when those defences are lowered, and the person has revealed themselves to be very vulnerable, they often find it difficult to face the person who saw them in that state again. I was determined to punish myself, however – and she finally did concede that for a client to disappear was slightly unusual. Perhaps I had got too close too quickly – so much for the advanced empathic response ...'

References

NACRO 1991 Race and Criminal Justice (Briefing Paper) London, NACRO

2 Organisation and structure of the probation service

There are two main reasons why an understanding of the organisation and structure of the probation service are important. Firstly because it is helpful to know 'Who's who' in the agency you are going to work in. Secondly because, in order to gain an appreciation of policy issues it is necessary to have some understanding of who is accountable to whom for what. This is by no means straightforward since probation is controlled, constrained and influenced by local magistrates, crown court judges, central government, civil servants, local authorities and, not least, by the professional management structure within the service itself.

It can be argued that this diversity is a strength in that management of the probation service can thereby reflect and balance the legitimate interests of:

- both central and local government;
- both the executive and the judiciary;
- both lay and professional perspectives.

The government green paper *Supervision and Punishment in the Community* (Home Office 1990) argues differently that, in the interests of a more efficient and standardised service countrywide, it is necessary that there should be greater central control of the probation service. This chapter offers information that will help inform your discussion of that issue.

There follows a brief digest on the function of:

- Probation committees;
- Probation liaison committees;
- The Home Office;
- Local authorities;
- The management structure within the probation service.

Probation committees

Within England and Wales there are 55 area probation committees that have responsibility for the local management of the probation service. Usually a probation area will be co-terminus with county or city boundaries and contain within it more than one, and frequently several, petty sessional divisions PSDs (i.e. area covered by individual magistrates courts).

The committee is made up of:

1. Magistrates (Justices of the Peace) representing the different PSDs within the probation area. (Most magistrates are 'lay magistrates' – i.e. they do not receive a salary. They are appointed by the Lord Chancellor. In some city areas there are paid or 'stipendiary' magistrates.)
2. One or more judge from the Crown Court.
3. Members whom the committee co-opt because of their particular knowledge or expertise relevant to the work of the probation service. Co-opted members may not excede one third of the total committee.
4. The secretary and treasurer to the committee will usually be officers from the local authority that is co-terminus with the probation area. (The case of Inner London is different in that officials from the office of the Receiver for the Metropolitan Police District will take on these functions.)

Probation liaison committees

Liaison committees have their origin in the days when individual courts appointed their own probation officer/s and when the service itself did not have the management and supervisory structures that it has today.

The function of liaison committees (or 'case committees' as they were originally known) was thus to oversee and support the work of individual officers.

The present day liaison committee is comprised of representatives from magistrates in a PSD. They may also co-opt members. The duty of the committee is to maintain links with the probation service that serves that PSD, to offer help and advice and share information. Liaison committees are a potentially useful forum for magistrates and probation officers to discuss issues of mutual concern.

The way in which liaison committees operate tends to vary from area to area. They may take the form of a 'round table' meeting with all, or in some cases just senior, members of the local service. Other models are one to one informal discussions between individual officers and a committee member.

The Home Office

The *Home Secretary* is the minister responsible to parliament for the work of the probation service

The *Criminal Department* of the Home Office is comprised as follows:

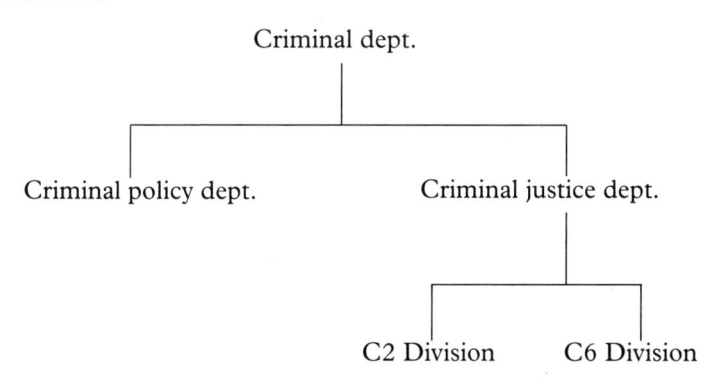

```
                    Criminal dept.
                   /              \
       Criminal policy dept.    Criminal justice dept.
                                      /        \
                                 C2 Division   C6 Division
```

C6 is the division most directly concerned with the probation service.

Within the Criminal Justice Department there is a *probation inspectorate* whose function is to:

1. Advise the Home Office on issues relating to the probation service.
2. Promote the efficiency of the probation service throughout England and Wales. This is done by way of:
   – consultation with, and advice given, to probation committees and chief officers;
   – periodic inspection of individual probation areas.

The Home Office provides 80 per cent of the funding for the maintenance of the probation service. Some expenditure (e.g.

salaries of probation officers seconded to prisons and some after care projects) is met in full by the Home Office.

The Home Office can exert control over probation committees via:

1. **Statutory instruments** which enlarge upon statutes by laying down procedures for local administration of the service;
2. issuing **circulars, letters or bulletins** which offer advice and guidelines;
3. having control over capital expenditure limits and the number of appointments that probation committees may make (in the case of chief and deputy probation officers the Home Office also has to approve the individual appointed to the post);
4. power to withhold grant from a probation committee.

The above considerations aside, the Home Office has no power to direct probation committees as to how the service should be organised at local level.

P2 Division of the Home Office is concerned with parole licences and is the division with which the probation service communicates about any breach of such licences.

Local authorities

Local authorities are required to provide 20 per cent of the cost of the probation service within their area.

Probation committees are required to submit their budget proposals to the relevant local authority, which, if it wishes to contest them, can refer the matter to the Secretary of State.

Many probation committees co-opt an elected member from their local authority and it is compulsory for them to do so in certain areas – North East, South West and South East London, Middlesex, South and West Yorkshire, West Midlands, Northumbria, Greater Manchester and Merseyside.

The secretary and treasurer to the probation committee are normally officers of the local authority.

Management structure within the probation service

For each probation area there is a **Chief probation officer (CPO)** who is accountable to, and offers advice to, the probation committee for the running of the service within that area.

Large probation areas may also have one or more **Deputy chief probation officers** (**DCPOs**) who may either share management functions across the board with the chief, or alternatively have responsibility for a particular geographical district area.

Most areas will have one or more **Assistant chief probation officers** (**ACPOs**). Again they may be delegated responsibility for general oversight of a district or, alternatively, carry responsibility for a specialist function throughout the whole area, e.g. training.

Senior probation officers (**SPOs**) manage teams or projects locally and constitute the middle management tier of the service. Seniors are directly accountable to whichever of the chief probation officer grades is designated for that area, be it geographical or functional. Seniors carry responsibility for supervision of all staff within their teams: **Probation officers** (**POs**): **Community service officers** (**CSOs**), and **Probation service assistants** (**PSAs**). PSAs are not normally professionally qualified and undertake such aspects of probation work as escort duties, overseeing money payment supervision orders, work in probation hostels, welfare rights or accommodation schemes and some elements of court duty.

The probation service also employs many other staff, e.g. secretaries, clerical assistants, domestic staff etc.

Some probation teams will have a pool of volunteers or **Voluntary associates** (**VAs**) upon whom they can call to assist in aspects of the service's activities, such as befriending and escorting clients.

At the end of 1988 the total numbers of staff employed by the service were as follows:

Probation grade staff	6,731
Ancilliaries (Probation service assistants)	1,721
Sessional supervisors on community service schemes	1,875
Administrative, clerical, secretarial staff, cleaners	4,000

(Source: Home Office 1990 *Supervision and Punishment in the Community.*)

Traditionally probation officers have worked in community based teams where their prime responsibilities have been provision of reports to, and service for the courts, supervision of probation orders and aftercare licences. Increasingly over recent years the scope of the work of the probation service has broadened and specialist teams have emerged as a result. These are teams that are solely concerned with community service, teams running probation or bail hostels, day centres and teams based within prisons or YOIs, liaison teams attached to crown courts, teams specialising in civil work or work with young people. Figure 2.1 shows a typical organisation structure.

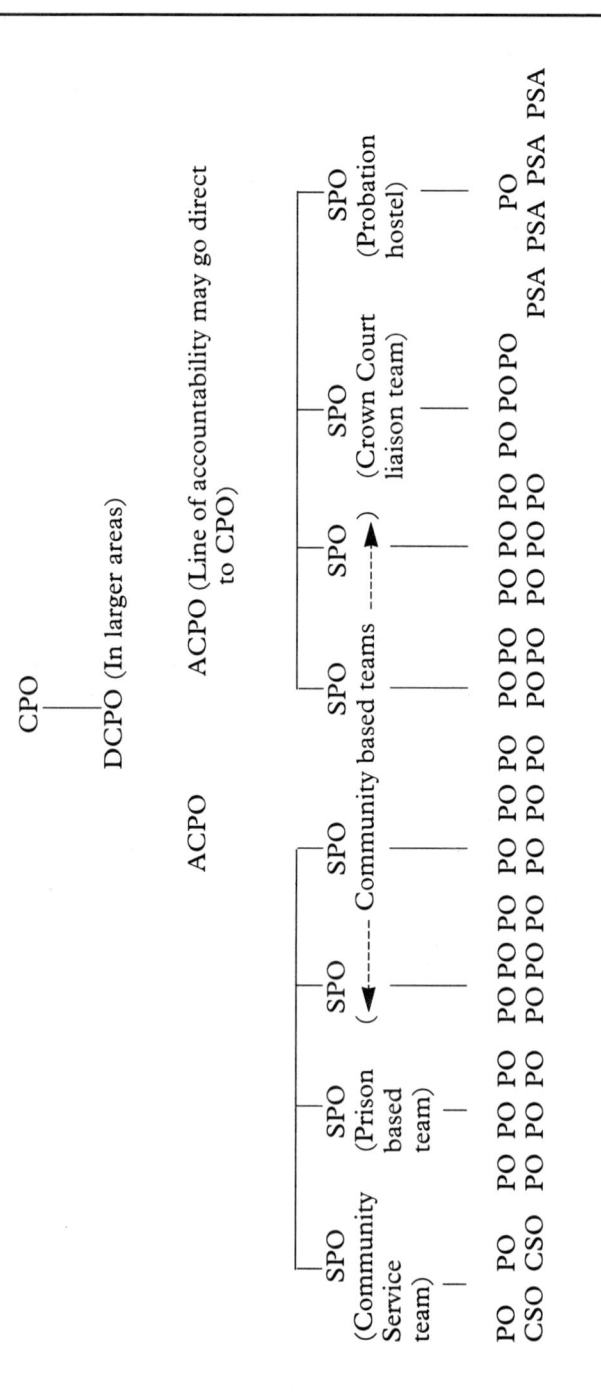

```
CPO
 |
DCPO (In larger areas)
 |
ACPO        ACPO (Line of accountability may go direct
                  to CPO)
 |
 ├─────────┬─────────┬─────────┬─────────┬─────────┐
SPO       SPO       SPO       SPO       SPO       SPO
(Community (Prison   (◄------ Community based teams ------►) (Crown Court (Probation
 Service   based                                              liaison team) hostel)
 team)     team)

PO PO     PO PO PO   PO PO PO PO   PO PO PO PO   PO PO PO PO PO PO   PO
CSO CSO   PO PO      PO PO PO PO   PO PO PO PO   PO PO PO PO PO PO   PSA PSA PSA
```

Figure 2.1 Organisation chart of probation grade staff in Little-Acop-on-the-Wold CPO

So much for the formal structure within which the probation service operates. There is a sense in which it provides a clear line of accountability: from officer to senior; senior through ACPO to CPO; from CPO to probation committee; from probation committee to the Home Office. And yet that is too simplistic a picture. In part it is so, because, even at *formal* level, there is not a direct chain of command in the usual sense. There are, for example, limitations on the extent to which the Home Office can exert *direct* control over what probation committees do. Committees, in their turn, comprised as they largely are of lay people, cannot prescribe the basis upon which the officers they employ should make their *professional* judgements. At an *informal* level there are also certain constraints on the degree to which hierarchical control can be effectively exercised because much of what a probation officer does is not visible to those to whom they are accountable. Most face to face work with offenders is undertaken away from the gaze of seniors, courts and Home Office. The combination of these factors has meant that probation officers have traditionally enjoyed a degree of autonomy in their work which they have greatly prized.

None of this need be problematic so long as all the elements that comprise the organisational structure (Home Office, probation committees, courts, probation service managers and officers etc.) share a unity of purpose. To an extent they indeed do. All would, for example, see it as the probation service's function to reduce the likelihood of offending. However, since this is not a straightforward and unambiguous task, it is inevitable that different people will attach different priorities to different aspects of that task and, furthermore, have varying views upon the most appropriate set of methods or strategies needed to succeed at it.

These varying perspectives are not so much a product of the idiosyncracies of different individuals (though at times they may be), but far more a consequence of the particular position they occupy within the organisational structure.

Probation officers will arrive in a post with a social work qualification. This is likely to have given them an orientation which places particular value on respect for individuals, and a commitment to 'empowering' those who are oppressed or disadvantaged. When this is translated into their practice as a probation officer, they will be inclined to attach high priority to addressing the social, emotional and welfare needs of their clients, arguing that, if these needs can be met, then the client is less likely to need to resort to offending.

Management grades within the probation service are usually promoted 'from the ranks' and to that extent may retain this welfare orientation, although, as Leonard (1966) points out, as managers, they become 'concerned with the maintenance of the organisation *as such*', and have 'responsibility for the decision making necessary to co-ordinate an organisation *as a going concern*, and so a professional social worker who becomes the head of an agency must focus on goals different from those of the practitioner'. For probation service managers such goals could include requiring basic grade officers to conform to organisational policies, which may, on occasions, be at variance with the dictates of 'professional' values.

For central government, the probation service is but one element within the criminal justice system, and its interests must be subordinate to those of that system as a whole. During the 1980s there was increasing government concern that the activities of the probation service should be brought into a closer alignment with national criminal justice policy. In 1984 the Home Office issued a 'Statement of National Objectives and Priorities' for the probation service which spelt out expectations of what should constitute the service's core tasks. Later the 1990 Green paper *Supervision and Punishment in the Community* asserted: 'First and foremost the probation service has to respond to the wishes of the courts. It is a criminal justice agency .... As officers of the court, probation officers must... implement programmes in a way envisaged by the courts and enforce firmly any conditions attached to orders.' There are moves to reinforce probation officers' attention to these concerns by the introduction of national standards for probation practice. (These will be concerned with such issues as the frequency of contact between probation officer and probationer, the production of clear plans for confronting offending in each case, routine checking of probation officer's records by senior staff etc.)

Faced with pressures to be a professional social worker, to be loyal to the employing organisation, to be an officer of the court and an instrument of national criminal justice policy, the probation officer could be forgiven for echoing King Lear's plaintive words: 'Who is it that can tell me who I am?' (Act I scene iv). S/he is indeed caught up in the sort of situation which, to use Merton's terminology, contains 'potential for differing, and sometimes conflicting, expectations of the conduct appropriate to the status occupant (in this case the PO) among those in the role set' (Merton 1957).

Merton is able to offer some comfort to the hapless 'status occupant' on the receiving end of these conflicting expectations, when he suggests that these need not be experienced as 'wholly

Organisation and structure of the probation service

private problems which must be coped with in a wholly private fashion'. By forming groups and alliances with others in a similar position it is possible to 'counter the power of the role set' and thereby achieve a position of 'being not merely amenable to its demands, but helping to shape them'. For probation officers, membership of the National Association of Probation Officers (NAPO) affords just this sort of opportunity.

NAPO is both a professional association and an independent trade union. Its constitution outlines NAPO's objects as follows:

(a) to protect and promote the interests of its members;
(b) to combat racism, oppression and discrimination;
(c) to promote full equality of opportunity for its members;
(d) to ensure collective action on matters affecting the interests of its members and to improve their salaries, conditions of service and superannuation;
(e) to formulate and execute policies which improve the work and development of the probation service and which address issues of criminal justice and social welfare;
(f) to co-operate with others in pursuit of the objects of the Association; and
(g) to collect, maintain and administer funds for all or any of the above purposes.

The NAPO negotiating committee serves as the staff side of the Probation Joint Negotiating Committee (JNC), a national body which formulates codes of conditions of service for probation officer grades. NAPO also negotiates their salaries. At a local level, in those areas where there is a union recognition agreement, joint negotiating and/or consultative committees exist which are made up of representatives of the union and employers, and which negotiate upon local interpretation of the codes of conditions of service and related matters. In this respect, membership of NAPO confers yet a further role on the probation officer – that of 'worker'.

In pursuit of objective (e) above, NAPO is continuously involved in the formulation and review of policy and guidelines for good practice in relation to all aspects of probation work and is actively involved as a national pressure group. In the year preceding Autumn 1991, NAPO issued 17 press releases (in respect of such issues as the Woolf Inquiry into prisons, the Criminal Justice Bill, sex offenders, juveniles on remand, racism and drug couriers) and 54 parliamentary questions were asked on NAPO's behalf in a range of criminal justice matters. During the passage of the Criminal Justice Bill, regular meetings occurred with MPs and Lords, and about 30 amendments were tabled on NAPOs behalf in both Houses. In addition NAPO drafted a bill to integrate the Prison Medical Service into the National Health Service. This was introduced in June 1991 with all party support.

Autonomous groups also exist which represent and address the specific needs of some probation workers: the Association of Black Probation Officers (ABPO); Lesbians and Gay Men in Probation (LAGIP); the National Association of Asian Probation Staff (NAAPS).

The structural complexity of the probation service, and the attendant tensions for the role of the probation officer, have led to successive generations of trainee and student probation officers being confronted with an essay question which is a variant on the theme of 'probation: care or control?' Most answers judiciously conclude that both elements inevitably feature in the probation officer's work. Echoing this view, Robert Harris, in his paper to the 1988 Madingley seminar for Probation Committee members, comments that, throughout its history, the probation service has:

> represented the maintenance of a necessary equilibrium between the interests of criminal justice and those of social welfare.

He goes on to suggest that:

> whatever the future role of the probation service may be, the maintenance of the equilibrium is a necessary aspect of its occupational identity.

Knowledge check

1. Who employs probation officers? A. The Home Office; B. area probation committee; C. the local authority. If you think A go to number 8; if B number 16; if C number 13.
2. Sorry wrong. Go back to 17 and try again.
3. Correct. Even though probation committees actually appoint, the Home Office has to approve the individual appointed. The same applies to chief probation officers. Next question – Apart from chief and deputy chief probation officers how many other probation officer grades are there? A. 3; B. 2; C. 5. If you think A go to number 12; if B number 7; if C number 23.

Organisation and structure of the probation service

4. Correct. A 'PSD' is the area over which an individual magistrates court has jurisdiction. Next question – Who appoints magistrates? A. the Home Secretary; B. the Clerk of the Peace; C. the Lord Chancellor. If you think A go to number 19; if B number 14; if C number 17.
5. No. Go back to 21 and try again.
6. No. Local authorities provide some but not the bulk. Go back to 13 and try again.
7. Not quite. Go back to 3 and try again.
8. Wrong I'm afraid. Go back to 1 and try again.
9. Wrong. Go back to 12 and try again.
10. No such department I'm afraid. Go back to 16 and try again.
11. No. Go back to 21 and try again. You're bound to get it right eventually.
12. Correct. Assistant chief, senior and main grade PO. Final question – Which of the following have power to withold funding from a probation committee? A. the local authority; B. the Home Office; C. both of them. If you think A go to 9; if B go to 25; if C go to 18.
13. Wrong I'm afraid. Go back to 1 and try again.
14. Wrong. Go back to 4 and try again.
15. No. Go back to 24 and try again.
16. Correct. Probation committees are constituted of local magistrates (representing each court within the probation area), crown court, judges and co-opted members with relevant experience – but not Home Office representatives. Now – What do the initials PSD, stand for? A. Petty Sessional Division; B. Penal Services Department; C. Probation Service Document. If you think A go to number 4; if B number 10; if C number 20.
17. Correct. Well done. Do you know where the bulk of the money for running the probation service comes from? A. the local authority for the area concerned; B. the Home Office; C. the Treasury. If you think A go to number 6; if B number 21; if C number 2.
18. No. Go back to 12 and try again.
19. He would probably like to but in fact doesn't. Go back to 4 and have another go.
20. You were guessing weren't you? Go back to 16 and try again.
21. Correct. The Home Office provides 80 per cent of the costs of running the probation service and 100 per cent of some specialist projects within it. The local authority provides the balance. Next question – A probation lisaison committee is A. a nationwide forum for representatives from individual

probation committees; B. a sub-committee of the probation committee which relates to the local authority over budgeting; C. a group of magistrates attached to each PSD who have general oversight of the work of the local probation service. If you think A go to number 5; if B number 11; if C number 24.
22. No. Return to 24 and have another go.
23. No. Not as many. Return to 3 and try again.
24. Correct. For which of the following posts does the Home Office have to approve the individual appointed? A. probation officers seconded to prisons; B. deputy chief probation officers; C. officers appointed without a recognised qualification. If you think A go to number 22; if B number 3; if C number 15.
25. Correct.

Exercise – role set of the probation officer

Probation officers do not operate in isolation. Their work brings them into face to face contact with a variety of bodies and groupings, each of which have some influence upon, or expectations of, what probation officers do and how they do it. This exercise invites you to give consideration to:

1. who expects what of probation officers; and,
2. the extent to which these expectations are compatible or contradictory; and
3. how probation officers might handle conflicting sets of expectations.

This exercise is not about getting 'correct' answers, it is an exercise in thinking. It can be undertaken on your own, collectively with a group of colleagues, or used as the basis for a supervision session.

Stage A

Figure 2.2 is a simplified diagram containing boxes which represent different members of the probation officer's role set. Each grouping or organisation shown will have its own views on what the probation officer's task is about. Use the blank space within each box to jot down a concise phrase, or maybe key words, which typify what you perceive those expectations as being.

In the centre of the diagram there is space for you (as the actual or prospective probation officer) to note *your* views on 'what probation officers should do.'

Organisation and structure of the probation service

HOME OFFICE	COURTS	OFFENDERS
Probation Officers should:	Probation Officers should:	Probation Officers should:

POLICE		VICTIMS
Probation Officers should:	**PROBATION OFFICER** Probation Officers should:	Probation Officers should:

PRISON SERVICE		MEDIA
Probation Officers should:		Probation Officers should:

S.W. PROFESSION	CPO	NAPO
Probation Officers should:	Probation Officers should:	Probation Officers should:

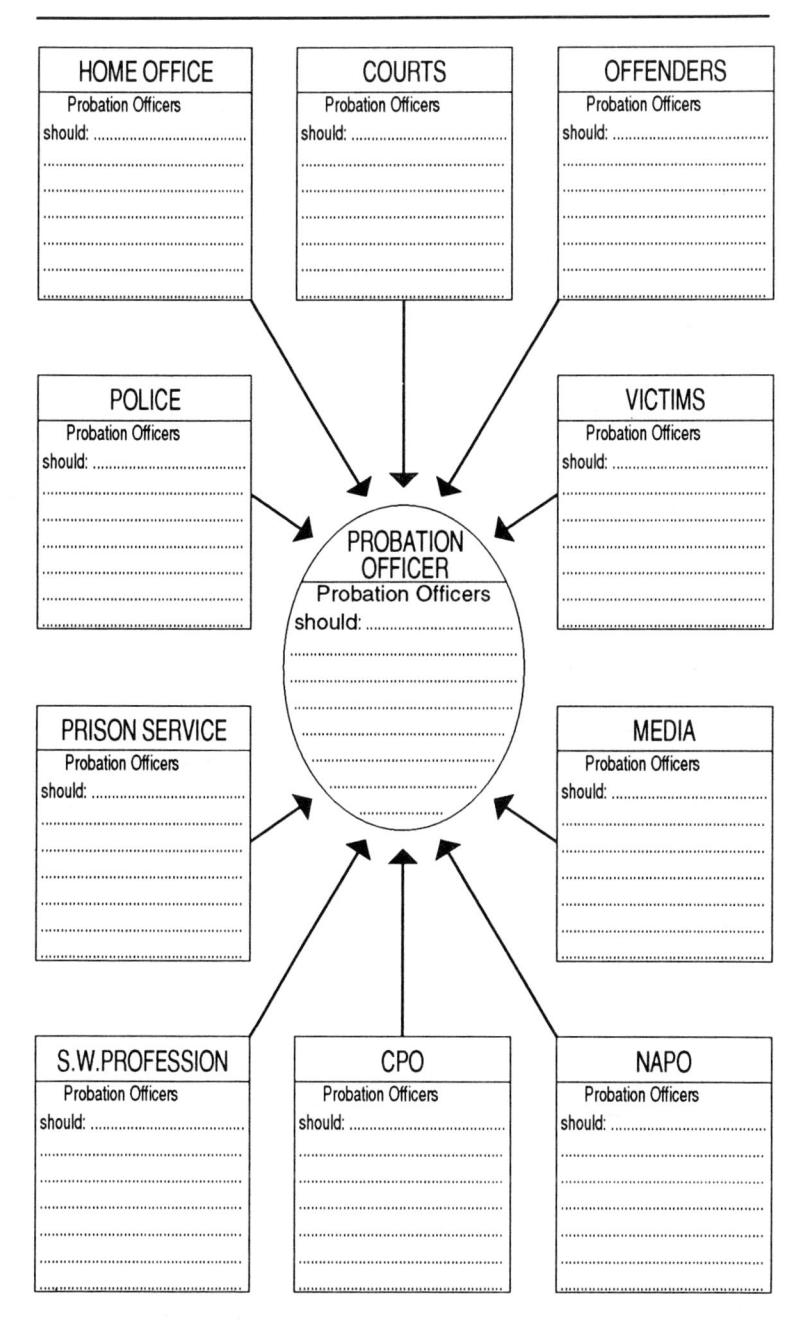

Figure 2.2   Expectations of probation officers

Stage B

Having completed your entries in the boxes, examine them to identify which sets of boxes contain:

- identical or similar expectations;
- differing expectations, but ones which are nonetheless potentially compatible with each other; and
- contradictory or conflicting expectations.

It is this last grouping which will be likely to pose problems for the probation officer. Issues raised by this are the focus of . . .

Stage C

Where box contents are contradictory (and in particular where there is conflict with *your own* box) think about:

- Why does the conflict arise?
- Is this conflict inevitable?
- Are there ways of avoiding it? or minimising it?
- If not, in what ways do you/might you cope with it?

References

Harris, R. 1988 'The place of the probation service in the criminal justice system,' in The Madingley Papers. University of Cambridge Board of Extra-Mural Studies.

Home Office 1990 *Supervision and Punishment in the Community* HMSO.

Leonard, P. 1966 *Sociology in Social Work* Library of Social Work (pp. 89290).

Merton, R.K. 1957 'The role set: problems in sociological theory' *British Journal of Sociology*, **8**.

3 Offenders and the courts

Anybody who wanders into the Old Bailey – that most famous symbol of British justice – on a busy day cannot help but observe that, despite the changes in British society during the 900 years over which the court system has been evolving, it remains a predominantly white, middle class, male institution. You could be forgiven for assuming you had wandered onto the set of a costume drama, moreover, one in which the performance has little relevance to the lives of those who appear in the dock. The language and procedures serve to baffle and mystify, and many leave unsure of exactly what has taken place.

It is important for probation officers to be familiar with how the court system operates, since a large part of their professional activity is either undertaken in, or for, the courts. This chapter will give an outline of:

- the variety of routes by which an offender may come before a criminal court;
- the way in which the courts are structured and organised, and the procedures they follow.

Routes by which an offender may come before a criminal court I

Paragraph numbers relate to the correspondingly numbered boxes in Figure 3.1.

1. The *commission of an offence* is the starting point of an offender's career through the courts. It may appear to be stating

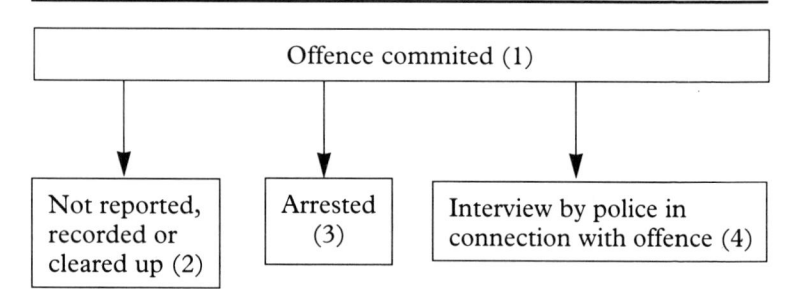

```
┌─────────────────────────────────────┐
│        Offence commited (1)         │
└─────────────────────────────────────┘
      │              │              │
      ▼              ▼              ▼
┌───────────┐  ┌───────────┐  ┌──────────────────────┐
│Not reported,│ │ Arrested  │  │Interview by police in│
│recorded or │ │    (3)    │  │connection with offence (4)│
│cleared up (2)│ └───────────┘  └──────────────────────┘
└───────────┘
```

Figure 3.1 Routes by which an offender may come before a criminal court I

the obvious that an 'offence' is some action that is against the law, but it has to be recognised that what is 'legal' in one time and place, is not always in others, i.e. behaviour is 'criminal' because legislation has defined it as such.

'Offending' covers a wide range of activities. The following table of notifiable offences recorded by the police in England and Wales in 1987 gives some idea of the range and extent of criminal activity:

Table 3.1 Indictable offences recorded by the police in England and Wales

Offence	Numbers (in thousands)
Violence against the person	141
Sexual offences	25.2
Burglary	90.1
Robbery	32.6
Theft and handling stolen goods	2052
Fraud and forgery	133
Criminal damage	589
Other offences	19.3

Source: Home Office Criminal Statistics

2. It is salutory to realise that only a small proportion of offenders are likely to be apprehended. Of all the crimes that it is estimated were committed during 1987, as few as 40 per cent were *reported* to the police. Of this number, only 64 per cent were officially *recorded* by the police; and of that number, only 27 per cent were *cleared up*. Thus as little as 7 per cent of all crimes committed were cleared up (*Source*: Home Office).

3. Police may make an *arrest* either:
   – when they have obtained a warrant for which they have

Offenders and the courts

had to make application to a magistrate; or
- if they have reason to believe that someone has committed, or is about to commit, an offence. In these circumstances the police have to explain the reason for the arrest.

4. Some people may be interviewed by the police without having first been arrested. If during the course of such an interview the police have reason to believe that the person concerned has committed an offence the police should formally caution them thus:– 'You do not have to say anything unless you wish to do so, but what you say may be given in evidence.' This caution is different from the type of 'caution' referred to in paragraph 5 below.

Routes by which an offender may come before the court II

The following numbered paragraphs relate to the correspondingly numbered boxes in Figure 3.2.

```
┌──────────┐  ┌─────────┐  ┌─────────────────────┐  ┌──────────┐
│Cautioned │←─│Arrested │  │Interview by police in│  │Cautioned │
│   (5)    │  │  (3)    │  │connection with offence(4)│ (5)    │
└──────────┘  └─────────┘  └─────────────────────┘  └──────────┘
                    │              │                      │
                    ▼              ▼                      ▼
         ┌──────────────────┐              ┌─────────────────────┐
         │ Charged by police│─────────────▶│ Report sent to crown│
         │      (7)         │              │ prosecution service (6)│
         └──────────────────┘              └─────────────────────┘
                    │                                │
                    ▼                                ▼
         ┌──────────────┐   ┌──────────────────┐   ┌──────────┐
         │Held in police│   │Decision to prosecute│ │No action │
         │ custody (8)  │   │                  │   │  taken   │
         └──────────────┘   └──────────────────┘   └──────────┘
                │                   │
                ▼                   ▼
  ┌──────────────┐ ┌────────────────┐ ┌──────────────────────┐
  │Appearance at │ │Bailed to appear at│ │Summons issued to appear│
  │magistrates'  │→│magistrates' court│ │at magistrates' court (9)│
  │court for     │ │     (11)       │ │                      │
  │remand (10)   │ │                │ │                      │
  └──────────────┘ └────────────────┘ └──────────────────────┘
        │                  │                    │
        ▼                  ▼                    ▼
  ┌──────────────┐ ┌──────────────────────────────────────┐
  │Remand in     │ │  Appearance at magistrates' court    │
  │custody (12)  │ │               (13)                   │
  └──────────────┘ └──────────────────────────────────────┘
```

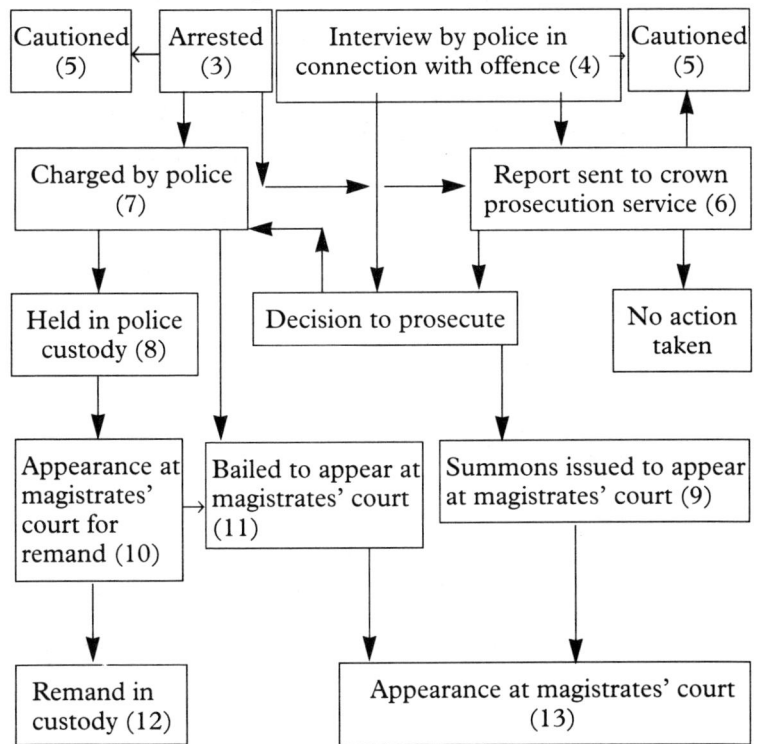

Figure 3.2 Routes by which an offender may come before a criminal court II

5. Police have some discretion about whether or not they institute prosecution of an offender. It is open to them to *caution* an offender thereby keeping them out of the judicial system and saving police time. Factors which might predispose the police to decide upon a caution are if the offence is of a relatively trivial nature and/or if the offender has no previous convictions. A caution cannot be administered unless the person concerned admits the offence.

Police inspectors have authority to administer an immediate caution at the stage of an initial arrest or enquiry. 'Formal' cautions would be administered after documentation has received further consideration (e.g. by the Crown Prosecution Service – see paragraph 6). It has long been the case where juveniles are concerned that the police may well consult with social services departments or the probation service concerning decisions about cautioning and may refer young people to these agencies. It is now becoming more common for such inter-agency collaboration and consultation to be utilised in relation to adults as well.

Some indication of the frequency with which cautions are used can be gained from the fact that in 1989 in England and Wales 136 000 persons were cautioned for indictable offences, whereas 449 000 were proceeded against (Home Office 1990).

6. ***The Crown Prosecution Service (CPS)***, as the name implies, is a central body, but has regional offices. It performs the functions (formerly a police responsibility) of evaluating evidence to decide whether it will support a case being brought to court, of conducting prosecutions in court and making recommendations to courts concerning the granting of bail. Crown prosecutors have discretion to discontinue a prosecution if it appears that it would not be in the public interest to proceed with it. Where such discretion is exercised it would normally be on the grounds that the offence is not a serious one or that the defendant is very young, or elderly and infirm. In some areas there are schemes in operation whereby the probation service can involved in making a 'public interest case assessment' (PICA) in order to provide the CPS with fuller information on a defendant's circumstances prior to a decision being made about the exercise of discretion not to prosecute.

The probation service can also be involved in bail information schemes which seek to provide the CPS with information relevant to recommendations to a court concerning the granting of bail.

7. When police ***charge*** an offender this consists of formally putting to them the offence they are alleged to have committed

and citing the statute it contravenes. After the charge has been read, the police are required to issue the following formal caution You do not have to say anything unless you wish to do so, but what you say may be given in evidence.'

11. Having charged someone the police may release them on *bail* to appear before a particular court on a particular date.

8. If the police decide not to grant bail to someone who has been charged with an offence, they may keep that person in *police custody* (usually in police cells) for up to 72 hours. Thereafter the person must be produced before a magistrates court – either for immediate trial, or for the court to decide upon the question of bail until such time as the case can be heard.

9. When someone has not been charged, the *summons* exists as an alternative means by which they may be brought before the court. The summons is a formal notification which is served upon someone, requiring them to be at a particular court on a particular date. Should they fail to turn up then the court can issue a 'bench warrant' for their arrest.

10/11. As indicated in paragraph 8 above, if there is a delay of more than 72 hours between the time a person is charged and brought to trial, it is the duty of a *magistrates' court* to determine whether or not *bail* should be granted. There is a presumption that bail should be granted unless there is reason to believe that the defendant will not subsequently surrender to bail, that they will reoffend, or that they will interfere with witnesses. Bail can be granted unconditionally or subject to sureties being given and /or living at a particular address (such as a bail hostel). Over recent years the probation service has become increasingly involved in informing courts about, and providing and supporting, bail facilities.

12. If a magistrates' court decides against granting bail, then a *remand in custody* would be made – usually to a local prison. If a defendant is remanded in custody, then they have the right to reappear before the court to make two further bail applications during the period that they are awaiting trial.

13. *A magistrates' court* represents the lowest tier in the judicial system. Most commonly such courts are presided over by lay magistrates (justices of the peace) who work part time without remuneration. A 'bench' usually comprises three magistrates. The

clerk of the court is legally qualified and is available to advise the magistrates upon matters of law. In some areas – more usually those in busy inner cities – the court may be presided over by a single stipendiary magistrate, who is legally qualified and salaried. Figure 3.3 illustrates the characters who are involved in proceedings in a magistrates' court. However, different courtrooms have different arrangements so positioning will not always be as shown here.

At present magistrates' courts are subdivided into three specialist areas:

   i. Youth courts (formerly known as juvenile courts)
   Prior to October 1992, these courts dealt with children and young persons up to 17 years who were accused of criminal offences. From this date jurisdiction is extended to include 17 year olds. Youth courts tend to be less formal than the adult courts, and the general public are excluded. The press are admitted but may not report names of the children or young people who appear before the court.

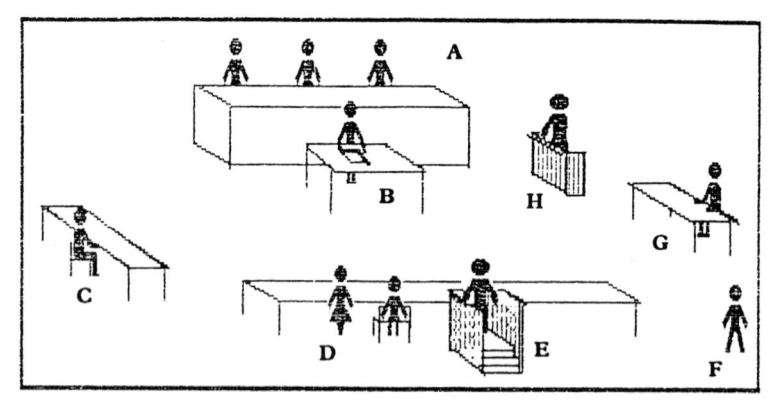

A Magistrates (or justices of the peace). Sometimes collectively referred to as 'the bench'. Most are 'lay' magistrates, although in large city areas there will sometimes be a paid or 'stipendiary' magistrate.
B The clerk, who advises the court on legal matters.
C The press   **D** Lawyers appearing for prosecution or defence.
E Defendant   **F** The usher
G Duty probation officer   **H** Witness

NB. Personnel in a crown court would differ in that in place of magistrates there would be a judge or recorder. (Sometimes the judge might sit with a magistrate who would be involved in sentencing decisions. A jury would determine guilt or innocence.)

Figure 3.3   Who's who in court?

Offenders and the courts

ii. Adult courts
From October 1992 every person of 18 or over, accused of a criminal offence, will initially appear before a magistrates' court, although ultimately they may be dealt with by a higher court (see paragraphs 14, 15 and 20 below). This is an open court to which the public are admitted. The probation service is expected to provide a court duty system and the duty officer is very much in evidence executing a range of different tasks (see Chapter 5 Working in the court).

iii. Family proceedings courts
These were created under the 1989 Children Act to deal with non-criminal matters relating to children. These include care proceedings, adoption, child protection, residence and contact. All applications relating to these orders (except in cases of divorce) begin in this court, but may ultimately be dealt with by a higher court, depending upon complexity and appropriateness.

Proceedings in the magistrates' court

The following numbered paragraphs relate to the correspondingly numbered boxes in Figure 3.4.

14. There are certain serious offences (e.g. murder) which cannot be tried by a magistrates' court and someone charged with

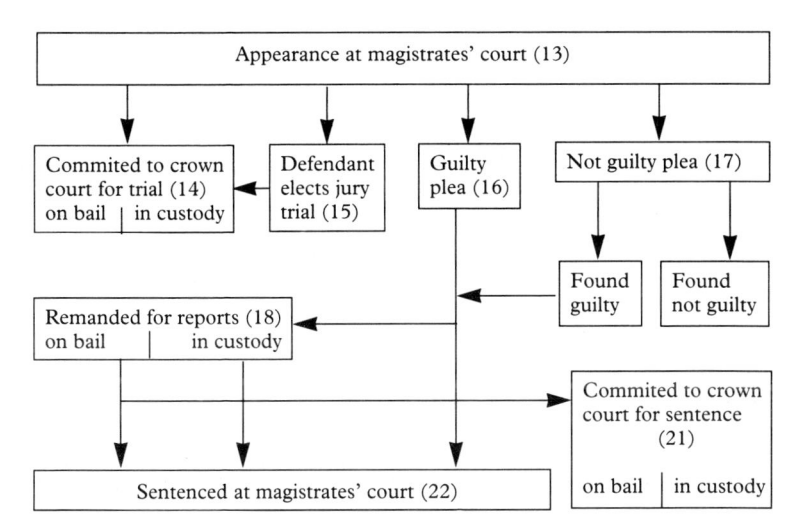

```
                    Appearance at magistrates' court (13)
                                     |
   ┌─────────────────┬───────────────┼───────────────┬──────────────────┐
   ▼                 ▼               ▼               ▼
Commited to crown  Defendant      Guilty         Not guilty plea (17)
court for trial (14) ◄── elects jury  plea (16)         |
on bail | in custody trial (15)                         ▼
                                                  ┌──────────┬──────────┐
                                                  ▼          ▼
                                               Found      Found
                                               guilty     not guilty
   
Remanded for reports (18) ◄──────────────
on bail | in custody
                                                  Commited to crown
                                                  court for sentence
                                                         (21)
                                                  on bail | in custody
        Sentenced at magistrates' court (22)
```

Figure 3.4 Proceedings in the magistrates' court

such an offence must be ***committed to the crown court for trial***. There are some relatively minor offences which can only be dealt with 'summarily' (i.e. tried at a magistrates' court). There is a third category of offences which can be tried by *either* magistrates' or crown court. These are sometimes referred to as 'either way' or 'hybrid' offences. Following application from the Crown Prosecution Service the magistrates' court may commit a defendant charged with such an offence to the crown court for trial. This would normally occur if the offence was a particularly serious one.

15.   Equally the defendant themselves may ***elect jury trial***. In either case the magistrates' court would receive depositions of the evidence before committing the case to the crown court. The defendant may be committed either on bail or in custody.

16.   If a defendant ***pleads guilty*** at the magistrates' court, the prosecution will read out brief facts of the case. There is no need for sworn evidence to be given or for witnesses to be produced. Some defendants may also ask the court for other, additional offences that they have committed to be taken into consideration (TIC). These are offences with which the defendant has not been formally charged. The incentive for the defendant is that all their offences can be cleared up, and they can leave the courtroom in the knowledge that they are no longer at risk of being arrested in connection with these other outstanding offences. Generally speaking, offences that are 'taken into consideration' in this way do not lead to a dramatically more severe penalty than would anyway have been imposed for the offence(s) with which the defendant is charged.

17.   If a defendant pleads ***not guilty*** then the prosecution has to attempt to prove the case against them. The procedure for this is for the brief facts of the allegation to be stated, and then for witnesses to be called to offer evidence as to the facts. The defendant or their legal representative has the right to cross examine witnesses on the accuracy of their evidence. When the prosecution case has been presented the defendant may themselves give evidence and call witnesses of their own, who can, in turn be cross examined by the prosecution. Alternatively a defendant may 'make a statement' that is not on oath in which case they cannot be cross-examined. A further option is for the defendant to say nothing. The onus is upon the prosecution to prove guilt, not upon the defendant to prove innocence.

18.   If a defendant has pleaded guilty or been found guilty, a magistrates' court may then adjourn the hearing in order that a

Offenders and the courts 55

PSR can be prepared, the purpose of these reports is to provide additional information about the defendant and their situation in order to assist the court in determining the most suitable method of dealing with the defendant before it. During this period of adjournment the defendant may be remanded on bail or in custody.

In adult courts the probation service would normally be responsible for the preparation of reports. In youth courts it would usually be either a local authority social worker or a probation officer, depending in local agreement.

For fuller details about the purpose, content and structure of reports for court see Chapter 6.

21. If, following admission of, or conviction for, an offence at a magistrates' court, the court feels it has insufficient powers to deal adequately with the offence because of its seriousness, then the court may ***commit the defendant to the crown court for sentence***. A crown court, for example, is able to impose a prison sentence of more than six months for an offence, which a magistrates' court cannot.

22. In Chapter 4 there is a discussion of the principles which govern ***sentencing at a magistrates' court*** together with a catalogue of the sentences and orders available to the court.

The crown court

The following numbered paragraphs relate to the correspondingly numbered boxes shown in Figure 3.5.

19. A defendant who has pleaded not guilty to an offence at the magistrates' court, but has been found guilty may ***appeal to the crown court against conviction at the magistrates' court***. A defendant who has pleaded guilty does not have this right.

This procedure is different from an appeal against ***sentence*** (for which see paragraph 22 below).

20. The procedure for a ***trial at the crown court*** is similar to that in a magistrates' court except that the court is presided over by a judge who determines any matters of law that may arise. S/he does not determine guilt or innocence of the defendant (or appellant); that is the province of the jury. However, it is the judge, and not the jury, who makes sentencing decisions.

There are far fewer crown courts than magistrates' courts – 94 in England and Wales, although many consist of several court

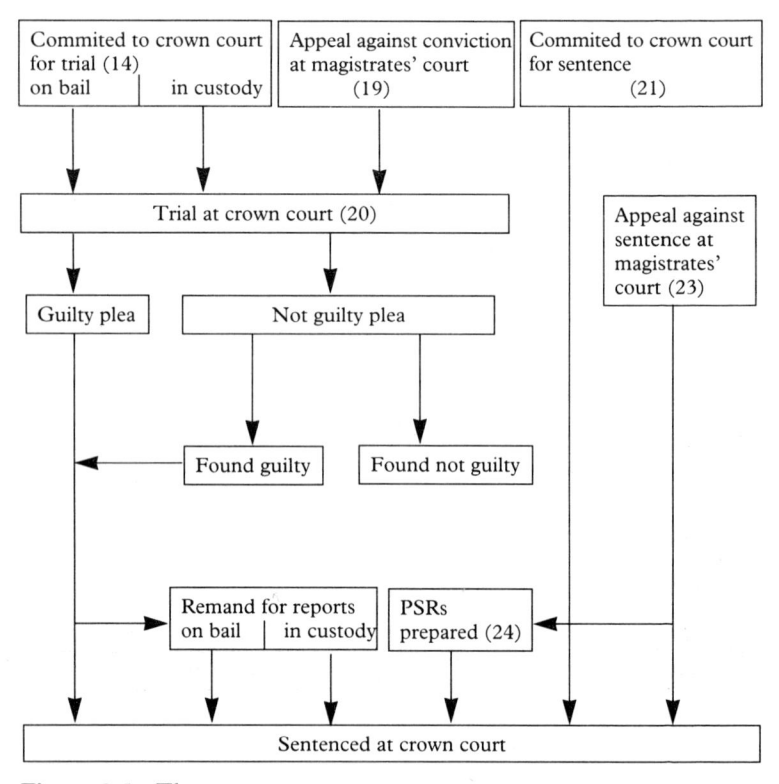

```
┌─────────────────────────┐ ┌─────────────────────────┐ ┌─────────────────────────┐
│ Commited to crown court │ │ Appeal against conviction│ │ Commited to crown court │
│ for trial (14)          │ │ at magistrates' court   │ │ for sentence            │
│ on bail    │ in custody │ │        (19)             │ │        (21)             │
└─────────────────────────┘ └─────────────────────────┘ └─────────────────────────┘
```

Figure 3.5 The crown court

rooms. They are generally more formal than magistrates' courts and both judge and legal representatives wear wigs and gowns. This is an open court to which the public are admitted. Once again the probation service usually provides a court duty service, although the officer may be less conspicuous than in the busy magistrates' court, as it is possible to conduct more of the tasks behind the scenes.

23. A defendant may *appeal to the crown court against the sentence* imposed by a magistrates' court.

24. If *pre-sentence reports* have not already been considered by the magistrates' court, then it would be usual for them to be prepared prior to the defendant's appearance at the crown court for sentence. Even if they have already been prepared they may need updating by the time that the case is heard at the crown court.

Figures 3.1, 3.2, 3.4 and 3.5 have been integrated into one

Offenders and the courts

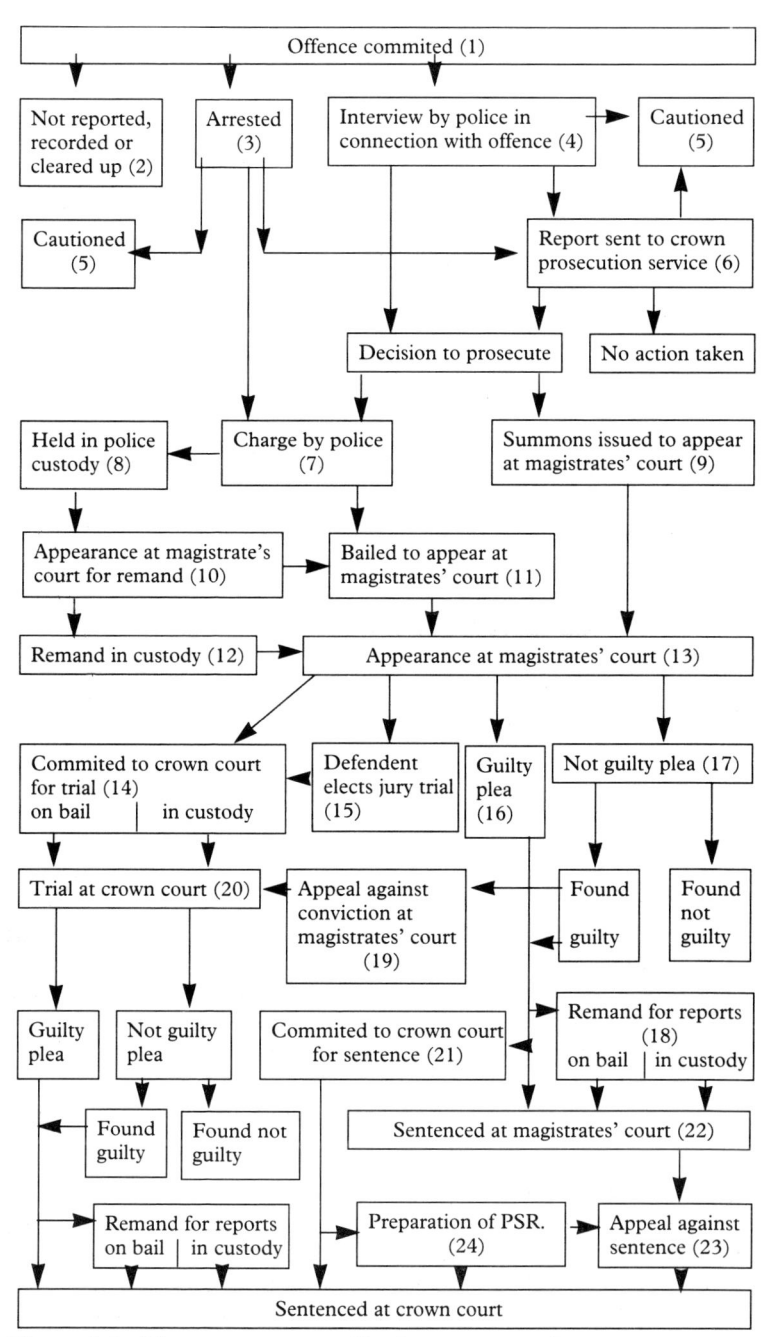

Figure 3.6 The processes an offender may experience

diagram, Figure 3.6, which offers an overview of the various permutations of processes an offender may experience en route to being sentenced.

Although it is with magistrates' and crown courts that probation officers have most dealings, there are other courts with which they may, from time to time, be involved. These are as follows.

The county courts

These are local courts, presided over by judges at the same level as those of the crown court. They deal with the vast majority of civil matters – contract and tort for example. Of most relevance for the probation service, they have jurisdiction in the same areas as the family proceedings court and, in addition, hear divorce cases. The probation service will be called upon to provide reports for the county court. These could, for example, relate to a child's residence or contact.

The high court

The high court is made up of three divisions:

  i. The Queen's (or King's) bench division, dealing with civil matters which are beyond the jurisdiction of the county court. This division also deals with appeals on points of law from the magistrates' court.
  ii. The chancery division, dealing with such things as tax, wills and trusts.
  iii. The family division, which has the same jurisdiction as the family proceedings and county courts.

The most famous high court is the Royal Courts of Justice in the Strand in London, but there are some 25 others around the country. They are presided over by the highest tier of the judiciary.

The court of appeal

The court of appeal comprises two divisions:

  i. The criminal division, of which the Lord Chief Justice (the country's senior judge) is head. This court hears appeals from the crown court.
  ii. The civil division, of which the Master of the Rolls is head. This court hears appeals from the county and high courts.

In making its decisions, the court of appeal does not hear

evidence from witnesses, but considers only written material. Its role is to interpret the law when it is unclear, and as a result, its decisions set legal precedents on which subsequent rulings are based.

The House of Lords

The House of Lords is the final arbiter, not only of English law, but of Scottish civil law as well. Matters may only be taken there with the permission of the court of appeal. It is unlikely that such permission will be given unless a significant legal point of public importance is involved. Matters are not heard by the full House of Lords but by five of the Law Lords.

The European Court of Human Rights

Judgements from the European Court of Human Rights will on occasions have implications for policy and practice in British courts.

References

Home Office 1988 and 1990. Criminal Statistics, HMSO.

4 Sentencing

This chapter will give an outline of the sentences and orders available to the courts in criminal proceedings, but as a prelude to the *what* of sentencing, we need to give consideration to the *why*: i.e. the philosophies which form the basis of sentencing decisions.

Listed below are some of the principles which have traditionally guided magistrates and judges when they are passing sentence upon offenders. You will see that there is a degree of overlap between some, whilst others are potentially in contradiction with each other:

Making the punishment fit the crime (proportionality – the justice principle)

The government white paper *Crime, Justice and Protecting the Public* (Home Office 1990a) asserts that 'punishment in proportion to the seriousness of the crime ... should be the principal focus of sentencing decisions' (para 2.2). One of the merits of this principle is its 'fairness' in that everyone convicted of a similar offence can expect a similar punishment. By focusing upon the offence itself however, little account can be taken of the individual offender.

Offenders may be more or less culpable and this has been recognised by the Home Office in its National Standards which require that a PO in assessing the seriousness of an offence for the purposes of a PSR (see Chapter 6) should pay due regard to aggravating and mitigating factors.

Deterrence

The 1991 CJA makes no specific mention of deterrence yet it is clear from the research of Howard Parker and his colleagues (1989) that the desire on the part of magistrates to deter people from committing crime is an important consideration in their sentencing decisions.

(a) *Individual.* A deterrent sentence is one that is designed to be sufficiently punitive to make an offender realise that 'crime does not pay'. It rests upon the assumption that offenders will thereafter be better able to link 'cause and effect' and be deterred from embarking upon criminal behaviour.

(b) *General.* Whether or not punishment acts as an effective deterrent upon individual offenders, it also serves the function of demonstrating the consequences of criminal behaviour to the public at large. On occasions courts will make this explicit when passing so-called 'exemplary' sentences by saying words to the effect of 'we wish to make it quite clear that this court will not tolerate behaviour of this kind' – a message that is targetted to the rest of us as much as to the individual offender concerned.

Protection of the public

Sentences designed to protect the public (although they might at the same time have a deterrent effect) are primarily concerned to make it impossible for the offender to re-offend. Typically this would entail custody, although community based sentences which place some restriction upon the offender's freedom of action could also be said to afford the public some degree of protection.

Compensation to the victim

In the past the victims of crime have had relatively little acknowledgement from criminal courts. The 1988 Criminal Justice Act requires courts to give priority to ordering the offender to pay compensation to the victim. There are occasions when this consideration could be in competition with the demands of, for example, deterrence or protection of the public in that a 'non-earning' prisoner is not in a position to pay compensation.

Reparation

This is an allied but more complicated concept than straightforward compensation to the victim. It involves 'payment to society' for an offence committed, but also embodies potentially therapeutic elements for the offender themselves in that they can expunge a sense of guilt by 'making good' the wrong that they have done. Typically this might occur under the auspices of a community service order where offenders perform some socially useful task and stand to gain satisfaction and a sense of self worth from the positive contribution that they are thereby able to make.

Rehabilitation

Many offences are the direct or indirect result of social disadvantage or personal difficulties that the offender experiences. Sentences can reflect recognition of this by offering the means by which the offender can be helped to function more effectively and thereby minimise the likelihood of their re-offending.

Not every sentencing decision will necessarily embody all of these principles. Sentencers use discretion in weighing up the seriousness of the offence and the suitability of the offender for the disposals available as to which considerations should take priority over others in any one instance. The personal preferences of the sentencer will obviously play a part in this.

Probation officers will have their own personal preferences concerning the principles they feel should determine sentencing decisions, and these preferences may be at variance with those of the sentencer. However, whether or not probation officers agree with the perspectives of the sentencers, it is nonetheless important for them to have an awareness of the pressures to which sentencers are subject, and the complexity of their task. The argument that the probation officer may put forward in a PSR is more likely to make some impact if it relates to the concerns of the sentencer, and addresses issues to which the sentencer attaches significance. (These issues are discussed further in Chapter 6.)

Sentences or orders available to courts in criminal proceedings

The range of sentences available to the courts is sometimes referred to as the 'tariff' since it represents a series of options (outlined here in approximately ascending order of severity) which the court may use in dealing with offences of varying degrees of seriousness. This 'sliding scale' is not necessarily adhered to in a rigid way by sentencers.

Sentencing

Absolute discharge

Effectively this means that a court is taking no action beyond registering the conviction or finding of guilt.

An absolute discharge would normally only be given when the offence is a 'technical' one or extremely trivial, and/or when there are compelling extenuating circumstances.

Conditional discharge

As with an absolute discharge, the court takes no action but this is upon the condition that the defendant does not re-offend during the period that the court specifies. The maximum period is three years.

In the event of a reconviction within the specified period the defendant is liable to be sentenced on the offence for which they had originally been conditionally discharged.

Bind over

For certain common law offences the court may require someone appearing before it to agree to be bound over to keep the peace for a specified period and a specified sum of money. Conviction for an offence within that period renders the person liable to forfeit the sum concerned.

A bind over is not a 'sentence' and it is not necessary for someone to be convicted before they can be bound over. It is for example possible to make a witness subject to a bind over if the court feels that their behaviour constitutes a potential threat to 'the peace'.

The 1991 Criminal Justice Act made provision for binding over the parent or guardian of a juvenile offender, by requiring them to enter into a recognisance to 'take proper care' and 'exercise proper control' over the child or young person. Unreasonable refusal to be bound over in this way renders the parent or guardian liable to a fine not exceeding £1000.

Compensation order

This is an order requiring the defendant to pay compensation for any loss, damage or injury incurred by the victim of their offence (motor vehicle accidents are not included in this category).

A compensation order can be used on its own, or in conjunction with another sentence; e.g. alongside a fine or conditional discharge.

There is a maximum of £2000 that can be ordered per offence.

In fixing the amount (and rate of payment) of compensation, a court is required to have regard to the defendant's ability to pay. Courts are also required to give priority to ordering compensation in preference say, to imposing a fine. This latter point has some implications for custodial penalties in that when someone is in custody they are less likely to be in a position where they can pay compensation.

Fine

A fine is the most commonly used of all the penalties that are available to the courts.

Each offence has a fixed maximum financial penalty and courts use discretion in fixing an amount up to that maximum. They may be guided in this by such factors as whether the offence was pre-meditated, the degree of loss or injury suffered by the victim, the degree of vulnerability of the victim etc.

Also relevant is the offender's ability to pay. If immediate payment of a fine cannot be made, courts will frequently enquire into the offender's means and order payment at a weekly rate.

The white paper *Crime, Justice and Protecting the Public* (1990) comments that 'it can be difficult to make it clear to the public and to offenders, that a particular fine is a fair punishment when another equally culpable offender is given a fine of a different level'. In response to this concern, the 1991 Criminal Justice Act has introduced the idea of a 'unit fine'. Under this system the number of units an offender is fined is commensurate with the seriousness of the offence, but the value of those units is determined by the offender's weekly disposable income.

Money payment supervision order

When a fine, compensation order or costs are imposed, and the court is of the view that the offender may need help in organising their finances and/or some additional incentive to meet their commitment, the court can make a money payment supervision order. This supervision would normally be undertaken by a probation officer or a PSA. The role of the officer is to oversee payments and ensure that they are made regularly and, should need arise, keep the court informed of any change in the offender's circumstances which have implications for their ability to pay their fine.

A money payment supervision order will normally remain in force until such time as payments have been completed or, alternatively, in the case of default, where the court has dealt with the matter in some other way.

Where someone subject to a money payment supervision order does not make payments it would be usual for the supervising officer to submit a 'means enquiry' report to the court before any decision is made to commit them to prison for default.

Supervision order

It is important to distinguish between supervision orders that arise out of care proceedings (S. 31 of the Children Act 1989) and those that can be made in juvenile *criminal* proceedings (S. 7[7] Children and Young Persons Act 1969).

In criminal proceedings a supervision order may be made in respect of a child or young person between the ages of 10 and 17.

The court can specify the duration of the order up to a maximum of 3 years.

The local authority social services department would normally be responsible for supervision. In some areas there is a local arrangement with the probation service whereby a probation officer may supervise young people aged 14–17.

It is not necessary for the child or young person to consent to the making of the order.

The normal requirements of a supervision order are that:

- s/he must inform the supervisor of any change of residence or employment;
- s/he shall keep in touch with the supervisor in accordance with such instructions as may from time to time be given by the supervisor, and, in particular, that s/he shall, if the supervisor so requires receive visits from the supervisor at home.

A court may impose additional requirements namely:

- to present him/herself to the supervisor or other specified person at a specified place on specified days for up to a maximum of 90 days;
- to participate in specified activity on specified days (Intermediate Treatment) up to a maximum of 90 days;
- to remain for specified evenings and nights at a specified place (night restriction) up to a maximum of 90 days;
- to refrain from participating in specified activities.

To this list of possible requirements, schedule 12 [23] of the 1989 Children Act added:

– a residence requirement which may last no longer than six months. For such a requirement to be made, the young person would have to have already been subject to a criminal supervision order, and the offence would have to be one that, for an adult, would be punishable by imprisonment.

Probation order

A probation order may be made on an offender aged 16 or over and requires them to be supervised by a probation officer for a specified period of between six months and three years. The terms of a probation order are outlined in more detail in Chapter 7.

Attendance centre order

This sentence is available for offenders up to the age of 21 for an offence that would be punishable by imprisonment in the case of an adult. The young person can be required to report at a local centre at specified times – usually at a week-end. They will participate in a programme of activity which might include physical education, work or sport.

The minimum number of hours that can be ordered is 12 and the maximum 24 for 10–15 year olds and 36 for 16–20 year olds.

Community service order

This order is available to courts for offenders of 16 years or over.

A community Service order serves 3 main purposes:

1. *punishment* of the offender, by requiring him or her to perform unpaid work, by the discipline of punctual reporting for work and by loss of free time;
2. *reparation* to the community by requiring the offender to do work which is socially useful, which repays the community for what the offender has done and which, if possible, makes good the damage done by offending;
3. providing work *of benefit to the community* which would otherwise not be done.

As a by-product of these aims community service can also provide offenders with a positive and stimulating experience which may help to re-integrate them into the community. However, the educative and rehabilitative aspects of CS work

should not take precedence over the need for the offender to comply with the requirements of a court order.
(Home Office draft circular, October 1988)

The minimum number of hours that can be ordered for community service is 40, the maximum is 240 hours. These hours should be completed within 12 months of the making of the order. Community service work would normally take place at week-ends and offenders would usually be expected to undertake it for an average of five hours per week.

The probation service is responsible for the management and administration of the scheme, and it would be a probation officer who has responsibility for reporting non-compliance with the order to the court. Courts may deal with a breach of a community service order by either (a) imposing a fine of not more than £400 or, (b) revoking the community service order and dealing with the offender for the original offence in some alternative way.

Combination orders

Following the 1991 Criminal Justice Act it is possible for courts to combine a probation order with a community service order. This would require the offender:

(a) to be under the supervision of a probation officer for a period of not less than 12 months or more than 3 years; and
(b) to perform unpaid work for not less than 40 or more than 100 hours.

Curfew order

This order, introduced by the 1991 Criminal Justice Act, is available for offenders over the age of 16, and can require the offender to remain for a specified period of time in a specified place. The 'specified period' may not be for less than 2 hours or more than 12 hours on any one day and cannot extend beyond six months from the date the order was made. It is not intended that the order should interfere with the offender's employment or education, or bring him/her into conflict with their religious beliefs.

Before the order can be made the offender has to express their willingness to comply with it.

In future a curfew order may include electronic monitoring of the offender during the curfew periods specified in the order.

Detention in a young offender institution

This is a 'unified' custodial sentence for young offenders which was introduced in 1988, replacing detention centres and youth custody which had previously catered for young offenders sentenced for short and medium terms respectively. The sentence is available for offenders over 15 and under 21. The minimum period for which this sentence can be ordered is 2 months and the maximum is 12 months.

Home Office Circular Instruction 40/1988 states that male juveniles and short term male young adults offenders:

> will generally be held separately from those serving longer sentences. The distinctive needs of ... short-termers require a regime which will differ in important respects from longer term male young adult offenders. They will thus undergo a busy, or brisk regime. The distinctive features of that regime will be a full and stuctured daily routine; a grade system, greater emphasis on education and physical education.... Young women do not normally respond well to regimentation and formal parades are not appropriate. Nevertheless, as with male offenders, inspections centred upon personal possessions and clothing may help to set and maintain standards of discipline and hygiene.

For longer term offenders the emphasis will also be on: 'education, training and work and will include physical education and acquisition, of social and life skills' (Home Office *op.cit.*) but there is greater scope for more individually tailored programmes.

Each offender will be allocated a 'personal officer' (drawn from prison officer grades) who will be responsible for preparation of a 'sentence plan', liaison with outside bodies on behalf of the offender and identification of any welfare problems.

All offenders serving more than 12 months will be subject to supervision on licence upon release (see Chapter 8).

Detention under section 53 of the Children and Young Persons Act 1933

This sentence is for juveniles who have been convicted by the crown court of murder or other serious offences (i.e. any offence for which an adult could be sentenced to life or more than 14 years). Juveniles so sentenced may be placed in a young offender institution, an adult prison, youth treatment centre, secure community home or a psychiatric unit.

Sentencing

Suspended sentence

When a court imposes a prison sentence on an adult over 21, it is possible to suspend this for a specified period. If during this period the offender does not re-offend, then they do not have to serve the sentence. As with a prison sentence a magistrates' court cannot order a sentence of more than six months on any one offence and may only order one concurrent sentence on a separate offence. The period for which a sentence may be suspended may not be for more than two years.

In the event of reconviction during the period of a suspended sentence a court would need to find special reasons not to activate the original sentence.

When suspended sentences were first introduced in 1967 they were seen as a means of cutting down the prison population. In the event the opposite was achieved and it is suspected that courts were using the sentence for offenders upon whom they would not otherwise have imposed an immediate sentence, and were thus drawing more, rather than less, offenders into custody.

Suspended sentence supervision order

This is a form of compulsory supervision by a probation officer alongside a suspended sentence. This order can only be made by a crown court since it relates to sentences of more than six months. The conditions are that the defendant (who does not have to agree to the order being made) should keep in touch with the probation officer in accordance with instructions, and notify any change of address.

In the event of non-compliance with the order, the supervising officer may apply for a summons or warrant to bring the offender before the supervising magistrates' court. If a breach is proved then the court may impose a fine whilst allowing the order to continue. Unlike the case of a probation order they may not sentence on the original offence.

Imprisonment

Most imprisonable offences have a fixed maximum term, and courts have discretion on the length of sentence they can order up to that maximum. The nature and circumstances of the offence and of the offender will influence this use of discretion.

A magistrates' court cannot order a sentence of more than six months on any one offence and may only order one concurrent sentence on a separate offence. A crown court is not bound by this limitation.

Hospital or guardianship order

This order commits an offender to a psychiatric hospital. It can only be made on an offender whose offence is punishable by imprisonment, and for whom two duly qualified medical practitioners have certified that the offender is suffering from mental illness that is of a nature and degree that is suitable for treatment in a hospital.

This order can be made by either magistrates' or a crown court. It is indeterminate, the medical authorities deciding upon when the patient should be discharged. The patient may apply for a review of the case after six months.

Restriction order

This can be made at the same time as a hospital order and places restrictions upon the discharge of the patient. The decision to discharge can only be taken by the Home Secretary or a mental health review tribunal.

This order can only be imposed by a crown court and would normally be used where there was a risk to the public if such a restrictions were not imposed.

Deferral of sentence

A court may defer a sentencing decision. Usually this would be to allow the defendant opportunity to find work or accommodation, to obtain treatment, or to assess response to a current order. In these circumstances the court would normally indicate the sentence they expect to pass if the defendants' plans materialise. Provided that they do, then it would be irregular, after the adjourned period, for a court to impose a harsher penalty than originally indicated.

Some indication of the relative frequency with which courts make use of the orders or sentences at their disposal, can be gained from Table 4.1.

Table 4.1 Number of offenders sentenced in England and Wales for indictable offences during 1990

Sentence or order	Numbers (in thousands)
Absolute/conditional discharge	59
Probation/supervision order	39
Fine	135
Community service order	27
Attendance centre	6
Care order*	–
Immediate custody	48
Fully suspended sentence	21
Other	7

Source: Home Office Criminal Statistics.
*Following the 1989 Children Act a care order can no longer be made in respect of children in criminal proceedings.

References

Home Office 1986 Circular 92/1986 HMSO.
Home Office 1988a Draft Circular PBN 88/316/1/40 HMSO.
Home Office 1988b Circular instruction 40/1988 HMSO.
Home Office 1990a *Crime Justice and Protecting the Public*, HMSO.
Home Office 1990b *Criminal Statistics*, HMSO.
Home Office 1992 *Probation Service National Standards*, HMSO.
Parker, H (1989) *Unmasking The Magistrates* Milton Keynes, Open University Press

Sentencing exercise

This exercise will give you an opportunity to check your knowledge and understanding of the content of the preceding chapter, and to explore the ideas that *you* bring to thinking about sentencing.

Below are brief pen pictures of four defendants. Having read each of these in turn you are asked to tick the accompanying grid to indicate:

(a) which **sentencing principle** you would consider most likely to influence sentencing decisions in each case.
(b) which **sentence or order** do you think a court would be likely to impose.

You can tackle this exercise on your own, but there would be advantages in sharing the results with others – colleagues, practice teacher, supervisor etc., as it is useful to get other peoples' perspectives on the issues involved.

Example one

A black British woman aged 37 who has pleaded guilty to stealing foodstuffs valued £35 from her employer. She has asked for five similar offences to be taken into consideration. She has no previous convictions.

She is single with no children and lives in council accommodation with her elderly and infirm mother who is housebound. The defendant lives a very isolated existence, does not go out in the day and works as a night cleaner at a factory. The offence occurred when she took food from the freezer in the factory canteen.

In court she broke down saying that life was impossible for her and she could not cope.

Example two

A 28 year old white male single parent of a 3 year old boy, who has pleaded guilty to theft of a car radio and handling stolen goods valued at £1500. He has six previous convictions for offences of dishonesty and has previously been dealt with by means of conditional discharge, fine (twice), probation order, community service order and a three month prison sentence.

He is unemployed and has never worked regularly. Police found a large number of car radios in his flat and the inference is that he made his living by stealing and selling them. He has considerable debts.

Example three

A 17 year old white youth who has pleaded guilty to two offences of taking a motor vehicle and driving without insurance. He has had two recent court appearances for similar offences for which he was fined on both occasions.

He lives with his parents who are materially well off, but with whom relations are strained.

Example four

A 23 year old white man who lives alone in a council flat, and is in regular employment as a clerical officer with the Civil Service. He was found guilty of malicious wounding. He had attacked a neighbour with a crowbar inflicting cuts and bruises about the face. He has pleaded not guilty on the grounds that the assault was justified because the neighbour had been using electronic devices

Sentencing

to spy on him to try to get him into trouble with the authorities. There appeared to be no evidence to substantiate these claims.

Sentencing Principle	Example 1	Example 2	Example 3	Example 4
Justice principle				
Deterrence-individual				
Deterrence-general				
Protection of public				
Compensation				
Reparation				
Rehabilitation				

Sentence or Order				
Absolute discharge				
Conditional discharge				
Compensation order				
Fine (how much?)				
Probation order				
Attendance centre				
Community service				
Combination order				
Curfew order				
Young offender inst.				
Suspended sentence				
Prison (how long?)				
Hospital order				
Restriction order				

5 Working in court

Court duty

The court is a legal stage where everyone has their allotted part to play. It is therefore important not only to know which part you are playing, but also to be wearing the right costume and to know your lines. Getting your entrances and exits right, and responding promptly and accurately to cues, are prerequisites of a professional performance. In addition, your role will not only be discreet in itself, but also represent the public profile of the probation service in action.

You will have a definite place in the courtroom (see Chapter 3 p.52) which will identify you as a member of the probation service. Although clearly part of the criminal justice system, you occupy the ground between the offender and the court – the court being theoretically representative of the wider community and upholding it's norms, values and laws. In this context, you will be assisting each to make sense of the other's position, and contributing to the sentencer's decision making. However, as we have already acknowledged, a visit to the majority of courts in Britain will immediately confirm that in terms of race, class and gender, they have a long way to go before they will adequately represent the communities they serve.

Assisting courts and offenders to make sense of each other and assisting with sentencing – It sounds a bit of a tall order, doesn't it? Needless to say, it is complicated.

It is probably fair to say that the role of the probation officer in court went unquestioned and unanalysed for many years. More recently probation services have made efforts to identify more clearly the purpose of court duty. Services vary slightly in their stated objectives about this area of practice, but the following are commonly held to be the core tasks:

Liaison

This element has a number of different strands. The court duty officer is the representative of her/his service, and as such is involved in the passing of information between colleagues and the court – for instance, informing the court verbally of the service's involvement with a particular defendant, informing colleagues of what has happened to their clients, or about a bench's comments, and of course presenting colleagues' PSRs.

In relation to this, there is an important additional task to be performed in checking reports that are to be presented to the court. The purpose of this is to ensure that they contain nothing which might reflect on the credibility of the probation service, such as an inappropriate proposal, the inclusion of obviously discriminatory material or some ambiguity.

The court duty officer also has a responsibility to liaise with other agencies – for instance, contacting a client's social worker in the event of a court appearance, and informing social services department in the event of an offence against children. For example, (see Chapter 1) when Ron first appeared before the court, the court duty officer would have written to the local social services department informing them of the nature of the charges, and what happened in court. They would also have been kept informed of the result of subsequent appearances. The court duty officer would, by the same token, inform the court of the involvement of other agencies if this seemed relevant – the mental health services, for example. When Claudette first appeared in court, having been in custody overnight, she was interviewed in the cells by the court duty officer, who was then able to confirm to the court, when the question of bail was raised, that she was seeing a drugs counsellor regularly.

Direct assistance for defendants

This may take many forms and can vary from court to court. The most obvious example of it is interviewing people who have just received custodial sentences, in order to ascertain whether some immediate intervention is necessary. Your role here could range from coping with someone's distress, to making arrangements for their children to be cared for or family to be informed. When Ron was sentenced the crown court duty officer rang his mother to break the news; Terry was given the fare to get to his probation hostel; when Dawn first appeared her case was not called until very late in the day, she was obviously in a state and so the court duty officer made arrangements for the friend with whom she had left the children to keep them for a bit longer (see Chapter 1). You will also need to notify the appropriate authorities if you consider that there is any risk of suicide or the presence of other factors that might place the client in a vulnerable position. At all costs avoid agreeing to look after pet pirrhana fish when a defendant is unexpectedly sent down.

Before the hearing, it will be necessary to ensure that all defendants on whom reports have been prepared are aware of the contents. This may entail informing the courts of anything with which the client disagrees, or of any factual inaccuracies. Defendants at this stage are often very anxious and may need both reassurance and some explanation of procedures.

At any stage during the proceedings, it may come to your notice that a defendant requires some advice or assistance, for instance about community resources, benefits or other services. After the hearing you may need to offer support to families, or explanations of the outcome.

Influencing the decisions of the court

There are three areas where the role of the probation service is crucial in influencing the decisions of court.

Firstly, in providing information about a particular defendant or facilities in the community – such as hostel accommodation – with a view to influencing decisions about bail, as in Terry's case. All decisions about bail are governed by the 1976 Bail Act, which has at its centre the presumption that everyone has a right to bail – that is, that a court should grant a defendant bail unless it is able to identify specific contra-indications. These are the likelihood of them committing further offences, interfering with witnesses or failing to appear on the next occasion. Despite the presumption of liberty, however, there are those who would argue that the spirit of the 1976 act has been slow to permeate the criminal justice system, and that as a consequence defendants may be denied bail unjustly. Black defendants are especially likely to experience discrimination in this regard.

In response to some of these concerns, and the unacceptably high remand population within the prison system, some probation services have established specialist bail information schemes to provide the court with corroborated factual information about the defendant's circumstances, as we have already mentioned regarding Claudette.

Throughout this process, considerable care must be taken that information to which the probation service is party must not

Working in court

either be passed on to other agencies or be used for any purpose other than to facilitate the provision of bail.

Secondly, intervening to encourage the court to use non-custodial options. Recognising that some groups of offenders are particularly vulnerable or disproportionately at risk of custody (black people, women, young offenders, those with mental health difficulties), many probation services have a policy of 'targeting' such defendants. This might involve interviewing and/or gathering information about those remanded in custody, prior to their appearance, in order to either reduce the likelihood of a further remand in custody, if bail is a possibility, or to suggest a remand for a PSR in order that all non-custodial disposals might be explored.

Thirdly, in providing the court with 'stand down reports'. These are verbal reports to the court based on an assessment of the need for a PSR, following a brief interview with the defendant outside the courtroom. 'Stand downs' are undertaken during the proceedings, either at the request of the court or at the suggestion of the court duty officer and have value both in terms of encouraging a remand for a report and eliminating requests for reports which are unnecessary, such as in the case of low tariff offenders. When Dawn first appeared, the magistrate was considering whether or not to dispose of the matter there and then and asked the court duty officer to 'have a word' and advise her. The 'stand down' interview revealed that Dawn had quite a few problems – her relationship with Clive, debts etc. – and so the duty officer requested the bench to remand the matter for a PSR.

It is considered good practice for court duty officers to take an essentially proactive stance – rather than simply waiting for the court to ask you to do something, you should actively intervene in order to fulfil the crucial role we have described. Likewise, an anti-discriminatory approach is essential and any instances of discrimination should be confronted either directly or by reference to your supervisor. Some court duty teams will be involved in monitoring the outcomes of hearings which can provide valuable statistical data concerning discrimination within the court process which can then be utilised to influence the future practice of other participants.

Administration and paperwork

For a court duty officer to accomplish her or his tasks effectively, a super efficient administrative system is an enormous help and if you don't get to grips with the administration and the paperwork it can all seem a bit of a nightmare, given the speed at which things move in court (sometimes, anyway!).

The systems and paperwork involved will vary considerably from court to court and service to service, as Kay discovered when she did court duty with Ned. You are likely to find that there are procedures for checking whether those on the court list are known to the service, noting the court process in respect of particular defendants and that there are forms for notifying colleagues of results, requesting various reports – PSRs, means, psychiatric, deferred sentence, community service etc. – advising on committal to crown court, and referring to hostels.

Courtcraft: how to play your part on the legal stage

Courtcraft, and the related art of court cred, is an essential skill in a probation officer's repertoire. Knowing your lines, and confidently playing your part on the court stage will enable you to perform to the greatest effect.

Before looking at some of the practicalities, here are a few points to remember

- Be clear about who you are and what you are in court for – are you representing the service as court duty officer? Are you there to present and be questioned on your own report? Are you there to prosecute a breach? Are you there to apply for a summons?
- Learn to feel comfortable and confident in the court setting – grit your teeth and get as much practice as possible, watch others, ask questions ...
- Be aware of and respond to court rules and procedure.
- Prepare! Learn your 'lines'! Think about what you are going to say before you say it, anticipate questions.
- Look the part.

Whatever you may think about the judicial system, with all its rules and conventions, it is unlikely to change its ways in the immediate future. The court game has to be played by the rules, whatever your feelings about them may be. This does not mean that you have to sacrifice your personal or professional integrity and individuality, but is often means that you have to compromise, particularly with regard to dress, and the way in which you communicate with other characters in this particular drama.

Forms of address

- *Magistrates* – collectively addressed as 'Your Worships'.
- *Chair of the bench/stipendiary* – addressed as 'Madam' or 'Sir'.
- *Crown court judges* – addressed as 'Your Honour'.
- *County court judges* – addressed as 'Your Honour'.
- *High court judges* – addressed as 'My Lady' or 'My Lord'.

Before Court...

Dress comfortably, but not casually – being inappropriately dressed can, and often does, unfairly jeopardise your professional credibility. Unfortunately, in this context, how you look can make a difference to how you are heard. Dress is of course to a large extent culturally determined, so a useful rule of thumb is to wear a formal version of your everyday attire.

By the same token, organise your papers in an orderly manner so that information you may need is readily accessible and you don't have to scrabble about in an unseemly manner. Carry them in something neutral and nondescript – not in a plastic carrier bag which serves only to give a supermarket free advertising!

If you are going to court for a specific case, for instance to present or speak to your own report, or to apply for a summons or prosecute a breach, assume you will be asked some questions and anticipate what these might be.

If you are going to court with a report, go through it carefully, asking yourself what you mean by certain phrases and expressions, so that you are ready to explain this to the court if necessary. Pretend you are 'out to get you', and challenge yourself on your assessment, observations and proposals, so that you can remind yourself about the process by which you came to your conclusions. Anticipate the possibility of hostile questions, or attacks (happily these are more likely to be verbal rather than physical), and prepare yourself to deal with them.

If the court is unfamiliar to you, get there early and have a good look round. If you have not managed to make contact with the duty probation officer beforehand, ask the usher where probation officers are supposed to sit and identify the witness box, in case you are called up to answer questions about your report.

Once you have identified these two crucial landmarks, work out you proposed route from one to the other, so that you can position your briefcase/umbrella/handbag/filofax in such a way that you will not trip over it en route...

Overture and beginners, please...

Everyone is expected to rise when a magistrate or a judge enters or leaves a courtroom. Legal personnel generally bow to the bench and there are a range of views about whether or not other occupants of the court should do likewise. Convention on this point may vary from area to area – if in doubt copy a colleague, or adopt a compromise that seems comfortable, be it a slight incline of the head, or a minor 'lean'.

If a magistrate or judge addresses you directly, you are expected to stand.

In the witness box...

In the witness box, you will be borne down upon by someone resembling a bat, who may be wielding a bible. Do not be alarmed – this is the court usher who will ask you to take the oath. There is provision in all courts for anyone of any religion to take an appropriate oath, according to their beliefs. Make a clear request for the appropriate religious text, or simply state your religion, and it will be produced for you. The oath will be written on a card and handed to you to read.

If you are an agnostic, an atheist, or just feel uncomfortable swearing an oath, then you have the option to 'affirm'. This excludes the mention of deities of any kind – you simply 'solemnly vow and affirm to tell the truth'. Ask the usher if you may affirm, you will be handed the appropriate card. Some people worry about affirming, fearing that to indicate a lack of religious belief will prejudice what they have to say. This is not the case.

Know thyself! If you know you are prone to trembling hands, grip the edge of the witness box to steady them. If you are prone to coughing fits, when you are nervous, ask the usher for a glass of water before you start. If you are prone to both, be careful when you lift the glass of water to your lips, with trembling hands .... But seriously, some degree of anxiety is not only natural, but necessary, if you are to perform well. Speak loudly and clearly and follow these basic guidelines...

- watch your body language – folded arms make you look defensive; downcast eyes convey lack of confidence in what you are saying;

Working in court

- think about what you are going to say before you say it;
- avoid jargon;
- back up what you say with evidence/examples;
- only speak from your own experience – do not be drawn into speculation;
- if you don't know, say so;
- if you don't understand a question, say so;
- never loose your temper or betray irritation;
- never argue with a magistrate/judge.

Most people find appearing in court an anxiety provoking experience – this is quite normal and nothing to be ashamed of. Anxiety often produces the adrenalin to do a good job, and provided that you have anticipated questions and prepared yourself to 'perform' nothing terrible should happen to you. However, just as defendants are likely to experience instances of sexism, and racism within the courts, so are probation staff and it is of the utmost importance that equality of opportunity policies are in place and all involved are clear about the implementation thereof.

Court psycho-babble exercise

You may be tempted to use some of the following phrases in court – please don't! Try instead to turn them into intelligible English:

1. He seems to have suffered from sibling rivalry.
2. She and her partner have an ongoing relationship.
3. Most of his previous offences can be seen in terms of peer group pressure.
4. She has taken on board the seriousness of her offence.
5. I hear what you are saying.
6. He has an ambivalent relationship with his mother.
7. He does not really seem to be in touch with his feelings about this.
8. She is not amenable to social work intervention.
9. He has an inadequate personality and is of low IQ.
10 I have been attempting to confront her offending behaviour.

6 Writing pre-sentence reports

What is a pre-sentence report?

Every year the probation service prepares approximately 200 000 reports for the youth, magistrates' and crown courts. With the advent of the Criminal Justice Act 1991 the social enquiry report [SIR] has been transformed into the pre-sentence report [PSR]:

The purpose of the PSR is to assist the court in deciding the most suitable way of dealing with a person who has been convicted of an offence(s). '... the features which distinguish it from other reports is that it should set the offending behaviour into the individual's social context, examine the offender's view of that behaviour and assess the likely effect of the range of measures available to the court on the offender or any dependants' (Home Office Circular 92/86).

PSRs are required when a court is considering a custodial sentence, a probation order, with any of the additional requirements contained in schedule 1 of the 1991 Act, a community service order, a combination order or a supervision order with additional requirements.

Basically then, the PSR will provide the court with some understanding of the circumstances of the offence and its seriousness, elements of the client's life and experience, either in the present or past, and factors which in your professional opinion, may have contributed to them getting into trouble. You will then need to examine what is likely to reduce the risk of your client getting into trouble in the future and in the light of this, to state what you consider to be the most appropriate community

Writing pre-sentence reports

sentence. In the case of a violent or sexual offence, it will be necessary to consider whether there is a risk to the public.

If the defendant appears to be in serious danger of a custodial sentence it will be important to outline any adverse effects of such a sentence for the defendant, for their family and significant others, for their employment or training prospects, their accommodation, their education and the likely impact of a prison sentence on their propensity to reoffend. Because the sentencing criteria of the CJ Act 1991 makes no reference to the likely positive effects of a custodial sentence, it is not legitimate to mention these in your conclusion and proposal.

You should avoid proposals which would push your client 'up tariff' for instance a probation order, community service order and combination order all involve a lot of commitment from the client and quite a curtailment of their liberty. It is arguable that it would be unjust to subject someone to this if they had been in little trouble before or their offence was a relatively minor one. In addition, the resources of the probation service are limited, and if such orders are being made in respect of clients who the court might otherwise have for instance fined, then they are not going to be available for clients in respect of whom there is no other option except custody.

You also need to consider the consequences if they were to breach either of these orders since this might hasten a premature entry into the prison system. These are important issues when you come to consider proposals for people who are generally discriminated against in the justice system, for example women – black and white – and black men, whom statistics show are disproportionately represented in the prison system (NACRO Briefing Paper 1991). There is a tendency among probation officers to portray women in stereotypical terms in PSRs– either as victims in need of social work help or as stalwart pillars caring for children and partners. Whilst this may win the sympathy of the court, one of the dangers already mentioned is that if such clients are given a probation order, they are immediately pushed 'up tariff', and get sent to prison at a much earlier stage in their criminal careers than men – especially white men. Additionally, women who do not conform to such stereotypes – lesbian women, black or white, or black women *per se* – could be more harshly dealt with. They will not only be punished for breaking the law but also for deviating from social norms (Raikes 1987).

'What if' we hear you cry 'the client has no previous convictions, the current offence is relatively minor but he/she has lots of personal and emotional problems? Ideally the solution to this should be available in the community – and here it is essential to explore what kinds of voluntary organisations there might be in your area which can provide advice, counselling, or family work, for example.

Why is writing PSRs such an important task?

In addition to being crucial in influencing the court and diverting offenders away from custody, the task of preparing PSRs is important for other reasons. A court appearance will represent a time of crisis for many people and your intervention may be particularly crucial in enabling someone to stop, take stock of their situation, examine their offending and the possible reasons behind it, and explore the possibilities for things being different in the future. This may prove not only helpful in itself, but can lay the foundations and form the basis of a contract for ongoing work in the event of a probation order being made.

Preparing pre-sentence reports

If your task is to provide the court with an understanding of what may have contributed to somebody getting into trouble, and whether or not they are likely to reoffend, it may well be necessary to gather a wide range of information about them, from several different sources, as well as asking them questions about key areas of their lives, as illustrated in Figure 6.1.

As you can see, these areas can be clustered according to the framework outlined in Chapter 12 (Critcher 1975), which enables us to look at the respective contributions of ***structure, culture and biography*** to a client's offending. Structural factors relate to the fundamental economic and material world of the client and would include housing, poverty, employment, income. Cultural factors relate to the way the individual has learned to operate within the limits of structure, and therefore could include offending history, attitudes, leisure, drugs, alcohol, gambling. These factors can also define or dictate what is possible in terms of opportunities. Biographical factors, not surprisingly, are what Raynor describes as:

> the multitude of contingencies or accidents of experience that distinguish one individual from another even within the same cultural or structural space　　　　　　　　(Raynor 1985)

and would include family background, experiences of oppression, mental health, physical health, personal relationships, child care and any significant life events of crises.

Writing pre-sentence reports

Figure 6.1 Causal factors in offending

Factors (clouds surrounding Client): Drugs; Alcohol; Prospects Hopes for the future; Family Relationships; Leisure; Previous Offences; Education; Pattern of Offending; Employment; Housing; Physical health; Experiences of oppression; Attitudes; Poverty; Child Protection Issues; Income; Debts; Mental Health; Gambling; Home Circumstances.

To collect all this information in every case would be an onerous task, and not a particularly economical use of time, so it is a good idea to start with a hunch/hypothesis and to test it. At the same time however it is equally important to avoid stereotyping on the basis of the offence or type of offender. Think of Ron for example – Kay found herself making assumptions on the basis of the stereotype of the sex offender, and although in some ways he 'fitted' it was equally important that she gave him the opportunity to be his other self as well (see Chapter 1).

Pay close attention to any information you already have from the Court – the court referral form is an obvious starting point and you may pick up some clues from previous convictions, and any comments made by the duty probation officer about the defendant. In addition you should study carefully the documentation received from the crown prosecution service (CPS).

- Example 1. This is the first time this person has been in trouble after a lengthy break – now charged with actual bodily harm. You'd wonder 'Why now?' and what has changed in their life. Is it a time of stress – a lost job, a broken relationship, a bereavement?
- Example 2. This is a first offence of theft of money from an employer but the defendant has insisted on an office appointment as he does not want his family to know – you'd wonder whether he might be in serious debt, gambling or leading a double life.
- Example 3. This is an offence of shop lifting and amongst the other goods there is a bottle of whisky – you'd wonder whether alcohol is a problem, and whether it has played a part in previous offending.

It is inevitable that at the end of your inquiries you will have a wealth of information, pages of notes and of course if you were to include all of it, your PSR would be the size of a small novel. In order to decide what to leave out, you should ask yourself 'What relevance does this have to the client's offending behaviour?' and having done this, try to work to a set of headings – which may well be the actual headings you use in the body of the report.

Basically, in the preparation of your reports, you are engaging in a particular form of assessment, since you are engaged in:

a perceptual\analytic process of reflecting, categorising, organising and synthesising data : it is both a process and product of our understanding.   (Coulshed 1988).

You are also involved in that other balancing act which assessment involves – that between **risk**, **need** and **resources** (Curnock and Hardiker 1979).

What follows is the usual format for a PSR.

1. Introduction

(a) A standard headline paragraph

For example 'This is a pre-sentence report as defined in section 3(5) of the Criminal Justice Act 1991. It has been prepared in accordance with the requirements of the Probation Service National Standards for pre-sentence reports.'

Writing pre-sentence reports

(b) Basic factual information

This should note the court, the date of the hearing, the full name, address, date of birth, and age of the defendant and the names of any co-defendants.

(c) Sources of information

This section should indicate who you have interviewed in connection with the report, where the interviews took place and how many times you saw them or spoke to them on the telephone. Other sources of information; crown prosecution documentation, social workers, doctors, psychiatrists, employers, lists of previous convictions, agency files etc. should be noted. Include details of the people or agencies you tried, but failed, to contact and any significant gaps in your information. You should also indicate whether the current offence constitutes a breach of an existing order.

2. Current offence(s)

(a) Circumstances of the offence(s)

In this section you put the current offence into context. You include any mitigating or aggravating factors but not details of previous offences unless you believe that the circumstances of previous offences are relevant to an understanding of the current offence. This is also where you present your own, and the offenders account of how and why the offence took place.

Peter Raynor (1985) says:

> Only by understanding the offender's own view of the offence and its circumstances can we begin to think about what he intended.

> You note, for example, whether your client meticulously planned the 'job' over months or 'just got caught up in the excitement of the moment'.
> Did the client know what she/he was doing and that it was wrong? Did she/he feel there was a choice (pressure from others, a dare etc. or any other reason. What do they feel about it now ... remember to consider not only what they say verbally but also what they say non-verbally, and use other people's comments (for example 'She/he came home in a terribly distressed state') ...

you have to highlight inconsistencies, or even a progressive change of attitude, e.g. initially she/he talked about it with bravado, but subsequently became quite shamefaced when she/he realised the implications ... Add the client's awareness or lack of it of the impact on victim, if any, and on significant others – family, partner, children etc.

The nature of the defendant's involvement in the offence and their attitude to it is very important in determining the seriousness with which the offence will be viewed by the court.

(b) The seriousness of the offence

The evaluation of 'seriousness' by the PO in the PSR marks the most radical departure from the format of the SIR which it replaces. This section should include the perceptions of the offender but the PO must assess seriousness in the light of all the accounts of the offence; the police, the prosecution, the defence and their own experience of the offender.

The seriousness of an offence can be established by a consideration of the following sorts of questions:

- Was the offence violent or sexual and, if so, was the violence sadistic and what injury, physical and mental was suffered by the victim[s]?
- Was a weapon carried or used?
- What actual damage, harm, cost or injury resulted from the offence?
- Did the offender gain from the offence, and if so, to what extent?
- Was the victim vulnerable, a child or an elderly person, and were they chosen because of their vulnerability?
- Was the offence racially motivated?
- Was the offender provoked?
- Was the offence pre-meditated or spontaneous.
- Were drink, drugs or other intoxicating substances involved?
- Did the offender intend the offence to cause the harm that it did?
- Do they express regret, indifference or a desire to make amends?
- What was their role in the offence, prime mover or 'just along for the ride'?

3. Relevant information about the offender

(a) Previous offending

Don't list all the previous offences ... you are telling the court what they know already ... don't discuss each and every one ... summarise them, commenting on anything significant about the nature of the offences and particularly the pattern of offending. For the purpose of a PSR, all previous convictions may be relevant and the rules about 'spent' convictions do not apply.

(b) Responses to previous disposals

Were fines paid (check)? What effect did prison have? Were conditions of licences fulfilled? What was the response to probation? Was community service completed? What is the client's view of the effects of previous disposals? What was the effect of previous disposals on the client's offending?

(c) Risk to the Public

In a case in which the current offence is a violent or sexual one you need to consider whether the public would be at serious risk from the offender if she/he remained in the community. In such circumstances you would need to offer a view about whether, and what type, of community sentence might reduce this risk.

(d) Relevant background

This can include personal history, education, employment, experience of discrimination, significant life events .... It's a tricky one – what is relevant in the case of one client's offending may be completely irrelevant as far as the offending of another is concerned, e.g. having been in care, turbulent relationships within the family, truancy, periods of mental illness, significant bereavement, many changes of address, divorce or separation

(e) Mitigating factors

What is happening in the present that contributes to the client's offending? Relationship problems, discrimination, finance, children, unemployment, illness, social isolation, environment, violence, loss, abuse, poverty, accommodation? Remember to include information about the present which may help clients to reduce offending behaviour – social networks, future prospects, imminent resolution of a worrying issue, for example.

4   Conclusion and proposal

In this section there should be a clear statement of what you believe the most suitable option to be and its duration. The purposes, methods and targets of your intervention should be spelled out and frequency of contact noted. Other agencies which constitute the change agent system should be identified and the nature and frequency of your own and your client's contact with them specified. You should also give a brief but very specific account of what you expect the impact of this intervention will be on the client's offending. In cases where probation, supervision or a combination order is proposed, you should present the court with a plan, agreed with the client, since these orders cannot be made unless clients state a willingness to participate and indicate that they understand the consequences of failure to comply with the conditions of an order.

Remember, however, that suggested headings are useful but not cast in tablets of stone, so be flexible... when you are doing your PSR interview, bear a broad range of headings in mind as an *aide memoir*, but do not allow them to trammel you in your questions/exploration of the client's world...every client is different and modification may be necessary ... for example, it might be most appropriate to start with the offence as this is why the client has come to see you. However, if the offence is a sensitive one, or the client seems particularly ill at ease, it may be better to start in a different area, before going back to the details of the offence. You may want to start the interview with a history, so you can put the offence in chronological context ... or you may suggest to the client that they start at the place they think makes most sense.

Guidelines

- Write your reports in simple, formal English , courtspeak is an art – it's about being concise, while bringing the client alive, and not sending the magistrate/judge to sleep.
- Avoid social work of jargon – judges in particular hate it. You will produce a more personal, live, vivid account by finding substitutes for ambivalent, sibling, peer group, sub-

culture, self image, ongoing relationship. Try to avoid 'take on board' – your client is not a ship. Remember also that your client will be reading this epic and needs to be able to understand what you are saying.

- Avoid slang and colloquialisms unless they are part of a direct quote and offered as such – indeed quoting what the client says can have a very powerful effect, and this is quite legitimate.
- Be sure to distinguish fact from opinion and avoid value judgements. If you are including opinion, it is important to be able to justify it if asked to do so.
- Watch the mixed message or negative inference, 'he claimed that', 'he maintained that' meaning 'that's what he said but I don't believe him'.
- Avoid discriminatory language and beware of labelling and stereotyping – there are great risks in describing a client as 'immature', 'inadequate', 'alcoholic', 'of limited intelligence' without explaining what you mean when you use these terms, thus leaving those who read the report to come to their own conclusions.
- Avoid the inclusion of irrelevant material particularly in relation to race, gender, sexual orientation. For example, the fact that the client is a good mother may have no bearing on her offending, and, as we suggested earlier in this chapter, to describe her as such in a report may serve to confirm the courts' stereotype about what women should be. Additionally, this may prejudice the view of the court about women who it is not possible to describe in similar terms.
- Balance negatives with positives. It is important to try to put what look like negative elements in context. There may be reasons for a poor work record (high unemployment, racism) or many changes of job (not enough money to care for family, confusion about work direction) or many changes of partner (fear of closeness, etc.). However, care should be taken to avoid a subjectively over positive or patronising tone.
- Be mindful of the impact on the client of reading or hearing what you have written. Share impressions along the way, if possible, so that this experience will not be too much of a shock.
- Finally, if you can, leave plenty of time to write your reports. If you have the chance to do a first draft, and to go back to it later, you will see much more clearly what may need changing or where the gaps lie.

Gatekeeping or quality control

The potentially powerful influence of the PSR in the sentencing process, coupled with an increasing recognition in recent years that all people are not treated equally within the criminal justice system, has resulted in the widespread establishment of formalised quality control systems. Gatekeeping involves the examination and discussion of reports prior to their submission in order to ensure that their content and proposals are consistent with the services policies in respect of anti-discriminatory practice and non-custodial disposals.

What follows is an example of one service's aims in respect of improving report writing practice:

  i. To improve the quality of service provided to offenders and the courts and other recipients in relation to reports written by the probation service.
  ii. To ensure that in their content, recommendation and general approach all reports reflect the services policies.
  iii. To eliminate racism, sexism, and any other form of discrimination.
  iv. To ensure that the merits and feasibility of all relevant non-custodial disposals have been properly considered.

(Inner London Probation Service 1990)

Models for gatekeeping vary, but it is generally considered good practice that gatekeepers are allocated formally and that all members of a team participate in order to avoid the risk of a collusive relationship whereby like minded officers always gatekeep for one another. In addition, reports should be scrutinised in draft form and allowing plenty of time for discussion and amendment.

In the event of a disagreement, there should be an established system for arbitration. In addition, all gatekeeping activities should be monitored and reviewed on a regular basis, in order to ensure that both objectivity and objectives are achieved.

PSR exercise

What follows is Seymour's draft PSR on Francis:

 (a) What is wrong with it and why?
 (b) How should it be improved?

Have a go at fixing it yourself and then turn to the end of the chapter to compare your thoughts with the comments of Seymour's practice teacher.

Little Acop-in-the-Wold Probation Service

Little Acop-in-the-Wold South office

Pre-Sentence Report

This is a pre-sentence report as defined in section 3(5) of the Criminal Justice Act 1991. It has been prepared in accordance with the requirements of the *Probation Service National Standards* for pre-sentence reports.

Name:	Francis Baker
Date of birth:	1 April 1973 (aged 20 yrs)
Address:	99 Dingly Dell, Little Acop-in-the Wold
Offence:	Burglary of private dwellings × 3
Court:	Little Acop-in-the Wold Magistrates' Court
Date of Hearing:	19/6/92

Sources of information

I have spoken to Francis twice and met his mother. His father did not make himself available, despite my request to see him. I have spoken to his solicitor.

Current offence

Francis told me that he was out one night with a friend younger than himself and was clearly trying to impress him with his bravado. They saw the front door of a house ajar and he broke into the house and stole a video recorder and a camera while his friend waited outside keeping watch. They then moved on to burgle two other houses in the same area.

During the third burglary his friend shouted that he could hear a car coming, they made a run for it across the sports field but the police, who know him well, picked him up in the High Street and took him and his friend to the local police station where he was charged. Francis told me that as the house was probably insured, he didn't think the people would lose anything by what he'd done.

The seriousness of the offence

Francis expresses genuine remorse about this offence, although he was reassured by the thought that the victims would probably be reimbursed by their insurance company. Francis feels sure that had it not been for the encouragement of his friend he would not have committed the offence.

Information about the offender

Previous offending

Francis has six previous convictions, two of which were when he was a juvenile and was convicted of theft of a bicycle and handling stolen goods, which, he tells me, was sports equipment. For these he was conditionally discharged and fined. When he was seventeen he broke in to a youth club and stole some tapes for which he was sentenced to an attendance centre order which he completed. Three months later he stole a BMW car and was sent to detention centre. While on licence, he committed two burglaries of private dwellings and served a six month custodial sentence in a Young Offenders Institution.

Francis did not mind being fined but he did not like having to get up and go to bed early at the Detention Centre. At the time this really brought him to his senses so it was unfortunate that he was convicted so soon afterwards. He liked the Young Offenders Institution better than the Detention Centre because it was not such hard work but he thought his sentence was a bit too long.

Risk to the Public

Francis is a good natured young man at heart and does not mean anybody any harm. However, he is not a very good driver and I would think that anybody who was in the vicinity of where he stole the BMW, when he was 17, was in considerable danger.

Relevant information about the offender

Francis lives with his parents and siblings in a three bedroomed, semidetached council house which is in a state of good decorative order. His parents – respectable, hard working and law abiding people who have had enough of his offending behaviour – are very keen that he should find regular employment. He has recently acquired a girlfriend and they are hopeful that she will prove a steadying influence upon him.

Francis tells me that relations between him and his parents are somewhat strained and he would like a flat of his own. Francis is in receipt of social security which is largely spent on social activities, although he was reluctant to say exactly what.

Francis was born and brought up in Little Acop-in-the-Wold, his parents having come to this country from the West Indies several years previously. He is the eldest of three children, having a sister of 16, Sandra, and a brother of 13, Tony. He recalls a happy and settled childhood. He attended St John's Primary School until the age of 11 years, when he moved on to Windemere Secondary School, a local comprehensive.

He tells me that he did not get on well with the teachers and he was excluded from school at 15, for disruptive behaviour. He enjoyed maths and science, but left without any formal qualifications, which was a pity as he is clearly very bright.

On leaving school, he did three months on a YTS scheme at an electrical factory but left because he said he was bored. Apart from short periods of casual work, he has remained unemployed since.

As stated in previous paragraphs, Francis is a nice young man who will probably grow out of crime. Not having a job can't help and if he got on better with his parents things might improve.

Conclusion

It seems that Francis' offending behaviour is related to his peer group influences. It is clear that Francis' unfulfilled educational potential has had consequences for his confidence, and as a result, his main source of self esteem is the commission of antisocial acts. It also seems that in late adolescence he is rebelling against the culture conflict between him and his parents.

In view of his very limited income, I do not feel that a fine would be appropriate. I have assessed him as suitable for community service but do not think that this would be of any benefit to him. I would therefore respectfully suggest that the court make him the subject of a probation order so that his offending behaviour might be confronted and the family offered some support at this difficult time.

Seymour Kleintz
Assistant Probation Officer

Comments of the practice teacher

What follows are the practice teacher's comments – how do they compare with yours?

Sources of information

'I have spoken to Francis twice and met his mother. His father did not make himself available, despite my request to see him. I have spoken to his solicitor.'

Francis is not a juvenile and so should be referred to either as Mr Baker or Mr Francis Baker.

What is the relevance of not having seen his father – it sounds as though you are making a negative suggestion. What point are you making?

Where did the interviews take place?

You should mention having had access to previous probation records and reports and to documentation from the Crown Prosecution Service.

Current offence

'Francis told me that he was out one night with a friend younger than himself and was clearly trying to impress him with his bravado. They saw the front door of a house ajar and he broke into the house and stole a video recorder and a camera while his friend waited outside keeping watch. They then moved on to burgle two other houses in the same area.'

You seem a bit confused about fact and opinion – in the first sentence are you making an assumption about Francis' wish to impress his friend or is that what he told you?

Have you checked with the arresting officer whether what Francis says about the means of entry and the items stolen is true. If so, you should mention that you have spoken to the arresting officer and this should be included in your 'sources of information' section.

'During the third burglary his friend shouted that he could hear a car coming, they made a run for it across the sports field but the police, who know him well, picked him up in the High Street and took him and his friend to the local police station where he was charged. Francis told me that as the house was probably insured, he didn't think the people would lose anything by what he'd done.'

You need to clarify whether the documentation from the CPS confirms or contradicts Francis' account of these events – your report must not simply be based on his account of what happened.

What Francis says about the victim being insured should come in the next section.

Seriousness of the offence

'Francis expresses genuine remorse about this offence, although he was reassured by the thought that the victims would probably be reimbursed by their insurance company. Francis feels sure that had it not been for the encouragement of his friend he would not have committed the offence.'

Try to be as objective and impartial as possible – what are the signs that Francis is genuinely remorseful? What is this about – the offence or being caught? Don't make judgements without being able to back them up.

This is the appropriate place for Francis' comments about the victims, both in terms of whether or not they were insured, and the degree of distress he considers they may have experienced.

You need to express your own opinion about the seriousness of this offence, and your assessment of Francis' attitude towards it.

Information about the offender

Previous offending

'Francis has six previous convictions, two of which were when he was a juvenile and was convicted of theft of a bicycle and handling stolen goods, which he tells me was sports equipment. For these he was conditionally discharged and fined. When he was seventeen he broke into a youth club and stole some tapes, for which he was sentenced to an attendance centre order which he completed. Three months later he stole a BMW car and was sent to detention centre. Whilst on licence, he committed two burglaries of private dwellings and served a six month custodial sentence in a Young Offenders Institution.

Francis did not mind being fined but he did not like having to get up and go to bed early at the Detention Centre. At the time this really brought him to his senses so it was unfortunate that he was convicted so soon afterwards. He liked the Young Offenders Institution better because it was not such hard work but he thought his sentence was a bit too long.'

There is nothing in this section that the court does not already know from his 609 (list of previous convictions). Is there any pattern to his offending? What does he say about the offences? In what context did they take place? What has been his response to previous disposals? How did he get on while being supervised on licence? Is there a link between his past offences and his current one?

How long ago was his last offence and are they getting any more or less serious?

I'm sure that Francis has lots of criticisms of the regime in penal establishments, but this is not quite what is required.... What you need to address is his response to the disposals – how did he respond to post release supervision ?... what effect did disposals have on his offending, his attitude or his behaviour?

Risk to the public

'Francis is a good natured young man at heart and does not mean anybody any harm. However, he is not a very good driver and I would think that anybody who was in the vicinity when he stole the BMW at the age of 17 was in considerable danger.'

Francis is neither a violent nor a sexual offender and so it is not necessary to comment on the risk he may pose to the public and, even if he were, it's an objective assessment of risk that is required, with supporting evidence rather than an anecdotal account.

Relevant information about the offender

'Francis was born and brought up in Little Acop-in-the-Wold, his parents having come to this country from the West Indies several years previously. He is the eldest of three children, having a sister of 16, Sandra, and a brother of 13, Tony. He recalls a happy and settled childhood. He attended St John's Primary School until the age of 11 years, when he moved on to Windemere Secondary School, a local comprehensive.'

The fact that his parents came from the West Indies is irrelevant and including it risks playing into racist stereotyping connotations.

Overall, this section on Francis' background needs to be linked more firmly to his offending or it's not relevant to include it. Was there a link between problems at school and the start of his offending? Has he tended to get into trouble when in or out of work?

'Francis lives with his parents and siblings in a three bedroomed, semidetached council house which is in a state of good decorative order. His parents – respectable, hard working and law abiding people who have had enough of his offending behaviour – are very keen that he should find regular employment.'

What is the relevance of the details about the house – they add nothing to an understanding of Francis and his offending. The description of his parents sounds patronising and contains value judgements, although their attitude to his offending is clearly important – try to focus on that, rather than their characteristics.

Colloquialism! 'Had enough of his offending behaviour'.

'He has recently acquired a girlfriend and they are hopeful that she will prove a steadying influence upon him.

Francis tells me that relations between him and his parents are somewhat strained and he would like a flat of his own. Francis is in receipt of social security which is largely spent on social activities, although he was reluctant to say exactly what.'

The comment about his girlfriend's influence runs the risk of reinforcing stereotypical sexist assumptions.

Strained relationships? What do you think this is about and what are the implications?

Colloquialism! 'Social Security'.

Saying Francis was reluctant to tell you what he spends his money on implies that he is up to no good – is this what you mean?

In general, there is quite a lot missing from this section – How does he spend his time? What is life like day to day? What about friends and other external influences? What are his hopes and plans for the future?

Mitigating factors

'As stated in previous paragraphs, Francis is a nice young man who will probably grow out of crime. Not having a job can't help and if he got on better with his parents, things might improve.'

Yes I can see what you're getting at but this is not quite the kind of thing the court if after ... here would be a good place to emphasise Francis' youth, the fact that he co-operated with the police on arrest, and readily admitted the offences. It would be appropriate to reinforce the fact that he responded well whilst on licence previously, and during the interviews for the PSR he showed signs of wishing to bring about some changes in his life.

Conclusion

'It seems that Francis' offending behaviour is related to his peer group influences. It is clear that Francis' unfulfilled educational potential has had consequences for his confidence, and as a result, his main source of self esteem is the commission of antisocial acts. It also seems that in late adolescence he is rebelling against the culture conflict between him and his parents.'

Jargon alert!! What sense is Francis going to make of this and what is this based on. Your assessment of his offending does not seem to link with the body of the report and you do not provide any supporting evidence.

Your reference to culture conflict – where is your evidence? This could be seen as racist stereotyping.

'In view of his very limited income, I do not feel that a fine would be appropriate. I have assessed him as suitable for community service but do not think that this would be of any benefit to him. I would therefore suggest that the court make him the subject of a probation order so that his offending behaviour might be confronted and the family offered some support at this difficult time.'

Given the seriousness of the offence, and the fact that there has been a pattern of this type of offending, it would be unrealistic to consider a fine, and you run the risk of undermining your credibility by mentioning it. Even if it were appropriate to suggest this, limited income is not an impediment to a fine *per se*, although it would dictate the level of financial penalty.

The rationale of CS is not rehabilitative, but punitive so whether or not it would be of benefit is irrelevant. However, you need to explain why you don't think it is appropriate, even though you say he is suitable.

Probation – what do you mean by support and do the family want it? Have you discussed it with either Francis or his parents? How are you intending to confront his offending behaviour? Should the order have any conditions attached to it – he is quite high tariff and the court are likely to be considering custody. If you are recommending a period of supervision, it is important to spell out the aims of the order, and how these are to be achieved, and of course to have negotiated these with Francis beforehand – his consent will he necessary before the court can make a probation order.

Finally – don't despair. These are traps we all fall into at times ... preparing a PSR is a very complex task, but it will get easier!

References

Coulshed, V. 1988 *Social Work Practice: An Introduction*, BASW Macmillan Education.
Critcher, C. 1975 'Structures, Cultures and Biographies' in S. Hall and T. Jefferson (eds) *Resistance Through Rituals*, London: Hutchinson
Curnock, K. and Hardiker, P. 1979 *Towards Practice Theory: Skills and Methods in Social Assessment*, Routledge and Kegan Paul.
Home Office 1991 Race and Criminal Justice (Briefing Paper) London: NACRO
Pitts, J. 1988 *The Politics of Juvenile Crime*, London: Sage.
Raikes, S. 1987 'When women offenders are not stereotypes' *Social Work Today* 28 January 1987.
Raynor, P. 1985 *Social Work, Justice and Control*, Blackwell.

7 Working with offenders I: The probation order

A lot of what can be said about probation orders is fairly straightforward. When one comes to consider what they are supposed to achieve, and what probation officers are supposed to do when supervising an order, things become slightly less clear cut.

This chapter will begin with the relatively straightforward part – an outline of the legislative framework of the probation order.

The legislative framework

Traditionally the probation order has been a device by which courts have been able to release an offender (subject to certain conditions) instead of sentencing them. Following the 1991 Criminal Justice Act the probation order became a sentence in its own right.

A probation order may be made on an offender of 16 or over. There is no offence for which an order cannot be made except those for which the penalty is already fixed by law, e.g. murder. However, the principle which underpins the Criminal Justice Act 1991, i.e. that restrictions upon liberty should be commensurate with the seriousness of the offence, make it unlikely that in the future probation orders will be made in respect of minor offences.

A probation order can be for any period between six months and three years. The standard conditions of a probation order are that the offender should:

The probation order

- be of good behaviour and lead an industrious life;
- notify the probation officer at once of any change of residence or employment;
- keep in touch with the probation officer in accordance with such instructions as may from time to time be given and in particular, if the probation officer so requires, to receive visits from them at home.

The frequency with which probation officers are to 'keep in touch with' those they supervise under a probation order is defined by the *Probation Service National Standards* (Home Office 1992): 'Where practicable twelve appointments should be made for an offender to see the supervising officer (or a person operating under his or her direction) in the first three months of an order; six in the next three months; and thereafter at least one each month to the completion of supervision. Where this is not practicable, a minimum level of six appointments in the first three months and one appointment monthly, thereafter, must be observed'.

As with a supervision order it is possible for courts to insert additional conditions into the probation order. These can include:

- *The requirement to undergo 'mental' treatment.* This can be as either an in- or out-patient. Before such a requirement can be inserted into an order the court must be satisfied on the (written) evidence of a duly qualified medical practitioner that the offender requires, and is susceptible to, treatment and that such treatment is available to them. The requirement may be for the duration of the whole order or some lesser part of it.
- *Requirements as to residence.* These can be:

    (a) Residence in an approved probation hostel. Such hostels may be managed by the probation service or by voluntary organisations. 'Approval' is undertaken by the secretary of state. It is the responsibility of the probation officer writing the PSR to initiate enquiries about the availability of a hostel place. It is usual for the offender to spend a trial period at the hostel. This may entail asking the court for a further remand. The requirement cannot be inserted into the order without the agreement of both offender and hostel, and may be for the duration of the probation order or for some lesser period.

    (b) Residence in non-approved institutions (e.g. a drug rehabilitation centre). A similar set of considerations

apply, although if a PO anticipates such a requirement being made they would normally be expected to consult with a chief (or assistant chief) probation officer, as probation committee funding may be involved.
  (c) A general requirement to 'reside as directed by the probation officer'.
- *Requirement to attend probation centres or other specified activities.* Section 4A(1) of schedule 11 of the Criminal Justice Act (1982) makes it possible for a probationer to be required to attend particular locations, e.g. education classes, or a drug dependency centre. Section 4A(1)b covers activities which may not take place at a fixed location. Section 4B concerns requirements to participate in activity at a day centre provided (or approved) by the probation committee. These centres offer an intensive training programme which may include elements of group therapy focusing on offending behaviour, craft activities, social skills training etc. As in the case of hostels it would be usual for the offender to visit the centre for a period of assessment prior to the making of the order. All of these requirements are subject to a 60 day maximum period.
- However, In the case of sex offenders, the Criminal Justice Act 1991 allows the court to insert a treatment condition which may be for the duration of the order without the normal 60 day limit.
- *Requirement as to treatment for drug or alcohol dependency* by any person, including a probation officer, recognised by the court as having 'the necessary qualification or experience' to work effectively with drug/alcohol misusers.
- *Negative requirements,* i.e. a condition which requires the probationer to refrain from a particular activity, e.g. attending football matches or frequenting particular public houses. Negative requirements of this sort are rarely used as they are difficult to enforce.

No probation order can be made unless the defendant agrees to the requirements. Although formal agreement of this sort may sometimes be given because the defendant is seeking to avoid some less palatable alternative, it is nonetheless seen as important to stress that probation can only really work if the probationer is willing to co-operate. Agreement once having been given, it is not possible for a defendant to subsequently appeal against the order.

Breach of a probation order

If a probationer fails to comply with the requirements of a probation order then the supervising officer can apply for a summons or warrant to bring the probationer before the court. Once that has happened, if the breach of probation is admitted or proved, then the probationer can be dealt with for the original offence. This will mean that the probation order then ceases to have effect. Alternatively, if the court decide to allow the probation order to continue, then it is possible to deal with the breach by: (a) imposing a fine not exceeding £1000; or (b) imposing up to 60 hours community service; or (c) if the offender is under 21, requiring attendance at an attendance centre. It is also open to the court to take no further action. If the breach is a particularly serious one, the court may decide to revoke the probation order and impose a different penalty for the original offence. The same option is open to the court if an offender is convicted of a further offence committed during the currency of a probation order. The court must take into account the extent to which the offender has complied with the terms of the order up to that point.

Discharge

A probation officer, or a probationer, may apply to the court to discharge a probation order before it has run its full course. This could be on the grounds of the 'good progress' that the probationer had made or, alternatively, because supervision had become impractical (e.g. if the probationer had emigrated). It is also possible to apply for the probation order to be substituted by a conditional discharge.

What are the aims of probation and who is the client?

Whilst the above provisions lay out the legal framework of the probation order, they give very little indication of what it is designed to achieve, or indeed the methods and procedures to be employed by the probation officer in attempting to achieve them. From the time of the police court missionaries (pre-cursors of the modern probation service) there has been considerable flexibility about this. Cooper (1987) says: 'the missionary could be whatever his magistrates and his conscience required him to be in relation to the pathetic individuals for whom he cared'. Thus, at an early stage, the community supervision of offenders combined the principles of surveillance, philanthropy and reclamation, and, moreover, the mix and manner of their mediation appears to have left much to the discretion of the individual supervisor. Since that time the 'welfare' component of supervision has variously placed emphasis upon ***psychodynamically*** based notions of 'treatment' of offenders; alternatively, stress has been laid upon the empowerment of oppressed and dispossessed clients through a process of ***advocacy*** and ***campaigning***.

'Advise, assist and befriend' is the well known catch-all description of the probation officer's role that was enshrined in legislation between 1905 and 1973. In the 1990 Government White Paper *'Crime, Justice and Protecting the Public'*, this has given way to a more hard headed formula. Here the aims of supervision of offenders are outlined as the:

- Protection of the public;
- Prevention of re-offending; and
- Successful re-integration of the offender in the community.

What is clear from this statement of aims is that the 'client' – the intended beneficiary of the probation officer's interventions – is 'the public' or 'the community' and not the probationer. This is a different emphasis from the one that has been traditionally held within the probation service where it is the probationer who has been seen and referred to as the 'client'. This is not to say that probation officers have not sought to encourage offenders to lead law abiding lives; nor is it the case that an approach which aims at 'protection of the public' and 'prevention of re-offending' discounts the possibility of offering 'help' to offenders. In practice the probation officer who sees 'the community' as client, and the PO who sees the probationer as client could be engaging in very similar types of tasks which are to do with meeting the practical, social and emotional needs of offenders. The difference would lie in their main reason for doing so.

For the one, the philosophical rationale would be that offenders merit help in their own right. If they benefit from this help, they may have been provided with the means of finding non-criminal solutions to their problems. The choice of whether they do so however, would ultimately rest with them. For the other, any help afforded is primarily instrumental. It is justified in so far as it minimises the risk of further offending.

Arguing in support of the former approach, Mark (1986) acknowledges its correctional limitations: 'The most anyone can do with offenders therapeutically is to increase the choices and control they have over their lives. This, of course, means that they may well change the type of offending they do, or even become "better adjusted criminals".'

Davies (1989) argues that 'such a persepective...does rather depend upon probation work being something which is, generally speaking, ancilliary to the correctional process itself, and more especially, independent of the punitive process .... The social work ethos ... is sustainable for only so long as the offenders allocated to probation officers are seen as being at the lesser end of the spectrum of seriousness.'

Interestingly, proponents of these two ideological perspectives tend also to espouse different theoretical bases in their working practices: the 'correctional' approach often being associated with use of **behavioural** techniques, directed in particular at modifying offending behaviour; whilst adherents to the 'social work' traditions of the probation service are likely to draw upon the more holistic or humanist ideas of **psycho-social** or **client- centred** theories to inform their practice. Whilst these theoretical preferences doubtless reflect different value bases, claims are also made for each on the more pragmatic gounds of what works best:

> Our experience leads us to believe that even if offenders are better equipped to deal with...problems in their personal lives, even if they do get jobs, manage their money better, and make better personal relationships, they may still go out and commit offences as well .... Rather than approach re-offending obliquely via all its allied difficulties, why not examine ways of avoiding becoming involved in actual offence behaviour? (Priestley et al. 1984)

In contrast Mark (*op cit*) asserts: 'the type of personality problems exhibited by the clients ... strongly suggests that their internalised view of themselves contributes strongly to their offending ... We can talk for hours on end to compulsive thieves about rational other ways of getting money and be surprised that they simply start stealing again ... Work with them, however, on a feelings level on issues of envy, guilt, greed ... and you begin to work on the very defences that they set up to protect them from influence and change.'

Important as it is to be clear, both about the moral purpose and theoretical underpinning of one's interventions, the argument surrounding these issues can often seem very remote to the probation officer confronted by a possibly distressed, possibly angry, possibly apathetic, possibly suspicious offender. The most immediate challenge here is to find some way of getting on with them, and working out what on earth can be done to fill up the time that you are going to have to spend together. For this, one draws very much upon one's own personal resources, and the key pre-requisite to any work being done, work of whatever type, is the ability to establish a relationship.

'When policies and procedures have run their courses, practice consists of human interaction between officer and offender' (Cooper 1987). Reiterating this same point, Hardiker and Willis (1989) comment: 'The interpersonal dimension cannot be denied. It may be possible to get social security benefits through a hole in the wall, but (so far) the banks and building societies have taken no interest in cash card social work. (Please press for advice, assistance or friendship!).'

Relationship Building

The diary entries in Chapter 1 illustrate ways in which the relationship between officer and offender can be a key element in the success (or otherwise) of supervision. Kay's confrontation of Ron in prison for example, could never have been effective if it had not taken place in the context of an accepting and understanding relationship. Without that, Kay's probing and challenging would have been experienced as intrusive, oppressive or blaming – and would have raised Ron's defences against reviewing his past or contemplating the possibility of future change.

Where relationships are problematic, this can undermine the possibility of any constructive work being undertaken. Seymour, in his first meeting with Dave, found himself at a loss when faced by Dave's evasiveness. At a stroke this pre-empted Seymour's pre-interview plans of 'getting to know each other a bit' and possibly sharing ideas on how they might 'do some work on controlling his (Dave's) temper and his heavy drinking.' The only place left for him to go after that, it seems, was to fall back onto (or was he pushed?) asserting the conditions of the order in a far more authoritarian way then he would have wished. Not surprisingly the experience left him feeling frustrated.

The pattern of this initial interview is one that many probation officers would recognise, and it is worth trying to identify some of the factors which contribute to this sort of outcome.

It is easy to say after the event but...one wonders if the groundwork for the probation order might have been more effectively laid at the report stage. In the preceding chapter we are

The probation order

reminded that, when a probation order is being considered: 'It is important to spell out the aims of the order, and how these are to be achieved, and to have negotiated these with defendants beforehand.' In the case of Dave, he gives no indication that such negotiation had ever taken place. Seymour was at something of a disadvantage because it was not he who had prepared the report and could not refer back to any prior discussions that may have taken place at that stage. It is a frequent occurrence that the supervising officer is *not* the one who prepared the report for the court. In these circumstances good communication between the report writer and the supervising officer is important. Such communication does not appear to have taken place in Seymour's case. He approached his initial interview with only the vaguest of ideas about what the order was supposed to be about. 'Do some work on controlling his temper and cutting down his drinking' is a pretty imprecise brief. We shall return to this later in the chapter when assessment and planning are considered. For the time being it is worth reiterating that clarity and agreement about what a probation order is *before* it is made, will forestall troubles later on. Failure to ensure this is (for all parties) akin to buying a used car without a test drive.

Having said this, even cars fresh off the assembly line, and bearing a three year warranty may sometimes perform disappointingly. More than one probation officer has encountered the probationer who, at the pre-sentence stage, acknowledged difficulties that had contributed to their offending, was motivated and welcomed the help of a probation officer. Then, but a short time later at the initial interview under the probation order, a transformation has taken place. The 'difficulties' have resolved themselves, or do not seem as important as they had done previously, or a way has been found of coping with them which need not involve the probation officer, or they are too intractable for it to be possible to do anything about anyway. The probation officer, who had been anticipating some rewarding work with a motivated client is suddenly faced with the prospect of a probation order which has lost its *raison d'être*. The next one, two or (perish the thought) three years loom like a yawning chasm that has to be filled with something purposeful. But what? and how do we understand this dramatic transformation?

It may be that the 'difficulties' were only ever a calculated device to attract the interest and sympathy of the PO conducting the enquiry. Clients cannot be unaware of the enthusiastic 'problem searching' to which probation officers are prone. It is, however, equally possible that no such cynical motive was at work. For many, most, or maybe all people who appear before a court it is something of a crisis. As we note when discussing **task-centred casework** in Chapter 13, in a state of crisis we are all much more open to contemplating change; the inadequacy of our habitual 'coping mechanisms' prompts us to search for new ones. We also know that, as a crisis subsides, the urgency to change diminishes. We regain, or find a new, equilibrium and there is no longer any necessity to contemplate the risks and uncertainty involved in altering our attitudes or behaviour. We should never underestimate the threat, effort and courage that is involved in the process of personal change. If we recognise this, we should not be too surprised, frustrated or disapproving at people's prevarications, denials and retreats when faced with the prospect of that change. In such circumstances the officer will be better served by patient and persistent responses rather than panicky or punitive ones.

Apprehension about the possibility of change may also be accompanied by ambivalence towards the probation officer. For the probationer the initial meeting with the probation officer will come hot on the heels of their court appearance. They may have found this stressful and humiliating. The probation officer, identified as s/he is with the court which has inflicted this unpalatable experience upon them, cannot automatically expect an open and trusting response: indeed they may be greeted with resentment, suspicion and mistrust. This may be overt and obvious, or masked beneath superficial politeness and compliance. Either way the probationer is unlikely to be a willing and co-operative partner in the planning of the 'work' that is to be undertaken during the order.

The reverse can also happen. The probation officer may be seen by the probationer as the champion of their cause, someone who rescued them from a harsh custodial sentence, and who will always be on their side. Gratifying as it may be for the PO to bask in the glow of such adulation, it is, in its own way, quite seductive and manipulative in that, to remain on this pedestal, the PO must divorce themselves from their role as agent of the ('bad') court.

Other factors will also impinge upon the relationship between the PO and the probationer. Differences (or similarities) in their racial or class origins, their gender and their age could affect the way in which they perceive and communicate with each other. The PO needs not only to be aware of, and deal with, any stereotypical views they themselves hold about particular categories of people, but also to openly acknowledge with the probationer such aspects which may affect the course of their relationship. There are many permutations, each of which will carry its own particular dynamic, that contain both pitfalls and potential for effective work being undertaken (see exercise 1 at the end of this chapter). Sensitive acknowledgement of differences, and the power differentials associated with them, does not, of itself, mean that these issues cease to be problematic, but it does pave the way for more open discussion between the parties involved.

The race, class and gender differences and similarities referred to above are undoubtedly crucial in determining how people perceive, communicate and relate to each other. It is also worth remembering however, that these may not necessarily be the issues which are foremost in the consciousness of all the people with whom probation officers work. For some, their view and judgement of the probation officer, and the way they relate together, will be determined by quite different criteria: the way s/he dresses, the type of car s/he drives, the sort of music s/he likes or who s/he reminds them of.

Whether the initial feelings between the PO and probationer are positive or negative, one can be sure that there *will be* feelings of some sort that derive from the probationer's experience of having been to court and/or of having been placed on probation, and/or the officer's race, class, gender, age, style of dress etc. These feelings will not necessarily be based in any reality of what the PO is actually like. To that extent they may get in the way of the probationer's willingness and/or ability to hear what is being said by the PO or to engage in joint planning on a realistic basis. As one of their 'opening moves' therefore, the PO needs to check out and acknowledge exactly what the probationer is feeling before a premature negotiation of a contract. This may be achieved by the simple expedient of some such question/statement: 'I expect you've got mixed feelings about having been put on probation.' More probably it will take more than just this before someone feels secure enough to admit to what they do feel, and to experience the PO as someone who can understand and accept this. We cannot in any case necessarily expect people to feel confident enough, or to be able to verbalise their feelings towards us, but we can be alert to when these are being expressed in other ways. Dave's testing of the limits of Seymour's authority, the way he winds Seymour up with sexist remarks, can be seen as Dave's method of finding out about, and, in his own way, negotiating, the sort of relationship he is going to have with his probation officer. Seen in this light, it could be as important to check out with Dave what lies behind his sexist remarks as it is to challenge the content of them.

Time spent on relationship building, on establishing honest communication, on creating a degree of mutual trust is seldom wasted.

Assessment, planning and contracts

This chapter has already given some consideration to the purpose of the probation order in general. In any individual case, however, there is the further question of 'what is the purpose of *this* particular probation order?' The answer to this requires careful and detailed thought and discussion with the probationer concerned. It has always been good practice for a probation officer and probationer to draw up an agreement, or 'contract', outlining what they are aiming to achieve, but the 1992 *Probation Service National Standards* make this obligatory

> If possible within two weeks of sentence (and within a maximum of four weeks) an individual supervision plan should be drawn up in writing for each offender, normally by the supervising officer. It should be based upon the requirements of the order (including any additional requirements) drawing, where appropriate, on the assessment and any outline proposals for supervision contained in the pre-sentence report .... A copy of the plan should be given to the offender and another should be held on the offender's case file.

It is, for example, important that, as far as possible, this planning is a genuinely shared process. The more that the probationer can be engaged in it, the more their perspectives can be acknowledged, their needs and concerns addressed, their motivation harnessed, the greater is the likelihood that the plans will bear fruit.

Engagement of the probationer does not however mean that the PO abrogates responsibility for their own contribution to the planning process. It is after all the PO who should have a greater understanding of what can reasonably be achieved within an order. It is not really good enough to confront the flummoxed probationer with such questions as 'what would you like to use the order for then?' or: 'Now what problems shall we work on?'. These questions are not in a form which will be meaningful to many people. Sitting in a room talking to someone is not what is generally understood by 'work'. The PO needs to take some initiative in explaining, better still demonstrating, the nature and purpose of this work that they might undertake together.

Quite apart from this, it does not always follow that a probationer's concerns and motivation are directed towards reducing their offending. Since offending is the reason for the order having been made in the first place, this may at times involve the PO in being pro-active in placing offence related

The probation order

issues upon the agenda. Seymour somewhat missed the boat on this in his initial interview with Dave.

In any work to be undertaken it helps to be clear about who the 'client system' is, i.e. who is intended to benefit as a result. This could be the probationer, the 'public', or indeed both. If issues can be found which do meet the requirements of both, then these would be the most promising areas upon which to focus attention. The officer should be prepared to engage in quite extensive exploration and negotiation with the probationer to secure agreement wherever possible. Figure 7.1 is a sample of the sort of alternative 'pathways' such exploration might follow.

Continuation of each of the dialogues would allow the probation officer to gain an understanding of the probationer's world, and at the same time allow him/her to offer for consideration alternative ways of viewing their situation – alternative ways in which they might handle things. The dialogue in the left hand column of Figure 7.1 might lead to work on understanding more about cause/effect relationships, the middle column about fatalism,

---

Asked to explain how the offence occurred the probationer says.

it just happened

'Why does it just happen to *you*?'	'So it could happen again at any time?'	'Didn't you have *any* control over what happened? couldn't you have walked away?'
'It doesn't. Everybody does it.'	'Maybe'	'You can't just walk away from things when your mates are around.'
'So why is that it's always you that gets caught?'	'Aren't you worried that you'll probably go down next time it happens?'	'What would they have done if you had?'
'Just bad luck that's all.'	'It couldn't be worse than being in this dump. Nothing to do. Can't get a job. You get treated like shit'	'You'd be a dead man. No one wants to know you if you bottle out.'

Figure 7.1 Sample explorations

depression and employment opportunities, the right hand column on ways of dealing with peer group pressures.

If an area of concern can be identified and agreed upon, then the next step would be to convert this concern into an objective. An objective should be capable of being expressed in the form of a statement which specifies as precisely as possible what the desired outcome is.

'To do some work on cutting down Dave's drinking' is not an objective because it does not describe an outcome, merely an activity – 'doing some work'. This may seem a pedantic point to make but unless an outcome is specified, there is no way of being sure *how* to work towards it.

For 'Dave to gain control of his drinking' *does* describe an outcome. It refers to a state of affairs that should be different as a result of the work undertaken. However it is not an altogether useful statement of an objective because it does not specify very precisely what 'gaining control' would consist of. Abstaining from drink altogether? – or on one day a week? – not mixing beer with spirits? – avoiding situations where there are social pressures to drink excessively?

The more concrete the terms in which an objective can be expressed the easier it will be to monitor progress towards it.

It is always important to select an objective that is realistically attainable. Something that is over ambitious risks failure. This is not only unfortunate in itself, but it can undermine confidence in any future efforts to bring about change.

The more ambitious aims may need to be approached in a series of sequential intermediate stages. If, for example, Dave's social life revolved around the pub, it might, as a first step, be useful for him to establish alternative social or recreational activities before making any attempt at modifying his drinking patterns.

It is useful to set (at least approximate) time limits for the achievement of any aims that have been identified. This helps to keep work focused.

Once an objective is established, the necessary next step is to identify *who* needs to do *what* in order to achieve the desired outcome, e.g. 'Before next week Terry will look through job adverts in the local paper and select ones for which he wishes to apply. PO will help Terry fill in application forms. Together they will practice how Terry might handle a selection interview'.

Useful concepts to aid clarity of thinking in the planning process are

Target system   The person/s or organisations who need to change if the aim is to be successful. This may be the probationer, but need not necessarily be. It may be key figures in the probationer's environment, members of their family, their school or work place. A 'system' encompasses the notion of interacting parts and one may conceive of a target system in terms of a *relationship*, e.g. a couple, where the target for change is not one or the other of them, but the way in which they communicate or make decisions.

Action system Many tasks to be undertaken will require the co-operation and assistance of people other than just the PO and probationer: other family members, club leaders, hostel wardens etc. Plans need to include who can usefully make a contribution and how they might best be 'recruited'.

The process outlined above has much in common with task centred work referred to in Chapter 13. The concreteness and clarity of this approach has much to commend it as a model for forming a contract for a probation order. It will not be applicable in all situations however. It does need at least a degree of willing participation from the probationer, and this may not always be forthcoming. There are moreover some areas of work the PO may wish to undertake which do not so easily lend themselves to the very precise, almost mechanistic processes of the task centred method. If, for example, the PO were to assess the key to all Dave's problems and offending as 'low self esteem' it would be quite feasible to attempt to use the supervisory relationship as a means of enhancing Dave's self image. But how do you build that into the contract? 'In discussion with Dave, the PO will use empathic responses and ego-supportive techniques to encourage Dave to build a more positive image of himself'? Making allowances for rather unfair and facetious use of jargon here, can one imagine Dave buying this? Would he understand it? If he did, would he not feel patronised by it? – and can genuine concern be so calculatingly 'operationalised' anyway?

Within any probation case load there are likely to be some probationers who do not seek change, do not acknowledge 'problems', who are not accustomed to the structured problem solving style of task centred work, who continually tussle with the probation officer over reporting and who, at best, merely go through the motions of co-operating. It can be demoralising for the PO, apparently left with no option but to also go through the motions of requiring compliance with an order that seems to be going nowhere.

And yet, ironically, it is precisely such orders that can sometimes go *somewhere* – not in spite of, but because of, the struggles surrounding the officer's authority. These, of themselves, generate material that can be worked with. The probationer's anger, fear or suspicion become immediate and accessible. In responding to these the PO may be getting to grips with the very issues which precipitated the offending in the first place.

Breach Proceedings

The probation officer's authority (referred to above) stems from the power (and duty) to return the probationer to court if s/he has failed to comply with the conditions of the order. This is a task about which many probation officers have mixed feelings. They may have misgivings about whether a re-appearance at court will have any constructive outcome, or reluctance to jeopardise a 'helping relationship' by invoking coercive sanctions. Against this, probation officers are also aware of their responsibility to ensure that court orders are carried out, and concerned that probationers should face up to the consequences of their own actions.

It is clear that, in the past, officers have used a degree of discretion about whether or not to institute breach proceedings, and that there has been some variation in practice, both between individual officers, and between different probation areas. The Home Office has taken action to redress these inconsistencies: the *Probation Service National Standards* (1992) requires that 'breach action should normally be taken after no more than three instances of non-compliance with the order. Further continuation without breach action, in limited circumstances only, may only take place if agreed with the sentencer in a particular case or if approved by a senior probation officer as being strongly in the interests of the objectives of the order'.

Instituting breach procedings involves the supervising officer in applying to a magistrate for a summons to bring the probationer before the court. If contact with the probationer has been lost and his/her whereabouts are unknown the PO would apply for a warrant for his/her arrest. In applying for this the officer has to give information on oath (or affirmation), and in doing so will need to have considered whether the warrant should be 'backed for bail' which means that, after the police have arrested the probationer, they may release him/her on bail pending the court hearing.

When the matter comes before the court the probation officer occupies the unfamiliar role of prosecutor. In complicated or controversial situations it may be necessary for the case to be presented by a solicitor but this is not a usual practice. The probationer will be asked by the court if they admit the breach. If they do the PO merely has to give an outline of the circumstances of it. If, on the other hand, the breach is not admitted then the PO must offer proof of it to the court. In presenting evidence to the court the PO must establish that the probationer is subject to an order and the date on which it was made, and substantiate the nature of the breach. In doing this the rules of evidence must be observed, i.e. 'hearsay' evidence is not permitted. Unlike in a pre-sentence report, opinions are not admissible. Evidence must be restricted to facts. The probation officer may produce any relevant documentary evidence, e.g. a copy and receipt for a recorded delivery letter instructing the probationer to report. She can also produce any witnesses who can offer evidence relating to the breach. Both the probation officer and any witnesses may be cross questioned by the probationer (or their legal representative). The probationer also has an opportunity to give their account, and, when this is finished, the probation officer has an opportunity to challenge the accuracy of the account by cross questioning. If the court find the breach proved then the officer can revert to the more familiar courtroom role of advising the court on the disposal of the case.

Endings

Just as we noted that the initial stages of a probation order might elicit particular sorts of feelings or reactions in the probationer, so there are characteristic reactions and feelings that may be provoked by the prospect of the order ending, particularly if the contact has had some significance for the probationer. The nature and intensity of such reactions may, in part, be determined by the way the probationer has experienced, and coped, with loss and endings in the past.

The reactions may include:

- a denial that contact will actually come to an end;
- reminiscence about what has been done together, and possibly a 'regressive' re-enactment of some of the earlier stages of the relationship;
- disparagement of the value of the order;
- idealisation of the value of the order;
- panic at the prospect of losing a source of support;
- premature 'switching off' (sometimes accompanied by non-reporting).

The fact that many probationers will be only too relieved to get the order over and done with, does not mean that they cannot experience any of these reactions. Such reactions are, after all, characteristic of anyone who is faced with impending loss or change. There is nothing particularly 'wrong' with them but the probation officer will need to be sensitive to what is happening and respond supportively.

Much can be done well in advance of the end of the order to ease the termination of contact. The plans of work should always be related to the time scale available, e.g. a six month order should not be used to tackle long term issues. From time to time it may be worthwhile to remind the probationer of the time-limited nature of the relationship, to give them full opportunity to anticipate its termination.

Perhaps most important of all, the probation officer should continually be alert to fostering the probationer's independence. It can be very tempting to prove one's usefulness to a probationer by doing helpful things for them. This does little to enhance their autonomy or capacity to cope once the order is completed. It is in these respects that probation can make the most lasting impact upon the prevention of offending.

Exercise 1: Differences and similarities

The respective race, class and gender of probation officer and probationer are likely to have implications for how they perceive each other and communicate together. This exercise invites you to consider how *your* race/class/gender position might present you with either *pitfalls* or *possibilities* in your work with offenders. Use the boxes in Figure 7.2 p119 to make notes about how you think your work might be affected when the probationer shares with you, or differs from you, in respect of race, class or gender. It might be useful for you to discuss the results with colleagues, practice teacher or senior.

Exercise 2: Planning

This exercise is designed to give you practice in being clear and purposeful in planning how you might work with someone under a probation order.

We are told in Chapter 1 that Dave has difficulty in controlling his temper. In this exercise you are asked to:

(a) Assume that you are embarking upon supervising Dave on a probation order.

	SAME AS YOU	DIFFERENT FROM YOU
RACE		
	SAME AS YOU	DIFFERENT FROM YOU
CLASS		
	SAME AS YOU	DIFFERENT FROM YOU
GENDER		

Figure 7.2

(b) Assume that his 'temper' is an issue you wish to address.
(c) Use the planning process described in the preceding chapter by working through the following list of questions.

1. For whose benefit would you be undertaking this activity (i.e. who is the client system?). Is it Dave? – exclusively? Or the court? – exclusively? Or both? – in equal measure? Your answer to this will inluence whether (and the extent to which) Dave might be expected to be a willing accomplice in the work to be undertaken.
2. Convert the concerns about Dave's temper into a goal statement, i.e. describe as specifically as possible the

outcome that you would expect to result from your intervention. Your statement should be realistic and concrete. (Ideally of course Dave himself should be involved in doing this with you, but for the purposes of this exercise you will have to make unilateral decisions.)

3. For the above outcome to be achieved *who* or *what* would need to change in some way? (i.e. who or what is the target system?)
4. Which people or organisations would need to be involved? (i.e. who would constitute the action system?)
5. Can the outcome you have identified in 2. (above) be attained directly, or would you need to work towards it in stages? If so, identify what they might be.
6. Having clarified what you want to achieve, and the steps by which you aim to achieve it, identify (a) the tasks that would need to be undertaken, (b) who should be responsible for undertaking them, and (c) the time scale within which the tasks should be completed:

Exercise 3: Knowledge check

Tick the appropriate column against each of the following statements

TRUE FALSE

1. One year is the minimum period for which a probation order can be made.
2. Once a probation order has been made, its length cannot be varied.
3. 15 year olds cannot be placed on probation.
4. Offenders under 21 do not need to consent to the conditions of a probation order.
5. Before a condition of psychiatric treatment can be inserted in a probation order, reports are required from two psychiatrists.
6. Twelve months is the maximum period for a condition of treatment in the case of a sex offender.
7. Probation committees are responsible for approving 'approved' hostels.

The probation order   121

		TRUE	FALSE

8. Probationers are obliged to receive visits from their probation officer in their own home.
9. Section 4B (CJA 1982) refers to probation centre requirements in a probation order.
10. A probationer may apply to the court for their order to be discharged.
11. It is possible for a probation order to be amended to a conditional discharge.
12. If a probationer is convicted of a further offence during their probation order then, for the offence for which they were *originally* placed on probation, they can be fined and the order allowed to continue.
13. If a probationer is found to have breached the conditions of their probation order then, for the offence for which they were *originally* placed on probation, they can be fined and the order allowed to continue.

Answer overleaf

Answers

1. False
2. True
3. True
4. False
5. False
6. False
7. False
8. True
9. True
10. True
11. True
12. False
13. True

References

Cooper, 1987 'Probation practice in the criminal and civil courts' in Harding, (ed.) *Probation and the Community* p.40.
Davies, 1989 *The Nature of Probation Practice Today*, Home Office, p.9.
Hardiker, and Willis, 1989 'Cloning Probation Officers', *Howard Journal*, **28**, no. 4.
Home Office 1990 *Crime Justice and Protecting the Public* HMSO.
Home Office 1992. *Probation Service National Standards* HMSO.
Mark, 1986 'Offending behaviour or better adjusted criminals' *Probation Journal* December 1986.
Priestley, et al. 1984 *Social Skills in Prison and the Community*, RKP, p.170.

8 Working with offenders II: pre- and post-release supervision

License supervision

Young offenders and adults

All prisoners serving a sentence of more than twelve months are subject to **automatic conditional release** on licence or **discretionary release** on licence and the probation service has a statutory duty to supervise these licences. The conditions of a licence are that the client must report on release to the supervising PO without delay; keep in touch with the PO as instructed, and receive visits from the PO at home; inform the PO of any change of address or employment; be of good behaviour and lead an industrious life'; not travel abroad without permission. Additional conditions may also be added (e.g. as to residence or medical treatment). Importantly, the period of post-release supervision is just as much a part of the sentence as the period spent in prison. Adult prisoners (18+) serving a sentence of less than 12 months are released unconditionally after half of their sentence and are not subject to statutory supervision. Young offenders serving less than 12 months in a young offenders' institution, or detained in a community home or youth treatment centre under section 53 of the 1933 Children and Young Persons Act are, however, subject to post-release supervision.

'Short-term' prisoners serving between 12 months and 4 years are subject to **automatic conditional release** on licence after half of their sentence and are supervised until three quarters of it has elapsed.

Long term prisoners serving *4 years or more* will be released on licence after two thirds of their sentence. However, the Secretary of State *may* release any long term prisoner (including young offenders) after they have served *half* of their sentence, if recommended to do so by the **parole board**. [C.J Act 1991, s, 35 (1)]. At whatever stage they may be released, long term prisoners are subject to their parole licence until three quarters of their sentence has elapsed.

Just to make things a little more complicated, there are a number of exceptions to these arrangements

(a) *Young offenders*: all young offenders under the age of 22 years on release will be subject to 3 months supervision if they are serving less than 12 months provided that this does not take them beyond their 22nd birthday.

(b) *Sexual offenders*: some may be supervised until the end of their sentence, if the sentencing judge considers this necessary in order to protect the public.

(c) *Fine defaulters/contempt of court*: these offenders will be released on licence but are not subject to supervision. As far as release is concerned the rules for short – and long-term prisoners apply.

(d) *Deportees*: they are also governed by the rules for short – and long-term offenders. They will also be released on licence but are not subject to supervision.

In the case of life prisoners the Secretary of State may order their release on licence, if recommended to do so by the **parole board**, and after consultation with the Lord Chief Justice and the trial judge (if available). The licence remains in force for life.

Discretionary life prisoners are those prisoners whose offences do not carry a mandatory life sentence and they may be released in a similar way, but not before they have completed the portion of their sentence which may have been specified by the trial judge.

The Secretary of State may release a prisoner on licence at any time if he is satisfied that exceptional circumstances exist which justify the prisoner's release on compassionate ground. In such cases the licence remains in force until completion of half the sentence for those serving less than 12 months, and until completion of three-quarters of the sentence for those serving more than 12 months and until death for those serving life sentences.

Sanctions for breach of licence conditions

Prisoners subject to **automatic conditional release** may be prosecuted for a breach of their licence in a magistrates' court

Pre- and post-release supervision

Category	Unconditional release	Automatic conditional release	Discretionary release on recommendation of parole board	Duration of licence
Young offender Sentence of less than 12 months	–	After half of the sentence	–	Until 3 months or three quarters of the sentence
Adult offender Sentence of less than 12 months	After half of the sentence	–	–	–
Sentence of more than 12 months & less than 4 years	–	After half of the sentence	–	Until three-quarters of the sentence
Sentence of over 4 years	–	After two thirds of sentence	After half of the sentence	Until three-quarters of sentence
Life sentence	–	–	No specific period	Life
Discretionary life sentence	–	–	After period specified by the sentencing court	Life
Release on compassionate grounds when sentence is less than 12 months	–	–	At any stage	Until half of the sentence
Release on compassionate grounds when sentence is over 12 months	–	–	At any stage	Until three-quarters of sentence

Figure 8.1 Release on licence, a summary

which has the power to impose a fine of up to £1000, order a return to custody for a maximum of six months or the outstanding period of the licence, if that is less, or both.

Whether, when and how sanctions are invoked will depend on whether the breach occurs:

(a) as a result of a further offence committed during the licence period; or
(b) other conditions, e.g. keeping contact with a probation officer, being breached.

In the event of a further offence, the court may, whether or not it imposes another sentence, return the licencee to prison. In this case, the additional period of imprisonment will amount to the number of days between the date on which the offence in question is committed and the date on which the licence would have ended.

If the period between the offence and the end of the licence exceeds six months a magistrate may commit the licensee to Crown Court for sentencing and the sentence may run concurrently or consecutively with the period the parolee spends in prison because of the revocation of parole. In the case of a long term prisoner released on parole (discretionary conditional release) breaches of the licence conditions are reported to the parole board (usually via a PO of chief officer grade) which will take a decision about whether or not to recall to prison.

Breach proceedings

When conditions other than by the commission of an offence have been breached, the most likely being a failure to keep an appointment, the PO will usually respond by writing a letter or making a home visit to express concern about the missed appointment and to remind the licensee of the terms of the licence and the time and date of an alternative meeting.

The *Probation Service National Standards* (1992) on supervision indicate that if the licensee fails to keep a second appointment a written warning should be sent or breach proceedings instituted and that on the third occasion proceedings should be instituted (Home Office 1992). In some 'limited' circumstances. POs may waive breach proceedings despite failure to keep appointments if this is approved by their 'manager' 'as being in the best interests of the objectives of supervision'. This might well be the case where you are working with licensees who, because of addiction, homelessness, a peripatetic lifestyle or mental health problems have difficulty in keeping appointments.

Failure, on the part of licensees, to keep appointments should be noted on part C records and the SPO kept informed.

In the case of offenders on **automatic conditional release** licences, breaches will normally be linked to licence conditions but for licencees on **discretionary release** the *Probation Service National Standards* (Home Office 1992) indicate that other factors should also be taken into consideration when considering breach proceedings. These are situations where:

(a) a licensee's behaviour is such that a further serious offence is likely to be committed;
(b) the safety of the public may be at risk;
(c) a licensee's behaviour, although not involving direct risk to the public, seems likely to bring the licence system into disrepute.

If, for example, Ron, despite warnings from the supervising PO, persistently sought opportunities to be alone with young children then (a) and (b) might be said to obtain. On the other hand, (c) raises some worrying ethical issues. For example, will POs be under pressure to breach licencees who are persistent, voluble, solvent intoxicated, public nuisances because of their offensive, but legal, behaviour?

The licensees

With the changes ushered in by the 1991 CJ Act POs will be dealing with a greater number of, often, more serious and more needy offenders than they have in the past. It is important to remember than post-release supervision constitutes part of the penalty imposed on the client and may well mean that many of the people we are supervising will be at least ambivalent about having to work with us, and possibly quite resistant to it.

Well over half of the people in prison have a history of institutionalisation. The majority will have spent some time, and some will have spent their entire childhoods, in the Care system. A study of the mental health of prisoners concludes that 17 per cent of male prisoners, 19.9 per cent of young adults and 32.6 per cent of women in prisons have been diagnosed as mentally ill (Gunn 1991). The majority will have had problems of addiction to drink or drugs which will have contributed to their offending. Add to this the fact that the overwhelming majority will come out of prison to financial difficulties and a sizable minority will be effectively homeless and we can conclude that throughcare is no job for softies (Pitts 1992).

Personal safety

POs will be meeting more violent and dangerous people than in the past. How safe you feel, and how safe you are, will be determined to some degree by your own skill and knowledge, but in large part by the policies and administrative and organisational initiatives taken by your office and service. You must find out what they are, discuss them with your senior, union representative and colleagues until you are satisfied that, in as much as it is possible, you are working in a safe environment. And remember, there are no prizes for heroics. The world is full of cowards; five of them wrote this book. So when in doubt, RUN.

Supervision and its discontents

Many ex-prisoners feel that compulsory post release supervision is an infringement of their liberty and they resent it. Failure to comply with conditions of licences not unusual and sometimes result in court action, fines and custodial sentences. However, this is a group of people who are particularly prone to unemployment, homelessness, alcohol and drug abuse, mental illness and HIV/AIDS and most of these factors are closely associated with reconviction and custodial sentencing. There is, therefore, a question to be answered about whether the probation service will attempt to maintain voluntary contact with the most vulnerable people and, if so, how this might best be done.

In the past, some probation officers have developed very successful 'drop-in' after care projects in which clients were able to talk to the PO they chose and were given practical help and support in job and accomodation hunting and education and training. Other officers developed 'detached' (street) after care which attempted to carry these services out to where the young people were and, in cases in which clients were vulnerable to infection because of their involvement in prostitution or drugs, the dispensation of condoms and syringes.

The tasks of the probation officer in pre- and post-release supervision

The Home Office locates the individual *sentence plan*, constructed by prison officers in conjunction with prison POs at the centre of effective pre- and post-sentence release supervision

(Home Office 1992). No mention is made of the contribution the prisoner might make to the plan but it is not unreasonable to assume that if they are party to it, they will be more likely to comply with it. It is intended that the sentence plan will inject greater coherence into the work of the field and prison POs and prison officers involved with the prisoner, and greater continuity between work undertaken in the prison and after release.

The *Probation Service National Standards* identify 'protection of the public', 'prevention of reoffending' and 'successful reintegration into the community' as the primary objectives of throughcare. It is, however, reasonable to assume that the public is best protected if re-offending is reduced and successful re-integration into the community is achieved. This will be more likely if the personal deterioration which more often than not afflicts people who are confined to prison can be ameliorated and prisoners' families, who often suffer great emotional and material stress as a result of the imprisonment of a partner or parent, can be supported.

We can therefore identify five key elements in the pre- and post-release supervision task

1. Reducing the risk of further offending.
2. Minimising personal deterioration.
3. Assisting and working with prisoners' families.
4. Assisting resettlement in the community.
5. Preparing pre-discharge and home circumstances reports.

Reducing the risk of further offending

In terms of government policy and the stated objectives of the service, this is the key throughcare task, not least because of escalating levels of recorded crime. Whether, in fact, England and Wales, are really besieged by lawbreakers (things are rather different in Scotland and Northern Ireland) is another question.

If we are working with our clients on the issue of future offending we will usually be working on their attitudes, their behaviour, or both. It is much less likely that we will be working on the question of restricting criminal opportunity although where this has been attempted the results have been very encouraging.

You will usually be working with your client towards an acknowledgement that they did, in fact, commit the offence/s for which they were sentenced. It should be noted however that if your client maintains that she/he didn't do it and, as we know from recent experience, some of them did not, then this approach will not work. Assuming that they acknowledge the offence/s, you will probably explore the fact that their offence/s had consequences for the victims and that their conviction and sentence had consequences for them and those closest to them. You will undoubtedly also raise the problem that, were they to commit similar offences in the future, they might well be arrested, prosecuted and imprisoned again, not least because they are now much better known to the police.

This seemingly straightforward encounter with reality is often very difficult to facilitate because of the very understandable tendency of our clients to defend themselves psychologically against their guilt and the grim reality of their predicament. This is done by denying, or clinging to a distorted picture of, the actions which brought them to prison and the impact of those actions upon themselves and others. Imprisonment compounds this tendency by placing together, in a confined space, people who share nothing but the fact that they are not very good at getting away with crime. Having failed at it in real life they must elaborate a fantasy of criminal success in order to keep up with the Joneses in the next cell. It is not for nothing that both Hollywood and Wormwood Scrubs are described as the 'dream factory'.

You may remember the first meeting between Kay the student PO and Ron in Chapter 1. Ron was adamant that what he was doing with his 'victims' was not improper. He denied that he had abused the children saying that what he had done was an expression of love which had been reciprocated by the children.

Kay was aware of Ron's feelings about his mother's death and felt that she should focus on this first. Thus she chose to help him express his grief and try to come to terms with his disabling feelings of loss and isolation. Nonetheless, she felt it was important to indicate to Ron that she did not accept his account of his offending and that she intended to return to it.

Challenging clients about their view of, and attitudes towards, offending can be uncomfortable for them and for us but change often involves a great deal of discomfort. This said, the PO must chart a careful course between a confrontation which debilitates the client with guilt and remorse or drives them into a stonewall denial, and an approach which skates over the important questions and changes nothing. As in all other areas of social work, active listening, empathy, reflection and the sensitive use of non-verbal cues constitute the basic skills of inter-personal work in throughcare.

You are working towards a recognition on the part of the offender that they had, and have, a choice in the way their lives unfold. You are, in addition, encouraging them to develop a realistic vision of what a life without crime would be like and an understanding of the steps they might need to take to achieve this goal. **Task-centred casework** indicates that the steps should not be so large that they cause the client to 'fall at the first fence', nor so small that no sense of achievement is gained.

This said, the choices available to the client will appear more plausible to them if they feel that they are in a position to effect such choices. To this end, the PO may well find themselves involved in some strenuous **advocacy** with statutory and voluntary agencies in the areas of housing, employment, education and training and state benefits in the first few weeks after the client's release.

Minimising personal deterioration

Initially at least, the experience of imprisonment tends to take a heavy toll on an individual's sense of personal dignity. For women, who are often the sole or primary carers for children, the impact of imprisonment is often even greater. It throws into question their adequacy as women and mothers both for themselves and for the individuals and agencies which may have assumed responsibility for their children.

Reactions to imprisonment for both men and women may range from a reckless determination to fight the system every inch of the way, on one hand, to silent withdrawal on the other. Whatever the strategy, the danger of personal deterioration in terms of institutionalisation, depression, detachment from reality or over-identification and the adoption of a 'convict' persona, are ever-present (Mathiesen 1964, Gallo and Roggerio 1991).

Prisoners who are vulnerable to harrassment and attack by other prisoners are in particular danger of personal deterioration. These are the sex offenders, those who have incurred gambling or other debts while inside, and 'informers', who are placed on 'rule 43'. This has usually meant that they have been segregated on a special landing in the prison but both the prisoners and prison officers are aware of the inadequacy of this strategy. Recently, the Home Office Prison Department has developed vulnerable prisoner units and this initiative was given added urgency during the Strangeways riot of 1991 in which rule 43 prisoners were attacked and tortured.

As we have noted, a substantial minority of prisoners have been diagnosed as mentally ill. Whatever we might think of the diagnosis we have to acknowledge that in most cases the suffering is all too real. In these cases POs strive to ensure that, in as much as it is possible, their client is receiving the best and most appropriate treatment available. The other side of this coin is that other prisoners, because their behaviour poses a threat to 'good order' or, more rarely, because it is regarded as subversive, are treated as if they were mentally ill. Women, gay and black prisoners are particularly prone to such mistreatment or mis-diagnosis. Sometimes, you may find that you will need to support a prisoner's application for a move to another prison.

Pursuing possible injustices of this sort will not make you very popular but it may well be very important to your client and, even in these 'hard-headed' times, working in 'the client's best interest' remains a cornerstone of good professional practice.

It is intended that from 1 October 1992 prison officers and prison POs will be parties to, and active in realising the goals of, the sentence plans of prisoners serving over 12 months. While the primary responsibility for the plan lies with the prison it is intended that the field PO will provide information about home circumstances and community resources. PPOs and prison officers, for their part, will be responsible for identifying problems and issues to be addressed by the supervising field PO and the prisoner after release.

In some prisons, PPOs run specialist groupwork programmes which focus upon forms of offending behaviour, including sexual offending, addictions or the social skills required by prisoners who are about to be released. These latter groups are often conducted with prison officers.

Assisting and working with prisoners' families

It is important in your dealings with prisoners not to think exclusively in terms of the 'traditional' family. Not all prisoners will be part of such families and yet their emotional bonds with, and their concerns and anxieties about those who are emotionally closest to them will be equally profound. In assisting and working with prisoners' families, it is vital that we take into consideration those who are referred to in social work jargon as 'significant others'. This might be a gay or lesbian partner, a particular member or section of an extended family network or a close friend. Such individuals or groups, will be equally, if differently, affected by the custodial sentence imposed by the court.

Working with loss, and subsequently with reunion, involves working with complex emotions. People on the outside may feel angry, guilty, distressed, lost or relieved when the person closest to them is suddenly removed from their lives. They may need help in coming to terms with the reality of the loss and their, sometimes ambivalent, feelings about it. Beyond this there are often pressing practical problems of money, accommodation and child-minding.

Having made the adjustment to the loss, the family is then required to receive the prisoner back into its midst. Often the family has changed. Children may have grown older or grown up. Partners may have developed new skills, found new friends or formed new relationships.

These are just some of the issues you may need to address in working with prisoner's families as the date of release approaches. An important question for you to consider is how to encourage and foster good, open communications; not only between yourself and the family and yourself and the client, but between the family and the prisoner. Unless this latter task is undertaken probation officers can find themselves ending up as the scapegoat in a highly-charged family conflict. Ultimately, the role of the probation officer with a prisoner's family is to enable them to effect realistic choices about their predicament and deal, as creatively as possible, with the debilitating effects that imprisonment has upon all those who are closely associated with the person who is imprisoned. From time to time it may be appropriate to refer some family members to other agencies or organisations, prisoners' wives' groups, Gingerbread, black prisoners support groups etc. This should, of course, only be done with the prior agreement of the people in question.

On a practical level, working with, or assisting, prisoners' families can involve negotiation with the Department of Social Security, for travel permits, and benefits; with the housing department about rent or liaison with the social services department over **child protection**.

Some families or significant others, may want very little to do with you, except when the possibility of home leave or parole is mooted. In such case, you have no option but to respect that choice.

Assisting resettlement in the community

In part, in pursuing the above three goals; reducing the risk of further offending, minimising personal deterioration and working with prisoners' families, you will have already begun to pave the way for the offenders' resettlement in the community. Immediately prior to release however you will be focusing on the fears, confusions and fantasies your client may have about their re-entry into the community. This will involve you in helping them to think clearly about the problems they will encounter in their attempts to re-establish themselves in their social network and lead a law-abiding life.

In Ron's case, for example, Kay might well encourage him to consider the wisdom of returning to the area in which he committed his offences. She would also be concerned to ensure that Ron was not looking for a job or a place to live which brought him into close contact with young children. Beyond this she would probably be confronting Ron with his need to undergo treatment in an ex-sex offenders' group.

At a practical level, your client may need up-to-date and accurate information about state benefits, social security, housing or hostel accommodation, jobs and training schemes in the locality, run by the government or voluntary organisations like NACRO or the Apex Trust. They will probably also need application forms if they are to use these resources and they may well require help in completing them.

It may well be at the point where your client's personal circumstances have stabiliised that they become aware of a void in their life which was once filled by the excitement and challenge of offending and/or heavy drinking or drugs. This was the problem that Kay tried to tackle with Terry when she visited him at the Young Offender Institution. Terry's previous drug-taking, his low self-esteem and lack of any sense of direction in his life rang alarm bells for Kay, suggesting that he could easily drift back into crime. Kay tried to present Terry with the reality of his predicament, to get him to think about it seriously and make concrete and achievable plans for his release.

It is largely as a result of a recognition of how difficult, and how important, the period immediately following release can be in determining whether a prisoner will 'go straight' or not, that temporary release schemes were introduced. These schemes allow prisoners to spend a few days 'at home' prior to release. During this period they register at the job centre, with social security, the housing department and/or other relevant agencies, to meet potential employers and spend some time talking with family and friends about their release. Some probation areas run temporary release schemes in which field officers and PPOs work with prisoners on what they want to achieve from their temporary release and what the experience has meant to them. This usually involves a small group of prisoners from the same area and they are able to compare notes and support one another when, for example, things at home are not quite as they had hoped.

Writing pre-release or home circumstances reports

In the case of an offender in the *automatic conditional release* category a pre-discharge report is prepared by the supervising officer. This will tend to be brief, simply stating the circumstances to which the prisoner is to return in the community and whether any other conditions in the licence would be advisable. For those in the *discretionary release* category a home circumstances report is required which will play a part in the parole board's decision-making.

In both types of report you would normally be expected to make some comment about:

1. The home to which the offender intends to return, who lives there, their relationship to the client finances and the offending histories, if any, of other members of the household.
2. The family's attitude towards the offender and his or her homecoming. The willingness of other members of the household to have the offender back and the nature and level of the contact which has been maintained during the sentence; Whether there have been visits and letters and the frequency of these. In doing this one is attempting to establish the stability and support the individual is likely to receive from significant others.
3. Alternative options if the offender cannot return home or has no home.
4. The attitude of people in the local community, including victims, towards the offender. This would be particularly important in a case, such as Ron's, which evoked both fear and outrage in the local community.
5. The offender's attitude to the offence. If you are arguing that this has changed in the period between their conviction and the present, this can be supported by citing what the offender is currently saying about their offence and comparing it with what they were saying at the time the SIR/PSR report was prepared, if one was available.
6. Response to previous periods of supervision. This could be established by reference to both previous records and the SIR/PSR.
7. Recommendations regarding special licence conditions. It may be that you think that release should be conditional upon the offender receiving treatment from a named psychiatrist or psychotherapist, or residing for a specified

period in a particular rehabilitation unit. If this is your view it is important that you (a) discuss it with, and gain the agreement of, the offender, (b) liaise, and make arrangements with the appropriate body, and (c) detail the conditions in your report. If your recommendation is followed, these conditions will form additional grounds upon which the licence might be revoked in the event of non-compliance. Conditions should therefore be used carefully and sparingly.
8. Views about the need for specialist provision when managing the offender in the community and its relevance to group work programmes and appropriate licence conditions.
9. A programme of supervision incorporating an assessment of likely responses to supervision and proposals for managing this, including frequency of contact. You might draw upon the offender's previous responses to supervision or licence, if applicable, and the views of the probation officer responsible for preparing the SIR/PSR if there was one. You will also have formed your own views from your knowledge and experience of the offender.
10. The prisoner's response to discussions of the objectives of supervision.
11. An assessment of the risk of re-offending.

Throughcare, properly resourced, can be a very rewarding area of work. As with many aspects of probation practice, if you establish a good beginning in terms of building a relationship and purposeful planning with a client, this will provide a solid foundation for what will follow.

Finally, never forget the first essential rule of throughcare – keep your I.D. card with you at all times, since attempts to gain entry to a high security prison on the Isle of Wight by producing a bus pass are rarely successful.

Throughcare knowledge check – questions

1. Claudette was sentenced to 15 months imprisonment, what is her earliest date of release?
2. Will Terry, who was sentenced to 12 months in a young offenders' institution, have to be supervised by a PO upon his release?
3. What are the conditions of a licence?
4. Under what circumstances can a client be said to be in breach of their parole licence?

5. Ron has been sentenced to 10 years imprisonment, what is his earliest date of release?
6. For how long after his release will Ron be subject to supervision under licence?

Answers

1. Claudette will be automatically released on licence after half of her sentence ($7\frac{1}{2}$ months) has elapsed. She will be subject to that licence supervision until three-quarters of her sentence ($11\frac{1}{4}$ months) has elapsed. So the period she will spend on licence supervision will be $3\frac{3}{4}$ months.
2. Because his sentence falls into the category of '12 months or more', he is subject to licence supervision until three-quarters of it has elapsed. Thus he will be automatically released on licence on completion of half of his sentence (6 months) and supervised until three-quarters of the sentence (9 months) has elapsed. Had he been serving less than 12 months, Terry would have been released unconditionally on completion of half of his sentence.
3. The conditions of a licence are as follows, the client must:
    (i) report on release to the supervising PO without delay;
    (ii) keep in touch with the PO as instructed, and receive visits from the PO at home;
    (iii) inform the PO of any change of address or employment;
    (iv) be of good behaviour and lead an industrious life';
    (v) not travel abroad without permission. Additional conditions may also be added (e.g. as to residence or medical treatment).
4. Technically, failure to comply with any of the above conditions constitutes a breach. Explanations must be sought for such breaches and the PO must decide if these are reasonable/acceptable. If they are not, breach action must be taken.
5. Ron's earliest date of release would normally be when two-thirds of his ten year sentence had elapsed, i.e. on completion of 6 years and 8 months. However, because Ron is serving a sentence of over four years, the Secretary of State, on the advice of the parole board, may release Ron on completion of half of his sentence (5 years).
6. If Ron were to be released when two-thirds of his ten year sentence has elapsed (6 years and 8 months) he would be

supervised under licence until three-quarters of his sentence (7 years and 6 months) was completed. Thus the period of supervision would be 1 year and 10 months. If he was released at the half-way stage by the Secretary of State, on the advice of the Parole Board, his period of supervision would be 2 years and 6 months. However, as he is a sex offender he can be supervised up until the end of his sentence if so ordered by the trial judge.

References

Gallo, E. and Ruggerio, V. (1991) *Custody as a Factory for the Manufacture of Handicaps* Enfield: Middlesex Polytechnic Centre for Criminology.
Gunn, J. (1991) *Meeting the Need* London: Home Office.
Home Office (1992) *Draft Probation Service National Standards* London: Home Office.
Mathiesen, T. (1964) *The Defenses of the Weak* London: Tavistock.
Pitts, J. (1992) 'The end of an era' *The Howard Journal* 31, No. 2, May 1992.

9 Child protection and the probation service

The probation service is not of course primarily a child protection agency. However, there are two sets of circumstances in which probation officers can become involved with child protection issues:

- When the service has an involvement with a member of a household where a child is considered to be at risk of physical, sexual, or emotional abuse or neglect;
- When the service has an involvement with a client who is identified specifically as representing a risk to children.

Between them, these categories embrace a range of possibilities including both statutory and voluntary clients, and those upon whom reports are being prepared. All probation services will have policies regarding procedures in such cases and it is important that you familiarise yourself with these.

In all cases, the welfare of the child is the paramount consideration and supersedes everything else, including the interests of your individual client. To this end, the objective of any work undertaken will be twofold:

- working with those who pose a threat to children to reduce the risk of further offending;
- working with other professionals to protect the child.

As probation students, or first year officers/new entrants, you should not be expected to take responsibility for child protection cases. However, as the whole issue of child protection is very much a feature of everyday social work, in all kinds of settings, it is important to know about the procedures and processes, as well as signs to look out for. It is not beyond the bounds of possibility that you will be the first to discover some cause for concern in a particular case.

The role of the probation officer

Because of the pressures on local authorities, there are situations where children are on area child protection registers but are unallocated to a social worker. If a probation officer has statutory involvement with the family, there may be pressure to undertake the role of key worker, out of human kindness as much as anything else. The key worker is the professional identified at the case conference as the one with overall responsibility for coordinating intervention aimed at protecting the child but is not necessarily the worker who has the most extensive contact with the family. It is generally agreed within the probation service that pressure to undertake the role of key worker should be resisted at all costs as the service has neither the statutory powers nor the resources to intervene appropriately. However, even though one may not be formally named as the key worker, it will feel a very grave responsibility to be the only worker regularly in touch with a family if there is no allocated social worker and you will certainly be expected to visit the home, see the child, and keep both the senior probation officer and the social services department fully informed. Where there is an allocated social worker undertaking the role of key worker, it is essential to establish from the outset your respective roles and maintain regular liaison – as Seymour in his work with Dawn discovered (see Chapter 1).(HMSO[1991])

There are specific duties and responsibilities relating to offenders convicted of offences against children. Particular vigilance is required here, and in all cases, consultation is necessary with the local social services department, to alert them to the presence of such an offender in the area. With regard to prisoners being considered for parole, full discussion should take place at the earliest opportunity and the views of the local authority included in any reports prepared. When such an offender is released from prison, the local authority will be notified directly by the prison department.

When supervising someone with convictions for offences against children, either past or present, the probation officer must pay close attention to their domestic, social and employment circumstances...with whom are they living? – are there children in the household? – are they attempting to gain work with children? Discussion with such clients must inevitably revolve around these issues, and home visits may be necessary. They should be listened to carefully...they will often indicate, in a roundabout way, that their feelings are becoming difficult to contain – expressions of loneliness, inability to make friends or an inability to forget about the past should ring warning bells and should be explored fully.

Procedures

What do you do if

1. There is evidence of child abuse, neglect or injury?
    - Ensure medical attention is obtained if required.
    - Consult either your practice teacher/SPO, or an ACPO depending on availability, as soon as possible.
    - Inform the local SSD immediately by telephone, sending a confirmatory letter as soon as practically possible thereafter so action can be taken. Outside office hours, contact the duty social worker via the police.
    - Record everything you have seen, done and discussed in full detail.

2. You have concerns about a child – think once again about Dawn's children (Chapter 1) – or you believe that a child may have been abused, neglected or injured.
    - Immediately discuss with your practice teacher/SPO, or ACPO as above, and record both your observations and the discussion. Don't wait for your next supervision session!
    - Contact the social services duty officer, ask if the family is or has been known to the department and check whether there have been any child protection concerns. If so, establish whether the child's name is on the Child Protection Register.
    - Remember that the probation service has the right to request that a case conference be called if suspicion still remains, or concerns are sufficiently grave.

3. You suspect an unborn child is potentially at risk of abuse, neglect or injury
    - It may be that because of social, emotional and

historical factors (i.e. other children in the family have been abused and removed) a child has to be protected as soon as it is born ... if you consider this is likely, again consult your practice teacher/SPO and decide whether to request a pre-birth case conference.

Guidelines and hints for practice

Some important watchwords: consult, report, record, refer, communicate, liaise, confirm, watch, listen, hear!

Use the agencies practice guidelines as a working tool, rather than a document to be read once and then put on one side. If all else fails, sleep with them under your pillow....

Procedural instructions and guidelines provide routes for action, and accountability and may also heighten awareness of what to look for. They frequently emphasise that abuse can happen to anyone in any family, and should provide a structure for thought and action, without making the officer feel de-skilled and a failure. However, they are no substitute for thoughtful, careful analysis and assessment.

Probation officers, have been involved in some of the well publicised child abuse cases, which have been the subject of official enquiries in recent years. These have highlighted the crucial importance of inter-agency liaison, and communication... never assume that the other agency knows what you know... better to tell them twice than not at all. Similarly, attention has been drawn to the importance of full, detailed and accurate records which will not only 'protect your back' but may provide vital pieces of the jigsaw which will enable a full picture to emerge. Discussions and observations are just as essential to record as action taken.

It is the policy of many probation services that records in child protection cases should be seen regularly by the senior probation officer who should confirm that he/she has done so. Similarly it may be policy that regular reports are sent to the ACPO who holds an internal register of such cases.

Beware of the rule of optimism. There is an understandable tendency to think the best of our clients and to unconsciously avoid seeing things that may have serious consequences. It is tempting to imagine that you see hoped–for improvements, or to attach greater significance to minor changes than they really warrant. There is an increased risk of this when the alternative might be the removal of your client's children. It is for these reasons, along with the personal stress and anxiety involved, that regular and frequent supervision is essential in child protection work.

Case conferences

If it is considered necessary to call a case conference, you will be expected to attend. It is the policy of many probation services that the SPO accompanies members of the team at least to the first of these. It is useful to prepare what you want to say in advance, including your involvement to date and any observations you have which are relevant to the protection of the child/children concerned.

The purpose of the case conference is to determine whether a child's name should be placed on the area child protection register, and if so to appoint a key worker, who should, generally speaking, be a local authority social worker. Having a different perspective, you may find that the probation service is a lone voice within the conference. Stick to your guns – your professional opinion is as valid as that of any other participant.

It is important that the respective roles of the agencies involved are clarified – particularly if there is to be no allocated social worker. It is a good idea to take your own notes on what is said and what decisions were taken – you will receive minutes but they usually take ages to arrive and may not be as detailed as you would wish.

Predictive factors: signs to look out for
(The warning bell checklist)

There are a number of indicators that a person may be likely to abuse a child and these are often referred to as predictive factors. The presence of several predictive factors does not mean that child abuse is inevitable but they should alert you to potential vulnerability. Many of your clients will have problems in the present, often determined by factors beyond their control. In addition, like all of us, they carry baggage from their pasts.

What follows is a list of what are generally considered to be 'predictive factors'. Their presence should make your warning bells vibrate slightly, rather than peal at full volume. However, just to make life even more difficult, it is important to bear in mind that some children are subject to ill treatment in situations where there are no predictive factors apparent, so never ignore signs from a child that cause you concern. Likewise remember that the presence of one or more of the following does not inevitably mean that a child is at risk of significant harm.

Factors in adults

- a parent was abused her/himself as a child;
- a parent is subject to depression, mood swings and/or violent outbursts;
- a parent is socially isolated;
- a parent is under severe economic or emotional strain or is experiencing stress from some other source;
- parenthood occurred at a very young age;
- a parent is emotionally immature;
- a parent is abusing alcohol and/or drugs;
- a parental figure is not the child's natural parent;
- there is a poor marital/partnership relationship which may also be violent;
- a parent has mental health problems;
- a parent is caring for several young children close in age;
- a parent has unrealistically high expectations of a child, coupled with ignorance of child development – assuming a child can do things which are not appropriate to their age, and then being angry and disappointed when they can't;
- a parent is unable to separate her/his own needs from the child's – for instance, the parent who makes decisions for the child based on what they want the child to want rather than seeing the child as a separate individual with wants of their own which may be different;
- there is impaired bonding, where in the early stages of infancy parent and child were prevented from forming a close attachment, either due to enforced separation through prematurity or illness, post-natal depression (this could apply to either parent) or to rejection for some reason;
- the child is presenting feeding problems – a source of great anxiety and frustration which often leads to feelings of rejection in the parent;
- a parent demonstrates jealousy of, or rivalry with, the child;
- a parent has considerable unmet needs and the child has to make up or compensate for everything that has gone wrong;
- a child who was unwanted, the 'wrong' gender or has a disability;
- a parent is unable to cope with some of the inevitable aspects of parenthood – dependence, discipline, confrontation etc.;

Child protection and the probation service

- a parent who has abused other children in the past;
- there is conflict between loyalty to a partner and responsibility to the child.

Factors in children

There are also certain kinds of behaviour in children which should make your warning bells begin to jangle, irrespective of whether any of the above predictive factors apply.

- 'frozen watchfulness' – a child who is wary, hypervigilant, unusually still and who jumps at sudden sounds or movements;
- a child who is timid, apparently afraid of saying the wrong thing, and displays difficulties with articulation for no obvious reason;
- a child who is reluctant or unable to play, perhaps as a result of lack of stimulation by the parents or due to the child's depression – it is not only adults who get depressed;
- there is evidence of indiscriminate attachment, for example when a child comes up to you on your first visit and tries to sit on your lap or a parent reports that a child often wanders off with complete strangers;
- there are signs of a negative attachment to the parent where a child constantly approaches a parent for affection and attention, ever hopeful but comes away disappointed – remember physical closeness does not necessarily mean everything is alright;
- a child who exhibits parental behaviour for example seeming anxious about a parent or worried about matters which should not normally concern a child of that age – for example a 4 year old who worries about the cost of something;
- a child who is pale, tired looking with dark circles under the eyes, unkempt, dirty;
- a child who is apparently accident prone, looks vaguely bruised and/or scratched;
- a child who is whingey, clingy, cries a lot and leaves you feeling irritated, frustrated and despairing;
- a child who is attention seeking;
- a child who exhibits obviously self comforting behaviour (rocking, swaying, thumb sucking at an inappropriate age, i.e. over 4/5 years, openly masturbating);
- signs of self mutilation;
- persistent running away from home;
- sexual precocity or promiscuity.

If you become aware of any of this kind of behaviour, stop for a moment and ask yourself what might account for it – it may be that some of the predictive factors mentioned earlier might provide some understanding or possible explanation. For instance, it is possible that a child who is wary or jumpy and demonstrating 'frozen watchfulness' may be witnessing an unpredictably violent relationship between the parents; a child who is constantly seeking attention and affection may have been unwanted, rejected for some reason or never had the opportunity to bond effectively.

Be aware of your own feelings, instincts, intuition; the chances are that if a child evokes certain feelings in you – despair, sadness, anxiety, fear – they may be feeling some of these things themselves.

Watch for:

- injuries which are inconsistent with the explanation offered;
- mixed messages from adults – the parent who tells you one thing about their relationship with their child but demonstrates another.

Listen to:

- the exit line, the throwaway remark;
- what the child says and take it seriously.

Beware of:

- racist, sexist and heterosexist stereotypes – discriminatory assumptions abound about family relationships; it is crucial to have an informed understanding about cultural differences in child rearing norms in order to gain an accurate perspective on what is happening in a family; similarly it is important to be aware of gender based inequalities and to challenge erroneous assumptions about gay and lesbian parents;
- personal issues which may impinge upon your work in relation to child protection – self awareness is crucial in this area of work;
- over identification with or protection of your adult client, at the expense of their child's welfare (remember this is the paramount consideration);
- the 'dither' factor – if in doubt, consult, don't sit on something for two weeks worrying about it;
- avoidance or numbness – sometimes we tend to blank out what an adult is telling us about their behaviour because we don't want to hear it or believe it.

Child protection and the probation service 147

Learn to:

- use what you hear and see to open up discussion with family members and constructively confront the issues;
- keep clients fully informed of the agency's concerns, responsibilities and any action that has been taken;
- anticipate clients' anger when action has to be taken as well as their feelings of betrayal;
- listen to and watch children.

This is difficult, taxing work and you, like every other professional, will need all the support and help you can get – in fact it's your right as a professional worker and your duty to your clients. So, use supervision to the full, and sign up for any training courses going – in most probation services basic child protection training is likely to be compulsory.

Child protection exercise

In order to start thinking about some of the issues we have been discussing and how they relate to 'real life', consider each of the following scenarios and note down:

1. What would your main concerns be?
2. What would you do?

When you have done this check your responses with the discussions of the scenarios which follow them.

Scenario 1

Mr A in his late twenties is on parole, having been convicted of indecent assault of young boys whilst working in a youth club. During an interview he reveals that he has formed a relationship with a young woman and is planning to live with her and her two boys aged 7 and 9. He is clearly delighted about the relationship. He says he has not told his new partner about his offences but will do so once they have been together a little longer. All he wants to do is put the past behind him – he sees this relationship as his chance to start again.

Scenario 2

Ms B has been remanded on bail for a PSR for offences of assault and criminal damage. During a home visit for the preparation of the report, her 6 year old daughter appears pale, with dark circles under the eyes and uncared for, with unwashed and uncombed hair. She climbs onto the PO's lap and asks if she can go home with him. Ms B says how much she adores her daughter, that she lives only for her and without her her life would be empty, despite the fact that she is clearly an intelligent, articulate woman currently doing a post graduate degree. The child keeps her distance from Ms B and when she interrupts the conversation, which she frequently does, Ms B is curt, critical and rejecting.

Scenario 3

Mr C is on probation for drug related offences as is his partner. He has failed to keep the last two appointments offered and so the probation officer decides to visit the home one evening. On arrival, the door is opened by the couple's five year old daughter, who says her parents are out and she is just giving the baby her tea. In the background can be heard the wails of the two year old.

Scenario 4

Mr D has been remanded on bail for a PSR in respect of offences of theft. Mrs D, from whom he has recently separated, phones one day to ask if she can come to see the person preparing the report. She reveals that she is very worried about Mr D having contact with his 5 year old daughter, because when they lived together and he used to bath her, he would insist upon locking the bathroom door. She used to hear laughter. When she complained about the locked door, Mr D taunted her about being jealous of a 5 year old.

Scenario 1: discussion

There is no doubt that these children could be at risk and social services will need to be informed about the situation and Mr A must be made aware of this. Although it is clearly important to assist his rehabilitation and 'new start', remember that the welfare of children is always the paramount consideration. As Mr A is on parole, he cannot in fact change his address without the approval of his supervising officer, and if he does so there are grounds for the ACPO to consider notifying the Home Office and making a recommendation about recalling him to prison, particularly if it is thought that somebody is at risk or he is likely to commit a serious offence.

Scenario 2: discussion

You will recognise quite a few of the factors in our 'warning bells checklist' here. Ms B seems to be socially isolated, arguably

Child protection and the probation service

unable to separate her own needs from those of her child, and there certainly seems to be some incongruity between what she says about her feelings for her daughter and how she behaves towards her. The child herself looks neglected and uncared for and exhibits signs of indiscriminate attachment. There are sufficient worrying aspects here to warrant a check with social services to enquire whether Ms B is known, and to discuss with the senior probation officer whether or not to request a case conference be convened.

Scenario 3: discussion

Prompt action is obviously required, as children this age are invariably at risk if left alone. It may be that if the PO waits with the children for a little while, the parents will return, in which case the parents would need to be confronted and social services informed. If however it seems that the parents are not likely to return in the near future, you have no option but to contact the emergency social services duty officer via the police, who will take immediate action and remove the children, having obtained an emergency protection order.

Scenario 4: discussion

This is a tricky one. On the face of it, it seems that there could not be any possible legitimate reason for Mr D's behaviour. But in the context of a marital breakdown, and a potential contact dispute, you need to bear in mind that it might not be so straightforward. If Mrs D is serious about her allegations and her wish to protect her child, then she should have no objection to sharing them with the appropriate agency – the social services department – who would then investigate fully.

References

HMSO 1991 *Working Together under the Children Act*, London: HMSO.

10 Keeping records

We were tempted to call this chapter 'Sex, drugs and rock n' roll' recognising that the mere mention of recording often has the effect of sending probation officers to sleep. If it's any consolation, however, once the rules of good practice in record maintenance are learnt, they should become second nature and you won't have to worry about them anymore, so it really is worth gritting your teeth and reading on .... If you still have doubts, then here is the cautionary tale of Ms Phoebe N. Blue who drove around with all her out of date records in the boot of her car, for fear of an unanticipated inspection... of course she fell foul of a passing TWOC specialist and car and records both were gone. Try explaining that one....

Why keep records?

1. Contrary to popular belief, keeping records was not devised as a form of torture, but is in fact a statutory requirement (Rule 31 Probation Rules 1984).
2. It is not much fun to be asked to see somebody else's client in their absence only to find that the records are out of date and you have to start from scratch. This is a waste of your time and irritating for the client.
3. Even the most perfect probation officer will have a memory which is fallible. It is impossible to keep the details of the lives of all your 40 clients in your head at the same time, with any degree of accuracy and it is of course this accuracy which is crucial when providing information to others, in the form of a PSR for example. In the case of breach proceedings, justice will only be served by a true reflection of the facts.
4. Be it in a widely publicised child protection enquiry or an

Keeping records 151

informal chat with your supervisor, how much easier to prove that you did what you say you did if it has previously been committed to paper.
5. The essence of good social work practice is that it should constitute a planned intervention on the basis of a thorough assessment and that the approach should be sufficiently flexible to accommodate amendments to those assessments and plans in the light of new information or changed circumstances. Reflecting on your records enables you to maintain a sense of direction by reminding you what has gone before, and assists you to retain an overview at times when you may be absorbed in minutiae of a client's predicament.
6. In most probation services, an officer's records will still be relied upon to a large extent as a reflection of their practice and as such will play a part in the process of supervision and evaluation.
7. The intelligence and research officer is often seen lurking around probation service headquarters. Where do they get all the information which forms the basis for the graphs, grids and venn diagrams of which they are so fond? Why, from probation officers of course and how much easier to supply such information if you can just flick back through your records.

The fact that we are expected to keep records, immediately raises issues about confidentiality. Who has access to them? What are the clients' rights? What about third party information – that is, information provided by somebody other than the client? How long are they retained? How securely are they kept? The whole issue of open records is a very current one, and whereas in some services it is policy that clients may have access to their records, this is not universal as yet. It is generally accepted that information provided either by, or about, a third party will not be shared with the client without the permission of that third party. Files are likely to contain highly sensitive and personal material. They should be securely stored and not taken out of the office if this can be avoided. The length of time for which a file is retained after the last contact and before destruction is five years.

What records do we keep?

The probation case record is made up of several parts. We are going to describe each element, followed by a written up version using Dave (see Chapter 1) as an example.

```
LITTLE ACOP-IN-THE-WOLD PROBATION SERVICE CASE RECORD          PBN. BLUE 1

SUMMARY INFORMATION SHEET                                      Number ..............
```

Date & Name of Officer Responsible for Entry				
	1. Surname(s)	CROOK		
	First Name(s)	David Albert		
	Address	33A, Casework Terrace Little Acop-in-the-Wold		
	2. Date of Birth	12.8.62	Ref. No.	
	C.R.O. No.	1234/5	Prison No.	
	3. Type of Case	Supervision		
	Other Current Summary Information Sheet(s)		Number(s)	
	4. Offences	Affray		
	5. Order or Sentence	Probation Order.		
	Made by	Little Acop-in-the-Wold Crown Court		
	Length	2 years From 3.5.92	To	2.5.94
	Special Requirements			
	Amendments			
	6. Significant Custodial Dates			
	EDR		Parole Eligibility Date	
	Home Leave		Actual Date of Release	
	7. Caseworker	Seymour Kleintz		
	PSD/Establishment	Little Acop-in-the-Wold		
	Dates:	From 3.5.92 To		
	8. Reason for Termination			

```
                                                                        P.T.O.
```

Figure 10.1 PBN Summary information sheet

PBN Blue 1: summary information sheet (Figure 10.1)

This provides basic information about a client and the nature of their contact with the service. It is completed by the court duty officer after the making of each new order (supervision, probation, community service) or when someone receives a custodial sentence.

Keeping records 153

Date & Name of Officer Responsible for Entry	9. Other Persons or Organisations With Responsibilities or Involvement	
	Name Ms. Dee Tocks Designation C.P.N. Address and Tele. No. Little Acop-in-the-Wold Health Centre, 23 Sanity Road, Tel: 0927 - 1234 Remarks	Name Designation Address and Tele. No. Remarks
	10. Circumstances of Referral Little Acop-in-the-Wold Crown Court. PSR Presented. Judge said very serious offence but she was prepared to take exceptional course of probation - any further offending or breach then custody inevitable.	

Figure 10.1 continued

PBN White 1: Part A personal information (Figure 10.2)

This is completed by the officer holding the order. It is a permanent record of personal information and should be amended as circumstances change. The Part A often duplicates much of what is in a pre-sentence report and for this reason might be considered a waste of time. However it is important to

LITTLE ACOP-IN-THE-WOLD PROBATION SERVICE CASE RECORD   PBN. WHITE 1

Part A PERSONAL INFORMATION

Date & Name of Officer Responsible for Entry

1.

Surname(s)	CROOK
First Name(s)	David Albert
Date of Birth	12.8.62

2.

Address	Description of Accommodation
33A, Casework Terrace, Little Acop-in-the-Wold	Privately rented bed-sit

3. FAMILY AND OTHER MEMBERS OF HOUSEHOLD

Relationship	Name	Age	Additional Information
—	—		Lives alone.

P.T.O.

Figure 10.2 PBN White 1: Part A Personal information

remember that this part of the record will be retained after the last contact when pre-sentence reports may be destroyed. In addition, completing the part A with your client is often of value both in terms of engagement and discovering elements of the client's life of which you were previously unaware.

This is one of the places where you can be a little more inventive in your recording, particularly in relation to the develop-

Keeping records

Date & Name of Officer Responsible for Entry	

4. EDUCATIONAL RECORD

Local Comprehensive School.
Suspended for fighting on several occasions.
Left at 16 with 3 C.S.E's.

5. WORK RECORD

Rarely unemployed.
Started apprenticeship as electrician on leaving school, gave it up after a year.
Electronics factory for 3 years. Then general labouring.
Carpet Fitter for past 2 years.

Figure 10.2 continued

mental history, where for instance you may find a genogram provides a far more vivid picture than a chunk of text.

PBN Peach: record of court appearances and convictions (Figure 10.3)

This speaks for itself and it is important that it is kept up to date.

> Date & Name
> of Officer
> Responsible
> for Entry

6. MEDICAL AND PSYCHIATRIC HISTORY

Physically in good health.
No history of mental illness.

7. USE OF LEISURE

An ardent fan of Little Acop United - goes to most matches both home and away.
Pool.
Evenings spent in local pubs.

P.T.O.

Figure 10.2 continued

PBN Pink: Part B

This comprises a 'supervision plan', which should be completed two weeks after sentence and quarterly reviews thereafter. The

Keeping records

8. DEVELOPMENTAL HISTORY

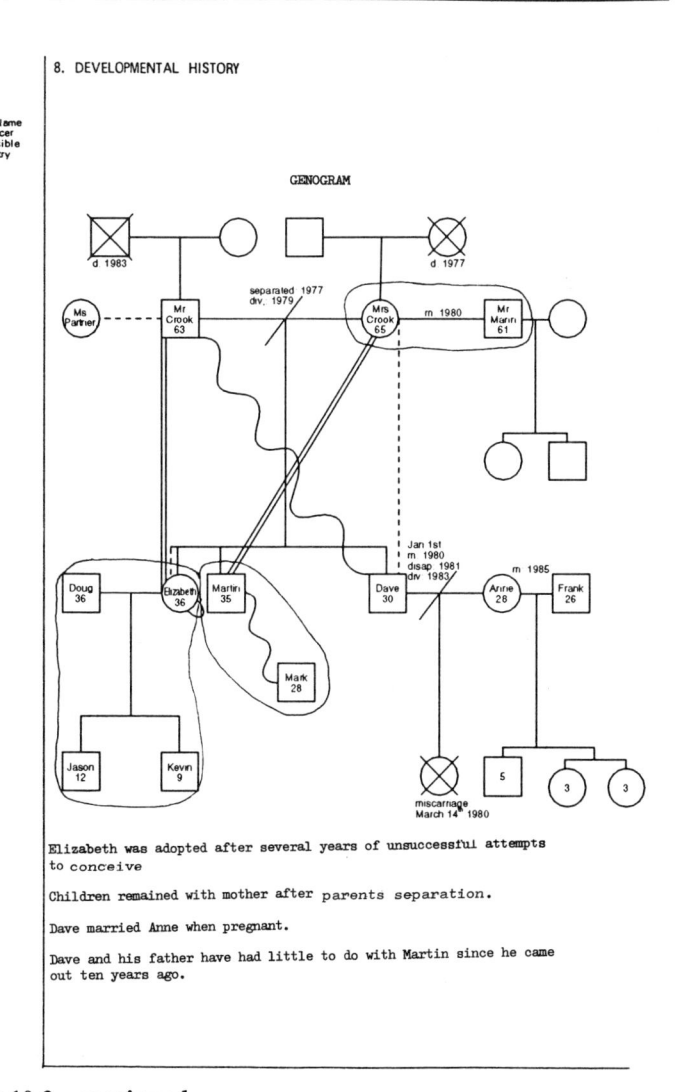

Date & Name of Officer Responsible for Entry

GENOGRAM

Elizabeth was adopted after several years of unsuccessful attempts to conceive

Children remained with mother after parents separation.

Dave married Anne when pregnant.

Dave and his father have had little to do with Martin since he came out ten years ago.

Figure 10.2   continued

supervision plan records the probation officer's assessment of the client and her/his offending behaviour, the objectives of their work together and the plans for intervention, i.e. how the objectives are going to be achieved. Quarterly summaries will review progress made, record any significant changes in the

LITTLE ACOP-IN-THE-WOLD PROBATION SERVICE CASE RECORD

PBN. PEACH

Name CROOK, David

Date & Name of Officer Responsible for Entry	9. RECORD OF COURT APPEARANCES OR CONVICTIONS			
	3.7.82	Little A-I-T-W	MC Criminal Damage	F. £50
	7.12.83	Socialworkville	MC Drunk & Disorderly	C.D. 12 Mths
	23.4.88	Hollisville	MC Assult Police	28 days Imprisonment
	17.5.90	Socialworkville	MC Threatening behaviour Offensive Weapon	F. £200
	9.7.91	Little A-I-T-W	MC Criminal Damage	100 hours C.S. £100 comp.
	3.5.92	Little A-I-T-W	CC Affray	Probation Order 2 years.
	9.8.92	Little A-I-T-W	MC Drunk & Disorderly	F. £25.

Figure 10.3 PBN Peach: Record of court appearances or convictions

client's situation and identify objectives and plans for the next quarter. If a case is transferred to another officer, you will need to do a transfer summary, reviewing your work with the client and drawing attention to anything of particular significance of which the new officer should be aware. Similarly the closing summary, when contact is at an end, is essentially a review of the work undertaken, and a prognosis for the future.

The supervision plan and summaries should be agreed where possible with the client, signed by both supervisor and client and copies should be held on file and given to the client.

Supervision plan: June 1992 Dave is on probation for two years for an offence of affray which took place at a local takeaway. He denies any racial motive. Violence and alcohol seem to be contributory factors in his offending both current and previous convictions. Several previous offences have been within the context of his support for Little Acop-in-the-Wold FC.

The PSR identified two main areas for intervention – anger management and controlling his drinking, but Dave now denies that either of these is a problem any more. It is agreed that each should be explored: 1) anger, by detailed analysis and discussion of situations in which Dave has lost his temper: 2) drinking, by monitoring Dave's consumption of alcohol by means of a drink diary. Dave is to attend the next alcohol education programme at the Sanity Road Health Centre.

Dave is to report each Wednesday at 6pm.

Date......................

Signed...................

Signed................... Date......................

Quarterly Review: September 1992 Little progress to date as until recenly Dave continued to maintain that the angry incidents in which he's been involved have invariably been the fault of others and deny that alcohol is any problem to him. He's tended either to forget his drink diaries or fail to complete them saying it was an atypial week.

Being freed for drunk and disorderly in late August has moved things on and Dave now acknowledges that he's been drinking too much and he's not so satisfied wiht his lifestyle as he'd previously stated.

It has been necessary to challenge racist comments made by Dave on two occasions and he has agreed to abide by the agency's Equal Opportunities Policy in future.

The Supervision Plan remains as previously but in addition it is agreed that there should be a focus upon which areas of his life Dave is satisfied with and which he would like to change. It is agreed also that there will be some discussion of issues of race and racism.

Dave is to report fortnightly on Wednesday at 6pm.

Signed.................... Date....................

Signed.................... Date....................

Quarterly review: December 1992 Dave disappeared and there is a warrant outstanding for breach of propation.

On the last occasion I saw him, he revealed much more of the real and vulnerable Dave than I had seen previously when talking of his alcoholic and violent father in whose eyes he could never do anything right. This certainly makes more sense of his defences, probably against the feelings of powerlessness and low self esteem and equally against people getting near enough to recognise these.

We did make some progress during this quarter, however. Dave had made some effort to cut down on his drinking, mainly by exploring alternative ways of spending an evening other than the pub – also he had been along to one meeting of the Alcohol Education Group at the health centre. His drinking is very much associated with the lifestyle of the group he hangs around with – football matches, and the pub – and this has been the only arena in which he gets kudos. If he is to give any of this up, then something must be substituted and this we had just started to talk about when he disappeared. I would certainly recommend that probation should continue if and when Dave turns up again or is arrested.

PBN White 2: Part C record of contact

This is the record of all that happens in relation to your client. It therefore will include letters, phone calls, interviews, visits, court appearances, discussions with others.

The example of one of Dave's Part C entries will be found at the end of this chapter where it forms part of an exercise.

Putting it down on paper

We don't have to remind you that good probation practice is all about making a relationship with your client and you won't stand any chance of finding anything out about them, never mind intervening to assist them unless you demonstrate that you are interested in what they say, that you are listening to them carefully and responding sensitively. This is all a bit difficult to do if you spend your interviews with your nose stuck in a notebook, scribbling furiously.

The whole issue of taking notes in interviews is, of course, a tricky one. It's important to get the facts right, but it will not be a very productive session if the client feels that everything they say and more is being taken down and may be used ... Apart from anything, you miss important non-verbal signals, and you are likely to get more from the client by looking at them than by writing about them. So, it's a question of balance – tell the client that it's important you get things right, so you may have to take a few notes during the session, but keep this to a minimum. If you take a few risks, you will probably find that your memory is more reliable than you think but make sure that you always allow time immediately following the interview to jot down everything you think is of significance.

It will also help a lot if your interview is well planned beforehand – having thought about what areas you want to cover will assist in recalling the content afterwards.

There are almost as many ways of recording facts, impressions, observations and opinions as there are probation officers, and you will be pleased that we are not going to present them all for your consideration.

Styles of day to day recording (Part C) will of course vary, depending on whether you are working with an individual, a couple, a family, or a group. You may find a structured approach with the use of headings a helpful way of organising your thoughts. For example, headings for recording work with an individual could include:

- Current situation/presenting problem;
- Areas discussed/assessment;
- Action/decisions;
- Plans for next session.

You may, however, feel more comfortable with the time honoured 'stream of consciousness' approach, in which facts, opinions and impressions are recorded as they occur to you, using continuous prose. The danger of this approach is that you may find yourself writing a short novel in respect of each of your clients, and with a full caseload, you are not going to have much of a life outside the office.

Many people adopt a style of very brief entries, in which virtually nothing of the content of the interview is recorded unless anything particularly significant has changed. However this approach would usually involve fuller and more detailed summaries at regular intervals.

Recording groups and families

Recording groups is slightly more complicated, since more than one worker is likely to be involved, and it may be useful to take it in turns to record, sharing your impressions with one another in between. You also have to find a way of recording both the contribution of each individual client, as well as both the group dynamic and the process. Some people find the use of diagrams a helpful tool – this is the easiest way to reflect where everyone was sitting, where the alliances were within the group and how these can change.

With regard to the content of what is recorded, once again headings can prove very helpful. These could include:

- date, time and duration of session;
- who was there and who wasn't;
- the aims of the session and plans for achieving them;

- contributions/responses/behaviour of participants – verbal and non-verbal;
- evaluation of workers intervention;
- conclusions/observations/plans for next session.

Process recording

You are probably familiar with the term 'process recording' and your response to it is unlikely to be neutral. People tend to love them or hate them, believing them either to be an invaluable discipline and working tool or a tedious waste of time. Process recordings, as you know, are detailed, blow by blow accounts of *everything* that happens in interview – not only what is said, but how it is said and what you and the client are doing and feeling when saying it. There are two main purposes, firstly, it may assist you to make sense in retrospect of what has happened during an interview and if you are particularly stuck with a client, discussion of the process recording in supervision can be very helpful in identifying the reason for this. Secondly, it is a valuable mechanism for training your powers of memory, particularly the ability to retain and recall sequences of words, feelings and actions.

There are two main ways of constructing a process recording, either the type of streams of consciousness or continuous prose referred to above, or the 'play script' method. This is written in the present tense, rather like dialogue in a play, with a column down one side to record the worker's thoughts and feelings and another one for analysis of what was happening.

Genograms

The genogram, or family tree, is a diagramatical representation of relationship patterns. It is a particularly useful mechanism for recording couples, or families. It is a very economical way of recording a complex personal history, and gaps in information become much more readily apparent than if material is presented in a more traditional manner. It vividly highlights transgenerational patterns, themes and links between family members or significant others.

An added bonus is the value of the genogram as a tool for working with clients. It is a useful means of engaging the client who may be ill at ease in face to face discussion and it captures the imagination. In cases where talking about the family is tricky, it is a less threatening way of exploring sensitive issues, and can be used to work through feelings about family members in a safe way. On a cautionary note, however, it is worth bearing in mind that, for some clients, this picture of their family could have a very powerful effect – it may remind them of painful experiences, and they may be confronted by links and patterns of which they have been previously unaware. It's a good idea to do your own genogram in private first to get some sense of how it feels – you might even go as far as asking if there is anyone there you would like to remove, or whether there are people you want to add. Who did you draw first and why? Will it be the same picture in 10 years time? Who did you forget to put in?

The survival guide to record keeping

- At all costs avoid a backlog of records – you can't afford the sleepless nights. Although it is tempting to let other things take priority, recording really is an integral part of good probation practice. A regular slot in your diary each week for recording is a must.
- It is useful to devise a system that enables you to identify when you need to complete records that are required on a regular basis; such as Part B reviews and reports on child protection cases. It can help to set aside a day a month for this purpose.
- Work jointly and negotiate with your secretary so that he/she understands your system of record keeping, and you can work as a team. Negotiate what is likely to be most effective – use of a dictaphone – personal dictation – copy typing?
- Keep a notebook with a page for each client, so that you can make quick notes after every interview and then record them more fully afterwards.
- Work out your own system of shorthand, for example 'OV' office visit; 'HV' home visit; 'F/A' failed appointment; 'PV' prison visit.

Before you drift off to sleep completely, let us end with a little homily. Getting a grip on recording as early as possible in your career will save you a great deal of unnecessary strain and anguish. There is nothing more draining than the knowledge of a stack of undone paperwork, and it will haunt you, getting ever larger both in reality and in imagination. Remember too that recording is a statutory requirement and failing to do it is as heinous a sin against a client as any other instance of poor practice.

Exercise: the blue pencil

What follows is Seymour's part C entry of his second interview with Dave. If he continues to record in such detail, as a matter of course, he is rarely going to have the opportunity to set foot outside the office, and neither is he going to be too popular with his secretary.

Have a go at précising the entry so that nothing of significance is lost, but it is more concise. You will find a suggested alternative below.

15.5.92 Dave arrived at the office on time but I was a few minutes late collecting him from the waiting room, as I'd been caught up on the telephone – he smiled benignly as I apologised! He was looking quite smart in neatly pressed jeans, leather jacket, shirt and tie. I started off by saying that I thought it would be a good idea to look back together at the PSR and the areas which had been highlighted to see whether he agreed or not and to give us some pointers for our work together. He said this was OK with him. Most of the report – family background, present circumstances, employment etc. – he agreed with but he said the bit about his temper and drinking were exaggerated and he felt his words had been twisted and he'd been misrepresented. He couldn't really answer when I asked why he hadn't really taken issue with this in court, if the report was inaccurate. Dave said that he was perfectly well able to control both his drinking and his temper, neither of which is a problem to him.

I asked him how much he does in fact drink and he replied that most nights he has a couple of pints. I was then able to ask whether it was just a couple of pints he'd had on the night of the offence or whether, as I suspected, he'd had considerably more to drink than that. Dave denied it and said it was nothing to do with alcohol – he and his mates had been to the match and as usual had a couple of cans of lager each, then later on 'fancied an Indian'. He said the guy in the takeaway over-reacted to their high spirits and asked some of them to wait outside, so they started moving some of his furniture around, because they didn't like his attitude and thought he needed to be taught a lesson. I said I'd been wondering about the fact that the guy in the takeaway was black and that he and his mates were all white.

Dave said 'I'm not a racist if that's what you mean' and that they'd have done the same if he'd been white and the same thing happened. I told him that I was not convinced, that the incidence of racist attack and abuse of black people who work in takeaways, restaurants etc. is high and that this was a subject I would want to return to.

I was similarly unconvinced by Dave's protestations about the amount he drinks and I gave him a drink diary and showed him how to fill it in, which he said he'd do by next week if he had time. I gave him another appointment in the office at the same time next week but he said his memory is not very good and asked if I could ring him at about 10 am to remind him. I said I didn't think this would be possible and he'd have to find a way of remembering himself. We shook hands and I showed him out.

Suggested alternative part C!

15.5.92 O/V Went through SIR. Says author made more of what he said than she should and that neither drinking nor temper were much of a problem – he can easily control both. Admits to a couple of pints a night. Denies offence was racially motivated or that alcohol played much of a part – explains it in terms of takeaway owner being stroppy, and their high spirits following match. Gave him drink diary to complete by next week. Asked if I could phone to remind of next appointment – I refused.

11 Survival

Starting a placement as a student, starting life as a first year officer/new entrant, or even taking over as chief probation officer will all generate the same kind of anxieties (if not the same kind of salaries). Will I cope? How am I going to survive? What will they think at the Home Office? Can I remember anything? This chapter will hopefully provide you with a survival kit to keep with you and assist you in most situations, except perhaps when lunching with the Home Secretary (no, we're not sure which cutlery to use either!)

As in all the best survival kits, you will need a map, a compass, an itinerary and a block of Kendal Mint Cake – or to put it another way, you will need a clear sense of where you are and where you are going, guidance along the way, a notion of the order of things, and a large dollop of whatever sustenance takes your fancy.

The map

Actually, you will stand more chance of people understanding what you are talking about if you refer to this as a contract, even though you may still find it difficult to avoid mountainous areas, deep ravines, and fast flowing rivers!

It is of crucial importance that you are clear exactly what is expected of you and what you can expect from your working environment.

As a student

These areas are likely to be clearly defined in a written contract which will ideally have been negotiated between student, tutor and practice teacher in a three way meeting at the very beginning of the placement. Although there are no hard and fast rules about what a contract or learning agreement, as they are sometimes called, should contain, it is generally considered appropriate to include the following:

- Hours of work. When should you start and finish? Are these hours flexible? What about time off in lieu (it's so lovely there at this time of year) and evening appointments?
- Agency policies. What is expected of you and what can you expect from the agency, for instance in respect of equal opportunities and health and safety policies and procedures?
- Frequency and duration of supervision. An hour and a half uninterrupted per week is the norm. Can you also see your practice teacher outside normal supervision times? What should you do when your practice teacher is not available? Are you expected to stalk the building, searching for an unsuspecting colleague, pin them to the wall, and question them mercilessly or is there a named person you can go to?
- Participation in meetings. How do you achieve a balance between operating as a member of a team, while at the same time getting your own work done within a limited period? Are there some meetings it would be more crucial to attend than others?

    What about meetings of NAPO (National Association of Probation Officers), ABPO (Association of Black Probation Officers) and LAGIP (Lesbian and Gay Men in Probation)? Is there a black workers' support group locally?

- Number and type of cases. If you have any special interests can these be accommodated? Remember numbers don't always reflect complexity and workload – a horrible case in the hand can be worth two in somebody elses' filing cabinet.
- Student's title while on placement. Student probation officer? Assistant probation officer? Trainee probation officer?
- Learning opportunities. Any chance of co-working or groupwork? what about court duty and office duty? How much contact with other agencies will there be? What about visits of observation to other parts of the criminal justice system? How are you to get to know all about the rest of the agency?
- Learning needs. What are the gaps in your knowledge, skills and experience and how are these to be addressed?

How are you going to tackle the process of integrating theory and practice?
- Methods of assessment. What combination of these is to be used? Audio tapes, video tapes, process recordings, live supervision, feedback from co-workers and/or colleagues, simulation, case discussion, supervision sessions, colour of socks, entrails of dead sheep, other?
- Role of the tutor. How often can you expect to see your tutor during the placement? Is this negotiable? Can the tutor be used as a troubleshooter in the event of any disagreements between practice teacher and student? Can either practice teacher or student ask for an unscheduled visit? Will practice teacher and tutor ever discuss the student other than in the student's presence? What are the boundaries of confidentiality?

As a first year officer/new entrant

It is equally important, before you start in a new office, to be clear about expectations even though these may not always be enshrined in a written contract. Workload is something which inevitably worries everybody and apocryphal tales abound of the 35 files waiting on one's desk, with a copy of Jarvis and a regulation plastic briefcase. It has always been recognised – especially by the NSPCPO (National Society for the Prevention of Cruelty to Probation Officers) that a first year officer/new entrant should be protected from the weight of a full caseload, in order that she/he has the opportunity and the time to make the transition from being a student, to be inducted into the agency and to consolidate and build upon what has been learnt during training. Many services have now drawn up guidelines which specify, for instance, a starting caseload of no more than 12, rising to no more than 30 by the end of the first year, and a maximum of 4 reports a month at the beginning, rising to no more than 8 at the end of the year.

Just as in the case of a student, a first year officer/new entrant needs to clarify how they are going to learn about the agency and the community resources, the frequency and duration of supervision, what training opportunities there will be in the first year, how they are going to be assessed and evaluated, and procedures for confirmation. In addition, as a first year officer/new entrant you will no doubt want some reassurance that the team which you are to join is able to demonstrate its commitment to anti-discriminatory practice and that you will have the opportunity to gain experience in all the core tasks and areas of probation practice. You may also have some questions about potential support networks – ABPO, First year officers/new entrants groups etc.

The compass

A compass is useful in several different ways, as the intrepid travellers amongst you will know, it can help you to find direction, to locate yourself in relation to your environment, and it can provide you with a sense of security and stability – without it you are lost. Yes, you've guessed it – the social work equivalent is supervision, the corner–stone of good probation practice.

Supervision comprises three elements, whose inter-relationship and relative significance will vary at different stages in your career.

1. Professional development – through discussion of and reflection about case material or practice issues, consideration of learning and training needs, and issues relating to career development.
2. Professional accountability – through continuous assessment of your performance in relation to agency policies and objectives. This will play a significant part in staff appraisal and evaluation.
3. Support – through allowing you the opportunity to let off steam, express anxieties, and explore any obstacles to your professional well being.

It is important to establish early on the timetable of supervision sessions, who has responsibility for setting the agenda, what the content should be, whether sessions are to be recorded and if so how.

The itinerary

There is one thing we can guarantee – irrespective of the setting in which you will be working, or the geographical location, you will at various times be extremely busy. Without an itinerary, our traveller runs the risk of missing connections, being at the wrong place at the wrong time, making very little progress and getting thoroughly confused about what to do next. So it is for the probation officer who has not learnt the art of time and workload management.

The secret of this is threefold – knowing what you have to do, how much time you have, and the relative importance of the tasks at hand. You are probably thinking that we are stating the obvious (and probably not for the first time... zzzzzzzz) but the thing about the obvious is that we often take it for granted and don't think about it. It is important to make a point of asking yourself these three questions at the beginning of each day/week/month. There is a lot of talk about prioritising but nobody actually tells you how to do it; here are a few ideas learned the hard way:

- Make a list of all the things you have to do, separating these into telephone calls, letters, reports, appointments, recording etc.
- Go through the list asking yourself what the consequence would be of not completing this task. This will provide you with a sense of their relative urgency – number them accordingly.
- Identify what absolutely must be done today and what could be done tomorrow.
- Look at how much time you have and allocate slots in your diary into which you can pop a phone call, a letter or a Part C. It is easy to despair and think 'I've only got 5 minutes free here, it's hardly worth doing anything' – it's surprising how the 5 minute slots mount up and how much you can fit in between interviews or meetings. Tick everything off as you do it.
- We hate to mention it, but when you make your list at the beginning of the day, don't forget the undone things from the day before, however tempting this might be.

This all sounds fine in theory – now have a go at putting it into practice!!

Time management exercise

When you arrive in the office on Monday morning, having been out for a couple of days the previous week, the following messages are waiting for you.

Prioritise and arrange your diary for the week, incorporating the other tasks (also listed below) which you have to undertake. Bear in mind that you already have the following commitments:

Monday	11 am	PSR interview
	2 pm	Team meeting lasting $1\frac{1}{2}$ hours
Tuesday		All day court duty
Wednesday	9.30 am	Supervision $1\frac{1}{2}$ hours
	pm	Reporting from 2 pm – 5 pm
Thursday	pm	Prison visit all afternoon
Friday	2 pm	PSR home visit

Survival 171

Note the reasons for your decisions and the factors that may have influenced them.

1. Five quarterly summaries (Part Bs) which are now a month overdue.
2. Phone call from court duty officer re one of your clients – please call back.
3. Phone call from social services duty officer re one of your clients who is on probation and has two small children – please call back.
4. Phone call from mother of one of your throughcare cases, sentenced to 18 months, 6 months ago. Please call back – URGENT.
5. Message from your SPO – please see about one of your PSRs in court today.
6. Phone call from prison PO re one of your throughcare cases (same client whose mother has phoned). Please call.
7. 16 year old client waiting to see you – parents kicked him out over weekend.
8. Home visit to client who missed last appointment and about whose children you have some concerns.
9. Finding a hostel place for client who is squatting and vulnerable.
10. Home visit to partner of client who is to be released from prison next week, having been inside for 9 months.
11. Dictating all Part Cs from last week.
12. Writing PSR due for beginning of next week.
13. Phone call from psychiatrist re client on probation with condition of psychiatric treatment. Please call.
14. Phone call from client – giro expected Friday still hasn't come – this is second time it's happened. Please chase up DSS for him.

Discussion

This has probably got a very familiar ring about it – and your heart is probably sinking, but remember what we've just said about the simple decision making strategies which can help considerably.

1. These are clearly important being a month overdue, and it's always tempting to put such paperwork at the bottom of the pile. All five don't have to be done all in one go remember, see if you can find five lots of 15 minutes this week to do them separately.
2. This has to be near the top of the list of priorities – it's

now or never. However as the SPO's message possibly refers to the same matter, it's sensible to see her/him first.
3. Anything to do with children can't afford to be left for long. It's useful to establish the degree of urgency straight away, and if it can be left, it's always possible to ring back at a later stage.
4. Whilst recognising that the client's mother sees the situation as urgent, you know from another of your messages that whatever is wrong, the prison PO knows about it, so you can probably afford to leave this until some of the more pressing matters have been dealt with.
5. As in No.2.
6. As in No.4, but perhaps it would be sensible to speak to your colleague in the prison before speaking to the client's mother.
7. There is clearly some degree of urgency here but there's no evidence to suggest that anything dreadful would happen if the client was given a cup of coffee and asked to hang on for a little while.
8. As in No.3, it would be of great assistance to you to get further information about the degree of urgency from other professionals who may be involved – SSD, nursery, health visitor. If someone is able to tell you that all is well, you can afford to wait a while; if not, a speedy visit must be made.
9. Ask yourself whether another day is going to make much difference, mindful of course of the fact that anyone homeless and vulnerable is in a bad way.
10. Is it going to make any difference if this is done later in the week – a phone call to reassure, and indicate that you will be round soon is a useful 'holding' mechanism.
11. As in No.1 – divide and rule!!
12. You're in luck – you have time on your side here but don't forget to negotiate with your secretary.
13. Ask yourself whether the psychiatrist would have indicated if this message was urgent or not.
14. Will it make any difference if you phone DSS immediately or later in the day?

The Kendal Mint Cake

We all know that social work is a stressful business and the roles of both student and first year officer carry additional tensions that

Survival

should not be underestimated. In both cases there is a feeling of being 'on trial', under close scrutiny for much of the time, expected to be full of new ideas, being fresh from training, but at the same time may be perceived as a threat for the same reasons. You may also encounter the office cynic who has seen it all before, and claims to have been just like you once, enthusiastic, idealistic, but rapidly became disillusioned – or the charming colleague who manages to undermine you at a stroke by saying that training cannot hold a candle to life experience. What you are probably encountering is colleagues suffering from 'burnout' – get yourself some Kendal Mint Cake, and fast.

Just as Kendal Mint Cake comes in different sizes, shapes and colours, you must find your own particular antidote to stress, of whatever kind. Support can come from various sources – kind encouraging secretaries, fellow students and first year officers – and can comfort – lunch away from the office, a drink after work with a colleague, a chat about something other than work. If all else fails, try chocolate. Don't keep it to yourself – if you feel fed up talk about it – everybody's been there even if you haven't spotted the T-shirt.

So, you've got your kit. Off you go – may the force be with you, to bravely go where no PO has gone before.

12 The origins of crime – criminological theories

Introduction

A major problem confronting probation officers who want to think about crime is the apparent lack of fit between ***criminological theory*** and ***practice theory***. While criminological theory tends to offer abstract explanations of the ultimate causes of crime, practice theory offers descriptions of practical techniques designed to stop people doing it. As a result, in their day-to-day work with offenders, probation officers can find few immediate practical applications for criminological theory. As Wilson (1975) observes:

> criminologists have shown beyond doubt that men commit more crimes than women and younger men more (of a certain kind) than older ones. It is a theoretically important, and scientifically correct, observation. Yet ... men cannot be changed into women or be made to skip over the adolescent years. (p.50)

On the other hand, a lot of practice theory either fudges the question of 'causes' or ignores them altogether. It concerns itself instead with 'solutions'. These 'solutions', part science, part 'common sense' and part guess-work are, as crime and reconviction rates suggest, at best partial.

The origins of crime

Criminologists generate one body of theory and social work theoreticians another. While both maintain that a relationship exists between the two, it is the usually the practitioner who is left to work out what that relationship is.

In this chapter we suggest that criminological theory does not, and should not be expected to, simply generate prescriptions for intervention. Instead it offers us different ways of thinking about crime and offending which can help us to make informed and coherent choices about our interventions. It requires us to think about the significance of socio-structural, cultural and biographical factors in a person's criminality. It asks us to ponder whether, in any given set of circumstances, anything can be done to bring about change and if so, whether we should intervene at political, administrative or face-to-face levels. Beyond this, it also tells us that popular or fashionable responses to crime and offending may not necessarily be the most effective and that such popularity may owe more to political convenience than the explanatory power of the theory or the effectiveness of the practice.

Ten criminological perspectives

Classicism

Classicism asserts that human beings, as rational creatures, are propelled through the world by a desire to maximise their pleasure (or ***utility***) and minimise their pain. Because, however, we live in society we must enter a 'social contract' with those around us. The rules which dictate how we should fulfill this contract are enshrined in law. Thus the job of the government is to 'referee' these contracts and provide a judicial and penal apparatus which will impose a measure of pain necessary to deter present and future wrongdoers and ensure compliance with the law (Taylor et al. 1973).

Subsequent revisions of pure ***Classicism*** have taken account of the fact that certain people, children and the 'mentally ill' for example, lack sufficient rationality to either enter, or be held to, a contract. This has ushered in the principle that in cases in which the offender cannot be held fully responsible for their actions, the punishment should fit the criminal rather than the crime (see Chapter 4 ***Sentencing Philosophies***).

The past twenty years has seen the renaissance of classicism in Britain in the form of a 'Back to Justice' movement. It has challenged the belief that there is a link between poverty and crime and that the provision of welfare or the administration of treatment can change criminals (Wilson 1975, Morris et al. 1980). It has stressed the essential rationality of offenders and championed their right to due process of law and, if necessary, punishment. Its influence can be seen in the development of the *'justice model'* in **intermediate treatment** in the mid 1980s, in the probation service in the early 1990s, and also in the importance the present government places on probation officers **confronting offending behaviour**.

Bio-genetic theories

This body of theory locates the drive towards criminality in the genetic or biological inheritance of the individual. At its core is a notion of behaviour as no more than the expression of the actor's chemical constitution or peculiar DNA. People afflicted in this way are seen to career through the world, bound for an inevitable collision with a victim. Bio-genetic 'man', like other animate species, *behaves* rather than *acts* and such behaviour can only be changed, it is argued, by the application of drugs, surgery or an elaborate process of reconditioning.

For Lombroso the delinquent was a throwback. Utilising Darwin's notion of *atavism* which describes creatures stuck at an earlier stage of development than other members of their species, he developed a taxonomy of 'criminal types'. In the 1940s William Sheldon devised a taxonomy of body types which was demonstrated to be statistically significant by the Gluecks in the 1950s. They ran extensive tests on groups of boys in reformatories to ascertain whether a relationship existed between body-type and criminality. They demonstrated that a disproportionately large number of inmates were hard and round (mesomorphs) and that far fewer were soft and round (endomorphs), or fragile and thin (ectomorphs). From this data they concluded that body type had a significant bearing upon a person's propensity towards criminality and that, as Lombroso had believed, criminality was geneticaly or biologically determined.

Critics pointed out that perhaps boys who looked 'tough' were more likely to be sent to a reformatory than those who looked, for example, like scholars. They also suggested that the realities of working class life, with its low protein diet and emphasis upon physical prowess and hard physical labour, meant that there were more short muscular boys in this traditionally arrest-prone population. Undeterred Hans Eysenck continued with this line of enquiry and in the 1960s demonstrated a relationship between biological type, personality (extraversion/intraversion), and criminality. Eysenck's project was to devise a scientifically informed 'technology of conformity' (Taylor et al. 1973).

The problems persist however. If criminality is simply a product of the actor's bio-genetic inheritance how do we account for the massive concentration of identified criminals in the lowest reaches of the social structure irrespective of height, weight or hat size. ***Social control theory*** (see below) cites self-report studies to demonstrate that undetected law infraction is a ubiquitous feature of social life. Indeed Belson (1968) indicates that the actual incidence of juvenile crime is over 90 per cent. Are so many of us 'programmed to offend', and if we are why do most of us grow out of it when we reach the age of 17 or 18 (Rutherford 1986)? Social disorganisation theorists (see below) have observed that the offending rates of social groups which move out of the inner city drop dramatically. If this is so, it appears that bio-genetic determinism can be modified or neutralised by social mobility.

While, these days, bio-genetic explanations of male criminality are out of fashion, criminologists, judges and magistrates are still prone to explaining female criminality as an effect of the menopause, pre-menstrual tension or impaired rationality brought on by the wayward demands of female bodies (Heidenson 1985, Gelsthorpe and Morris 1990) (see ***feminist criminology*** below).

Learning theory

Learning theory proceeds from the assumption that any and all behaviour, criminal and non-criminal, is learned. ***Behaviour*** refers to any activity, mental, physical or emotional which is 'observable' and acquired as a result of experience. Learning theorists, or behaviourists as they are sometimes known, are not interested in speculating about events and activities which cannot be observed.

The process of 'learning' is explained somewhat differently by different theorists. The idea of ***classical conditioning*** is usually associated with Pavlov and his justly famous salivating dogs. Pavlov observed that the presentation of a stimulus (dog food) caused his dogs to salivate. When the stimulus was consistently accompanied by a 'conditioned stimulus' (a ringing bell) over a period of time, the presentation of the conditioned stimulus on its own would eventually be sufficient to cause the dogs to salivate. The dogs were then said to have learned a 'conditioned response'. Throughout this process the dog remains an involuntary and passive subject.

Operant conditioning, by contrast, is a process in which learning takes place as a direct result of actions initiated by the actors themselves. Skinner's rats were confined in a cage. In this cage was a lever which, when depressed, released a food pellet. Initially the rat depressed the lever by accident but eventually came to 'learn' that there was a cause and effect relationship between depressing the lever and the arrival of the food pellet. In this scenario the rats who 'make the connection' are not credited with having 'worked it out' for themselves since the learning is seen to be an almost inevitable consequence of the environment in which they are placed.

When we translate this argument into the realm of human criminality it follows that such behaviour will not have arisen as a result of a deliberate moral choice on the part of the actor but as a conditioned response to their environment. As such, attributions of blame are irrelevant.

Other learning theorists ascribe a more active role to the learner's ***cognitive*** processes. Thus in Thorndyke's experiment a caged ape was confronted with a banana which was outside its cage and a stick which was inside. At first the ape could see no relationship between the two objects. When, however, the stick was placed in a line of vision between the ape and the banana, the ape was able to work out that the stick could be used as a tool to hook the banana and drag it into the cage. Such 'conceptual' learning has been shown to be enhanced by opportunities to observe others and to imitate or 'model' oneself upon them. In this perspective, criminality is seen to be learned by exposure to models who illustrate criminal solutions to problems.

The assumption that animal and human behaviour are essentially similar and may be changed in similar ways and the utilisation of the protocols and methods of the 'natural', rather than the social, sciences have exposed learning theorists to telling criticism. Nonetheless, learning theory in general, and 'cognitive' versions of learning theory in particular have, somewhat paradoxically, served as the major theoretical support to those who advocate 'confronting offending behaviour' or the 'justice model' (Priestly et al. 1985, Denman 1982).

These approaches involve offenders in a close analysis of their offending and the identification of the points at which they might have behaved differently. They are helped to recognise the factors which trigger their criminal responses and to learn a repertoire of social skills which will enable them to avoid or resist involvement in crime and participate more readily in non-criminal activities.

Psychodynamic theory

Freud believed that the development of a healthy civilisation and the development of a healthy individual were both predicated upon the successful resolution of the conflict between an individual's instinctual drives, their id, and the demands of the social world. For Freud the arbitre between these two sets of demands is the ego. In his view the development of a healthy ego is dependent upon positive, formative, experiences in the first five years of life. In this connection he attributes particular importance to the satisfactory resolution of the Oedipal conflict in which the child struggles with the parent of the same sex for possession of the parent of the opposite sex. Without these experiences, Freud suggests, psychological illness may follow.

The remedy Freud offers for such illness is psychoanalysis. The aim of psychoanalysis is to discover experiences which haunt the patient's memory but are so painful that they have been *repressed* into the *unconscious*. The psycho-dynamic theories of criminal motivation which draw their inspiration from Freud and his followers tend, therefore, to regard criminal behaviour as a symptom, or *acting out* of unresolved conflicts or traumas rather than freely chosen rational action.

In *Forty-four Juvenile Thieves* Bowlby (1946) locates the need to steal from others as an attempt on the part of boys who experienced 'maternal deprivation' to symbolically reappropriate the breast. Subsequent commentators have suggested that boys from fatherless families who steal cars are, in fact, engaged in a form of compulsive masculinity in order to repress the homosexual impulses they have developed as a result of the lack of opportunity to resolve the oedipal struggle with their fathers and over-identification with their mothers.

A major problem with psychodynamic explanations of crime is that they fail to account for why similarly neurotic or traumatised people do not turn to crime, and why so few women who are, presumably, equally vulnerable to psychic disorders, are involved in crime. Beyond this, if crime is simply a symptom of individual pathology we can only account for the significant differences in levels and patterns of crime between nations in terms of the differential capacities of parents of different nationalities to rear their children effectively.

This said, it is also the case that probation officers meet a disproportionately large number of troubled people whose formative years were disrupted or traumatic and whose behaviour cannot easily be explained in terms of rational choice (see Chapter 13 – Psycho-social casework).

Social reaction theory

Social reaction theorists locate the ***irrevocable stigmatisation*** associated with the ***dramatic*** and ***public*** attribution of ***deviant labels***, a court appearance for example, as the process which ***spoils identity and projects the person so labelled into a deviant career*** (Goffman, 1961, Cicourel 1968, Becker 1963). Thus labelled, the actor is forced amongst those who are similarly stigmatised and their predicament is compounded by increased surveillance from ***agents of social control***, the police, probation officers or psychiatrists, which serves to ***amplify*** their deviance by reinforcing the label and closing off non-deviant options (Young 1971).

The world depicted by the social reaction theorist is made up of a multiplicity of ***normative ghettoes*** the behaviour of whose residents may be at variance with that of the members of other subcultures or social groups but is, nonetheless, supported within their own ***ghetto***. Things go wrong however when a member of a powerful ***normative ghetto*** enters a less powerful one and calls into question behaviour, like marijuhana smoking or gambling, which the residents regard as both normal and proper. This 'laying' of a law and order 'trip' 'on' another social group which is just getting on with its subculturally supported 'thing' is attacked by Schur (1974) in his book *Radical Non-Intervention* which enjoins us, whenever and wherever possible, to 'leave the kids alone'.

There are a number of problems with social reaction theory. While describing the processes whereby offenders, once apprehended, are inducted into a 'deviant career', it fails to explain why they might commit offences in the first place. It explains ***secondary*** not ***primary*** deviance. It also exaggerates the impact of official ***labelling***. It is simply not true that everybody who appears in court, for example, is inducted into a deviant career. The vast majority of people who appear in court only do so once. Its level of analysis forces us to focus on the activities of low-level operatives within control systems rather than the reasons why these systems exist in the first place. Social reaction theory also fails to address those factors in the social structure and in the biographies of individuals which might push some actors into a 'life of crime' more readily than others. By its insistence on the primacy of 'normative ghettoes' it ignores the existence of overarching social norms and laws, like the formal and informal prohibitions on robbery, murder and incest, of which virtually everybody is aware. Beyond this is the highly dubious implication at the heart of this perspective that crime would cease to be a problem if state officials stopped reacting to it.

The origins of crime

This said, probation officers are often required to work with people to whom a *deviant label* has been successfully applied and who are, as a consequence, unable to break out of a self-defeating pattern of behaviour which can often involve frequent institutionalisation. In such cases the *deviant* label Con, Blagger, Nutter etc. has become, in Goffman's term, their *master role*. The problem for the probation officer is to help the person discover alternative roles and a non-stigmatised identity.

(Social) control theories

Box (1983) argues that were it not for moral and normative constraints upon our behaviour and the fear of getting caught, most of us would break the law far more often. Conformity, he argues is ensured by normative control and surveillance. Thus the question of why people desist from crime is as important to control theorists as the question of why some people engage in it. Control theorists identify the loosening or neutralisation of moral and normative constraints as the factor which allows the actor to *drift* towards a universally available *sub-culture of delinquency* which coexists with, and indeed, constitutes the 'flip-side' of, the conventional moral order.

Matza (1964) notes that for 23 hours a day, six days a week, the 'delinquent' leads a completely conventional, law-abiding life. He contends that in circumstances in which a young person needs to assert some control over their lives and when their peers help them to neutralise the usual moral and normative constraints, a young person may be put into a state of drift where he or she may eventually make a commitment to the deviant enterprises.

Whereas most of the other perspectives presented here view the criminal as radically different from the law-abiding citizen, control theory believes that the terms 'criminal' and 'law abiding', when applied to people, refer to moments in their lives rather than enduring characteristics.

The problem with social control theories is that they fail to account for the fact that radical differentiation is a reality. In the real world a small minority of people are persistently involved in serious, and sometimes highly dangerous, crime and the overwhelming majority of people are not.

The fact that we may all misappropriate the firm's paper clips gets us nowhere nearer to an understanding of the aetiology of persistent child molestation, rape or aggravated burglarly. It seems evident that something more than a temporary loosening of the moral bind is at work in these cases. Social control theories offer us a useful insight into the nature of rules, but as an account of deviant motivation they leave much unaccounted for.

Social disorganisation theory

Social disorganisation theory emerged from the University of Chicago in the 1920s as an explanation of the persistence of higher levels of recorded juvenile crime in districts, **zones of transition**, inhabited by successive waves of new immigrants. Park (1936) and his colleagues depicted the city as an ecological system in which symbiotic (interdependent) social and economic relations existed between social groups who occupied different zones of the city. Thus a structure, a socio-economic pecking order, was elaborated on the basis of wealth, race and length of time in the country.

They saw the zone of transition as a place peopled by groups which were losing the norms, mores and mechanisms of social control of their culture of origin but had yet to take on those of their new culture. Thus norms were in a state of suspension and they were unable to effect a symbiotic relationship with their social environment. This resulted in **social disorganisation**. The Chicago School's argument was however circular since in contending that high rates of recorded juvenile crime were both the primary indicator of social disorganisation and a consequence of it, their thesis was irrefutable. The higher levels of recorded juvenile crime in the zone of transition were a reality but social disorganisation was an inference made on the basis of this reality. Whether they were observing social disorganisation or the coming of age of a group of people who responded to being debarred from status conferring roles by criminal *innovation* remains an open question (Taylor et al. 1973).

Matza (1969) suggests moreover that there is no such thing as social disorganisation, only sociologists who can't work out how a given form of social organisation actually works. It is also possible that as members of a low-status social group, residents of the zone of transition were prone to higher levels of formal intervention by **agents of social control** and, as such, were prone to **labelling** by them.

Perhaps the major contemporary significance of the work of the Chicago School is their observation that the movement from the zone of transition signalled upward social mobility and was invariably accompanied by a reduction in the rate of recorded juvenile crime amongst the socially mobile group. Put another way, the crime rate appeared to be a function of the zone rather than of its inhabitants and this has important implications for the race and crime debate in contemporary Britain.

Social strain theory

Merton posits a world in which a fantasy of an 'open society', *'The American Dream'* masks the reality of an **enforced division of labour** and lack of access to **legitimate opportunity**.

In such a situation, argue Cloward and Ohlin (1960), people trapped at the bottom of the social structure who are enjoined to achieve socially valued material goals but denied legitimate opportunities to do so, will experience *strain*. Their response to this strain will be to form *sub-cultural* groupings in which *solutions* to the problem of *status frustration* can be elaborated. These solutions can take a variety of forms, but for *slum* youth they tend to coalesce around property crime, if a sufficiently *organised* criminal infrastructure exists, violent inter-group rivalry if it does not, or a retreat into drink or drugs.

Strain theories underwent a revival in the wake of the inner-city disturbances of 1981 since it seemed clear that the young black and white participants in these events were exactly the kinds of people that Cloward and Ohlin had been talking about twenty years before (Lea and Young 1984).

A major problem with strain theory, in its most familiar guise of *opportunity theory*, is that it fails to account for social 'differentiation'. In other words, given that so many young people are the subjects of oppression, status frustration and hence 'strain', how is it that so few of them effect a persistently criminal, violent or retreatist adaptation to it? As Matza (1964) has pointed out, while these young people may possibly 'drift' in and out of crime depending upon how they are feeling about their predicament at any given time, they are not, he argues, inextricably wedded to a *delinquent subculture* in the way that Cloward and Ohlin suggest.

Conflict theories

Conflict theorists maintain that in advanced capitalist societies, there is an inevitable conflict between the owners of capital and the state on the one hand, and those who must sell their labour on the other (Taylor et al 1973, Platt and Takagi 1981). The criminal justice system, they argue, represents the repressive arm of state power which acts in the interests of the *ruling* class (Mathiesen 1974), Box and Hale 1986). Crime perpetrated by working class people may be, on the one hand, a form of resistance to oppression, and on the other, particularly if it is committed against other working class people, a manifestation of *false consciousness*.

This analysis has led to some fruitful work. In *Policing the Crisis* Stuart Hall and his colleagues (1978) explore the origins and political function of the 'mugging' panics of the early 1980s. Taylor and Taylor (1971) also utilise a class analysis in locating 'football hooliganism' as a product of the hijacking of the game by big business. In a similar vein in *Skinheads and the Magical Recovery of Community* John Clarke (1976) locates the emergence of 'skinhead' as an attempt by groups of dispossessed working class young people to symbolically resuscitate a real working class community which has been eroded by economic recession.

In *The Empire Strikes Back* Paul Gilroy (1982) argues that the criminalisation of black young people as a result of unwarranted intensive policing and prosecution must ultimately be explained in terms of the need of a capitalist state in crisis to transform economic crisis into racial conflict, thus displacing the problem and dividing the working class. In a rejoinder to Paul Gilroy, John Lea and Jock Young (1984) argued that by denying the reality that in some places at some times, black young people are disproportionately involved in crimes of poverty, robbery, hustling etc., Gilroy et al. deny both the oppression of black young people and the suffering of their victims, a disproportionate number of whom are also black young people. Lea and Young enjoin conflict theorists to abandon their **Left idealism**, which they define as an engagement with the world as it ought to be, in favour of a **Left realism** which engages with the world as it is, politically inconvenient warts and all (Matthews and Young 1986, 1991).

Left realism is in part a rejoinder to a group of highly influential American right-wing commentators of whom James Q. Wilson (1975) is the best known. Wilson noted that those most likely to be victimised by crime were the poorest and most defenseless members of society. Because of this these people, whom socialist parties had traditionally viewed as their natural constituency, had the biggest investment in the election of a party which took crime itself, rather than the behaviour of the agents of the criminal justice system, seriously. A major influence on left realist criminology has been **Feminist Criminology**.

Feminist Criminology

In the 1970s and 1980s feminist criminology showed us that women and children were far more prone to criminal victimisation than men and that, contrary to popular opinion, for many women, home was a very dangerous place. Indeed, had it not been for the research undertaken within feminist criminology it is unlikely that the sexual and physical abuse of children, police responses to the survivors of rape and sexual assault and sexual harrassment in the workplace would have assumed the heightened political profile they did in the 1980s.

Beyond this rediscovery of the victim and the exploration of the ways in which female crime is pathologised by both criminologists and agents of the justice and penal systems, feminist criminology asked a central, but previously unasked, criminological question. **Why don't women and girls?** More specifically, why do women seem to commit so few crimes, appear in court and enter prison so much less than men? Why, if they are subject to social strain, do they not form **delinquent subcultures** or **drift** into crime when normative constraints are weakened or surveillance reduced. Why do they not **learn criminal responses** to criminogenic **stimuli** (Gelsthorpe and Morris 1990, Heidenson 1985).

And, of course, the answer is that girls and boys are socialised differently, encouraged to express, or not express, anger frustration and disappointment differently. Rewarded or not rewarded, covertly and overtly, for sallying forth to take what they want from the world. What emerged from this analysis was that gender socialisation was the key variable in all of the theoretical explanations of crime discussed in this chapter. Indeed, in most of them, the explanation only works if one is not a woman. More than most of the other explanations, Feminism offers us an account of crime the sophistication of which mirrors the complexity of the phenomenon it strives to explain.

Levels of explanation

There are, of course, conflicts between these theoretical schools. Psychodynamic Freudians who contend that 'it's all in the mind' will never be able to find a point of accommodation with learning theorists who dispute the very existence of an entity called mind. Similarly, classicists who celebrate the possibility of human autonomy cannot compromise with the inexorable determinism of Mertonian strain theories which regard human intentionality as an illusion.

Yet to see these theoretical schools simply as conflicting explanations of the same phenomenon is an over-simplification. They do not merely give different answers to the same question

Table 12.1 Levels of explanation

	Structure	Culture	Biography
Classical	★		★
Bio-genetic			★
Psychodynamic			★
Learning			★
Social reaction		★	★
Social disorganisation	★	★	
Social control	★	★	★
Social strain	★	★	★
Conflict	★		
Feminism	★	★	★

but, as Table 12.1 indicates, they attempt to answer different questions, directed at different levels of the phenomenon of criminality and thus the explanations they offer may, in fact, be complementary.

For example, it is not inconceivable that an actor who experiences *social strain* may nonetheless be kept on the 'straight and narrow' by the strength of the normative *social control* exerted by family and friends. It is also the case that if the actor is black, young and lives in London, he may be subject to more intensive surveillance by the police (Smith 1984), and will therefore be more likely to have a criminal identity, or label thrust upon him. Should family and friends respond to this with condemnation which confirms unresolved feelings of guilt he has about his mother's recurrent depression, he may well internalise, and then proceed to act out, the deviant label. The way in which he does this will be shaped in no small part by his bio-genetic inheritance. A successful forger *draws* other peoples' signatures. This requires motor skills and hand-and-eye coordination of a very high order, and in this field, as in some others, hard work is no substitute for talent. Similarly, the proverbial 'seven stone weakling' would rapidly find 'sand scuffed in his face' if he tried to make a living out of violent street crime.

Chas Critcher (1976) maintains that to understand the nature of the criminal act we must view it simultaneously at the levels of *structure, culture and biography*. He writes:

> For us biography is the network of personal circumstances, decisions, and (mis)fortunes which occur within a situation already highly structured and with a limited number of available cultural options . . . .. It may ultimately be that

The origins of crime 187

biographical factors (including some conscious choice) are crucial in the final thrust towards criminal activity, but the problems which the crime 'acts out' have been set by the interaction of structural and cultural factors over and above the individual. (p. 170–1)

In Table 12.1 we indicate the levels of explanation at which the theoretical perspectives we are discussing are directed.

Structure, culture and biography exercise

Use the information you were given in Chapter 1. about Claudette, Dawn, Dave, Francis, Terry and Ron to answer the following questions.

Structure

(a) Has the law, or the way the law is administered, contributed in any way to Francis' plight? *Classicism.*
(b) Has the social class, racial gender and group of which Claudette is a member succeeded in achieving high status social and vocational roles in the city in which they live. *Social disorganisation/conflict/feminism.*
(c) Have Ron's norms and values, surveillance by others or his fear of being caught served to contain his criminal behaviour at all? *Social control.*
(d) Can you find any evidence that Francis is debarred from vocational or educational opportunities because of his position in the social structure? *Social strain/conflict.*
(e) To what extent could Claudette's predicament and her criminal behaviour be said to be 'political'? *Conflict.*

Culture

(a) Do you think that Dawn's criminal behaviour would be accepted as 'normal' by her peers, her parents or other people in her neighbourhood? *Social reaction.*
(b) What facets of Francis' culture/sub-culture could support him in leading a law-abiding life? *Social reaction.*
(c) What facets of Dave's culture/sub-culture could support his continued involvement in crime? *Social reaction.*
(d) Are Francis and his parents confused about the values, norms, laws and rules of our society? *Social disorganisation.*
(e) Matza says that young people who offend are often in a state of drift; somewhere between deviance and con-

formity and that the peer group, through a process of *sounding* (bragging about their exploits) neutralises the moral bind. Is there evidence to suggest that this is true for Dave or Claudette? *Social control/feminism.*

(f) Do you think Francis' ***delinquent solution*** is part of a collective response, by young people in his position, in his neighbourhood, to status frustration? *Social strain.*

Biography

(a) Do you think that Claudette calculates the potential costs and benefits of her criminal deeds before she embarks upon them? *Classicism.*

(b) Is Terry an ectomorph, an endomorph or a mesomorph and what, if anything, might this suggest about his propensity towards involvement in crime? *Biogenetic.*

(c) From what you have learned about Ron's background, in what ways could his offending be understood as an ***acting out*** of unresolved inner conflict or trauma? *Psychodynamic.*

(c) Can you identify any behavioural ***triggers*** or ***reinforcers*** which might account for the persistence of Dawn's criminality? *Learning.*

(d) Do you think that Ron has taken on a ***deviant identity***, i.e. has the role of ***criminal*** become his ***master role***? *Social reaction.*

(e) How do you imagine Claudette understands her social, economic and educational position; as the result of a 'conspiracy', as 'her own fault', as natural/normal, as regrettable but inevitable, as an achievement, etc. ? *Social strain.*

References

Belson, W. A. 1986 'The extent of stealing by London boys and some of its origins' *Advmt Sci Lond* 25.
Becker, H. 1963 *Outsiders. Studies in the Sociology of Deviance* New York: Free Press.
Bowlby, J. 1946 *Forty Four Juvenile Thieves* Harmondsworth: Penguin.
Box, S. 1983 *Power Crime and Mystification* London: Tavistock.
Cicourel, A. V. 1968 *The Social Organisation of Juvenile Justice* New York: Wiley.
Clarke, J. 1976 'Skinheads and the magical recovery of community' in Hall, S. and Jefferson, T. (eds) *Resistance through Rituals* London: Hutchinson.
Cloward, R. and Ohlin, L. 1960 *Delinquency and Opportunity* London: Routledge & Kegan Paul.
Critcher, C. 1976 'Structure, culture and biography' in Hall, S. and Jefferson, T. (eds) *Resistance Through Rituals* London: Hutchinson.

Denman, G. 1982 *Intensive Intermediate Treatment with Juvenile Offenders: A Handbook of Assessment and Groupwork Practice* Lancaster University Centre for Youth Crime and Community.
Freud, S. 1980 *Introductory Lectures* London: George Allen & Unwin.
Gelsthorpe, L. and Morris, A. (eds) 1990 *Feminist Perspectives in Criminology* Milton Keynes: Open University Press.
Gilroy, P. 1982 'Police and Thieves' in Centre for Contemporary Cultural Studies *The Empire Strikes Back* Birmingham: CCCS.
Goffman, I. 1961 *Asylums* New York: Doubleday.
Hall, S., Clarke, J. Critcher, C. Jefferson, T. and Roberts B. 1978 *Policing the Crisis* London: Macmillan.
Heidenson, F. 1985 *Women and Crime* London: Macmillan.
Lea, J. and Young, J. 1984 *What is to be Done About Law and Order* Harmondsworth: Penguin.
Mathiesen, T. 1974 *The Politics of Abolition* London: Martin Robertson.
Matthews, R. and Young, J. (eds) 1986 *Confronting Crime* London: Sage.
Matthews, R. and Young, J. (eds) 1991 *Realist Criminology* London: Sage.
Matza, D. 1964 *Delinquency and Drift* New York: Wiley.
Matza, D. 1969 *Becoming Deviant* New York: Prentice Hall.
Morris, A., Giller, H., Szued, M., and Geech H. 1980 *Justice for Children* London: Macmillan.
Park, Robert E. 1936 'Human Ecology' in *American Journal of Sociology* 42 (1) July 1.
Platt, T. and Takagi, P. 1981 *Crime and Social Justice* London: Macmillan.
Priestley, P., McGuire, J., Flegg, D., Hemsley, V., Welham, D. and Barnett, R. 1985 *Social Skills in Prison and Community* London: Routledge.
Rutherford, A. 1986 *Growing Out of Crime* Harmondsworth: Penguin.
Schur, E., 1975 *Radical Non-Intervention* New York: Prentice Hall.
Smith, D. 1984 *Police and People in London* London: Policy Studies Institute.
Taylor, I. and Taylor, L. 1971 'Soccer consciousness and soccer hooliganism' in Cohen S. (ed.) *Images of Deviance* Harmondsworth: Penguin.
Taylor, I., Walton, P. and Young, J. 1973 *The New Criminology* London: Routledge & Kegan Paul.
Wilson, James Q. 1975 *Thinking About Crime* New York: Basic Books.
Young, J. 1971 'The role of the police as amplifiers of deviancy' in Cohen, S. (ed.) *Images of Deviance* Harmondsworth: Penguin.

13 Responding to crime – practice theories

Introduction

Most social workers and probation officers are aware of a range of methods which may be utilised in face-to-face work at the level of individual 'biography'. The feature of social work practice which has attracted most criticism from 'progressive' opinion, however, is its tendency to work exclusively at this level (Walker and Beaumont 1985). Thus, it is argued, social workers individualise what are, in fact, political and administrative problems and fail to seize opportunities to transform 'private troubles' into 'public issues' (Mills 1959).

Political, administrative, and face-to-face Intervention

In fact, of course, workers can intervene at *political*, *administrative* and *face-to-face* levels and Pincus and Minahan (1973) offer us the concepts of Client System, Change-Agent System, Target System and Action System with which to think about our interventions at each of these levels.

The *political* level is where legislation and policy which determine the availability of resources and opportunities is decided. These decisions may be made in parliament or in our own agency but if we wish to work in the best interest of our client, we will sometimes need to make an impact upon such decisions. At this level our client system may be all the offenders, or indeed suspects, who are the subjects of a particular piece of legislation or policy, or the victims of a lack of particular resources or opportunities. Our *target* for change may be a particular group of decision-makers or resource holders. The *change agent* may be the probation officer who may convene a meeting of representatives of local agencies and campaigning groups to form an *action system* or indeed the National Association of Probation Officers acting in its capacity as a pressure group (Beaumont 1985).

The *administrative* level is where we address the operation of the local criminal justice system, and the agencies which constitute it, including our own. This level may be addressed by adopting strategies of systems management or systemic intervention (Thorpe et al. 1980). At an *administrative level* our *client system* may be a category of offenders within the local criminal justice system who are subject to a particular type of disposal and, because of this, have been made the objects of our agency's monitoring/systemic interventions. These interventions *target* key decision-makers in the system and attempt to change their behaviour. In this scenario the *action system* is the agency or office which has usually been galvanised into action by one or more individual *change agents*. Racial monitoring of magisterial decision-making and intervention by main grade probation officers at magistrates' meetings or probation committees is an example of an administrative intervention.

At a *face-to face* level our *client system* may be group, family, or individual we engage in counselling, problems-solving casework or social skills development. In these interventions the *target* for change is usually the attitudes or behaviour of an individual client, the relationships between members of the client system or the relationship between members of the client system and those beyond it. The *action system* tends to be the interaction between the group, family or individual and the *change agent* but may also involve coworkers and volunteers.

These are not mutually exclusive levels of work. Indeed, often, effective work at any of these levels will only be possible if attention is paid to each of them. The criminological perspectives outlined in the previous chapter suggest that effective intervention to prevent crime or reoffending should be directed at the levels, indicated in Table 13.1.

Having identified the most appropriate level/s of intervention we proceed to choose the most appropriate practice theory or method/s of intervention. In Table 13.2 we have linked levels of intervention with methods of intervention. This is, of necessity, somewhat simplified and so the distinction between methods and

Table 13.1 The implications of criminological theory for levels of intervention

	Political	Administrative	Face-to-face
Classicism	★	★	
Bio-genetic			★
Psychodynamic			★
Learning			★
Social reaction		★	
Social disorganisation		★	
Social control	★	★	
Social strain	★	★	★
Conflict	★	★	
Feminism	★	★	★

levels appears clearer here than it will in real life. Some methods, like social crime prevention, appear at more than one level and where this is the case they will be dealt with in the narrative at the first level at which they appear.

Table 13.2 Methods and levels of intervention

Political/policy interventions
    Community action
    Pressure group activity
    Social crime prevention
    Systems management and intervention

Administrative interventions
    Advocacy
    Community organisation
    Coordination of resources
    Social crime prevention } See political/policy interventions
    Systems management and intervention

Face-to-face interventions
    Community development
    Family work
    Group living
    Group work:
        Reciprocal groups
        Remedial groups
        Social goals groups
    Individual work:
        Behavioural casework
        Client-centred counselling
        Control
        Psycho-social casework/counselling
        Task-centred casework

Methods of intervention

Political/policy level

Community action: Community action is, as it were, the political arm of social work. As such it could involve probation officers as individuals and as members of a pressure group or trades union in political alliances with grass roots organisations of prisoners, prostitutes and other subjects of the justice system who are agitating for reform (Beaumont 1985).

The Association of Community Workers (ACW) argues that community action is necessary because:

> the organisation and structure of society causes problems of powerlessness, alienation and inequality. To achieve greater equality and social justice, resources and power must be redistributed [and] collective action is a proper and effective method of working for social, political and economic change. Community work is a process which promotes such collective action.

In so saying, the Association is espousing a view of society very similar to that articulated in the **strain, conflict** and ***feminist*** perspectives discussed in the previous chapter. Its statement proceeds from an analysis of the social structure to the conclusion that in order to redistribute power in favour of the socially disadvantaged the community must initiate collective political action (Alinsky 1970). Within this strategy, social goals groupwork of the type discussed below, in face-to-face methods, is a central building block.

Two of the most effective pieces of community action in the sphere of crime and justice in recent years have been the campaign to repeal the 1834 Vagrancy Act (SUS), in the early 1980s, and the campaign to have the Broadwater Farm murder convictions reviewed in the late 1980s and 1990s. Both of these campaigns arose as a result of sustained pressures from black grassroots organisations which forged alliances with politicians, interested journalists and academics and pressure groups within the justice system. Thomas Mathiesen's *The Politics of Abolition* [1974] remains a key point of reference on campaigning for change in the justice system.

Pressure group activity In Britain there are a number of organisations [Radical Alternatives to Prison, the Howard League, the Prison Reform Trust, National Association for Care and Resettlement of Offenders, the National IT Federation, the Association for Juvenile

Justice etc.] which campaign on issues of crime and offending. For its part, the National Association of Probation Officers [NAPO] acts simultaneously as a trades union, a professional association and a pressure group. As such, many probation officers have their own built-in pressure group whose job it is to turn *private troubles* into *public issues* (Mills 1959). It does this by contributing to public debate via the media, contributing to parliamentary debate by providing evidence for, or membership of, relevant enquiries and working parties and forging alliances with other organisations to bring issues to the British and European courts. In the recent period NAPO has been involved in campaigns to expose brutality in detention centres, reduce overcrowding in prisons, end the practice of remanding juveniles to adult remand facilities and decriminalise minor drug offences.

Clement Atlee, the post-war Labour prime minister, maintained that the social worker should play two roles. They should, he believed, act to alleviate the suffering of their clients and gather together information about these private troubles in order to create the empirical basis for the development of progressive social and criminal justice policies. It is certainly the case that the NAPO campaigns mentioned above have drawn heavily on the accounts of the private troubles encountered by probation officers and their clients.

Social crime prevention In France in the 1980s the Mitterand administration initiated a national programme which aimed to improve the living conditions of the French North African Community, to open up educational and vocational opportunity for its children and young people and to prevent crime and victimisation among them. By the mid-1980s each major French town had a crime prevention committee made up of young people, local residents and representatives from local agencies and political parties. These committees are chaired by the mayor who, in turn, attends a national committee on crime prevention chaired by the deputy prime minister.

This strategy was initiated after riots in the poor North African suburbs of many French cities in 1981. It was these disturbances which saw the emergence of SOS Racisme under the leadership of Harlem Desir and the social prevention programme which emerged was designed jointly by government ministers, SOS Racisme, the managing director of Club Mediteranee and a Maoist student leader.

The programme, which appointed local people as *animateurs sociale* and used techniques of community action and community development, was a central strand in Mitterand's anti-racist strategy. It was paralelled by the establishment of committees of children and young people aged between 9 and 17 years on town councils. Thus, the use of the term *prevention* in this context means not simply *crime* prevention but the prevention of social, cultural and economic marginality, of which juvenile crime and civil disorder were seen to be symptomatic. This approach to the problem of crime derives from the analyses developed by strain and conflict theorists (Cloward and Ohlin 1960). In France the concepts of *social prevention* and *social insertion*, which concerns the need to locate young people in appropriate social, educational and vocational roles, are often used interchangeably (King 1988).

The tone of the programme is captured well in the title of the Bonnemaison Report on the causes of the 1981 riots: *Juvenile Delinquency, Repression or Solidarity* and expresses the political committment behind the social prevention programme.

In Britain, in recent years there has been a growing political committment to crime prevention (Bright and Petterson 1984, NACRO 1988, Pitts 1991). As yet, however, the emphasis has tended to be on target hardening; better lighting, anti-climb paint, closed circuit TV, and the introduction of 'neighbourhood watch' schemes, rather than social intervention. Government crime control policy in the recent period has tended to ignore the 'social causes' of crime and it is only comparatively recently, as the, sometimes, very positive results of the French programme have come to the attention of decision-makers, that government and opposition have felt able to reopen the debate about social deprivation, crime and civil disorder.

Crime Concern, an agency sponsored by the Home Office to promote crime prevention, has identified the three major ingredients and ten principles which, they believe, promote successful social crime prevention.

The three ingredients are:

1. effective law enforcement;
2. target hardening; and
3. community organisation

The ten principles indicate that:

1. Programmes should be located in high crime areas.
2. Local residents should be involved from the start.
3. The quality of policing, repairs, social and recreational facilities etc. will emerge as a primary issue and can often be the catalyst which brings residents and young people together.

4. As a result, crime prevention worker must be prepared to demand additional resources from existing agencies.
5. Action should be collaborative, involving local people and all relevant local agencies.
6. Targetting should be precise and accurate and, in the case of youth crime, should focus on young people identified as problematic by a range of people and agencies in the area.
7. Beware of over-reaction. Sometimes it is sufficient to allay the anxieties of complainants by giving them accurate information.
8. Young victims of crime, including bullying, need support.
9. The victimisation of young people and youth crime prevention both need to be given a high public profile in the area though the media, leaflet campaigns and talks/video presentations in schools, tenants associations, social clubs etc.
10. Equal Opportunities considerations are very important if the credibility of the project is to be retained.

The Kirkholt Burglary Prevention Project (Forrester et al. 1988, 1990) offers an interesting example of a remarkably successful initiative in Rochdale based on inter-agency action involving the probation service, the police, social services and local residents.

There is some evidence that successful social crime prevention reduces demands on the police, housing departments, social services and the probation service. Yet professionals involved in crime prevention recognise that only policies which get to grips with the core problems experienced by residents will gain their support. These, characteristically, are problems of access to *opportunity* for young people; problems of regenerating badly neglected neighbourhoods and estates; the need for support for parents and teachers in their attempts to create a safe, clean and decent environment for children. To work at this level requires resources and a high level of inter-departmental cooperation and it is for this reason that, in a similar way to the French experiment, successful projects often emanate from the chief executive's department of the local authority.

Systems management and intervention The White Paper *Crime Justice and Protecting the Public* (1990) expresses the present government's commitment to systems management and intervention in the adult justice system. This committment has been inspired in no small part by the success of systems management initiatives in the juvenile justice system in the 1980s. As a result of the DHSS Intermediate Treatment (IT) Initiative (1983), between 1984 and 1990, the annual population of Young Offenders Institutions was reduced from approximately 7500 to 2000 (Bottoms et al. 1990).

A *justice system* is the interdependent network of agencies and agents which identifies, apprehends, prosecutes, assesses, treats, punishes or rehabilitates offenders. Its systemic nature flows from the fact that the actions [inputs] of one system agent will affect the operation [outputs] of the others. For example, the prejudice of a police officer may mean that their description of an offence allegedly committed by a black person will differ from the description they would give of the same offence if it were committed by a white person. Thus their system *input* will be presented to the court differently (Tipler 1988, Shallice and Gordon 1990). As a result the system *output*, the sentence of the court, may vary, according to the race of the defendant (Pitts 1988). Yet the stated goal of a justice system is to treat all defendants equally irrespective of 'race, colour or creed'. This will, in turn, have an impact on the demands placed on the alternative-to-custody or prison to which the offender is consigned.

Systems management and intervention derives its theoretical rationale from cybernetics or systems theory, as it is usually known (Bateson 1975). This theory suggest that all systems, ecological, biological, mechanical and social, have a tendency to move away from a state of optimal functioning towards a state of entropy or chaos. When social systems, called organisations, which are created by human beings, are moving out of equilibrium, the original goals are displaced and a process of organisation *drift* occurs. In this process the organisation/system generates output which are increasingly at odds with its stated goals.

In the justice system, pressure to manage the system more effectively comes from a variety of sources. In recent years the police have supported the development of cautioning schemes for juveniles in order to govern their input to the juvenile court which was tying-up an inordinate amount of scarce police resources. Similarly, the government, through the DHSS IT Initiative (1983), strove to govern inputs to the penal system in an attempt to alleviate, and defray the costs of, the prison crisis.

Systemic interventions usually combine four, inter-related, elements

1. Systems analysis and monitoring As its name suggests, this is an analysis of all the inputs and outputs of a local justice system and it enables the analysts to identify key points at which 'disfunctional' decisions are being made. Computer software packages for undertaking such an analysis have been developed by Information Systems (Lancaster) and NACRO.

2. *Policy change* As a result of the systems management exercises undertaken by Lancaster University with social services departments in the 1980s many of them decided to reduce,. and in some cases abandon, their residential provision for young offenders. They often decided to place limits on the professional autonomy of their social workers as well by requiring them to submit their court reports to senior officers for 'gatekeeping'. Similar policy changes are being ushered in by the Home Office and in the past few years an awareness of the need to keep offenders *down-tariff* and to target recommendations has infused the probation service at all levels.

3. *Administrative change* In the short term systemic analyses usually lead to the installation of 'gatekeepers'; people who monitor the decisions of system agents. Thus the recommendations made by probation officers in their PSRs will be **gate-kept** in an attempt to ensure consistency and support an organisational strategy to promote the use of community-based, as opposed to penal, responses to offenders. Such strategies may involve the use of **risk of custody scales**. These scales offer probation officers a method for calculating the likelihood of a defendant being given a custodial sentence. As such they are said to be useful indicators of the type of alternative disposal a probation officer might need to recommend to avert imprisonment. Opinion is divided about the usefulness of **risk of custody scales** because sentencers and sentencing can be unpredictable (Parker et al. 1989). As followers of the horses will be painfully aware, knowing the odds is one thing, getting a 'result' is quite another.

4. *The development of alternative provision* Where systemic interventions have been used to limit the use of custody, they have usually been accompanied by the development of alternative provision. In the adult system, **day centres** are the most obvious examples of such alternative provision. The success of this provision is, according to Bottoms et al. [1990], contingent upon the magistrates having confidence in the people who operate it (Curtis 1989).

As we have seen, the proponents of systems management and intervention can point to successes in the juvenile justice system. Whether such success can be replicated in the adult system with a group of older, and possibly more persistent, offenders who have patently not grown out of crime (Rutherford 1986) is another question. Beyond this we have to ask whether the justice system can actually be made to respond rationally and consistently by the application of systemic technology.

Administrative interventions

Advocacy Most of the offenders sentenced by the courts come from the social groups with the lowest incomes, who live in the poorest housing and have least access to educational and vocational opportunities. Many may lack the confidence, experience or ability to make claims upon welfare services or resources. It has always been a part of the work of the probation officer to use the status of the service, their authority and knowledge of 'the system' to negotiate, or make representations, on their client's behalf to the courts, welfare agencies and creditors. Whether poverty causes people to offend is an open question but advocacy on behalf of a client can be justified both on the grounds of promoting social justice and on the more pragmatic basis that it is difficult to engage clients in 'work on their offending behaviour' while they are preoccupied with their material needs.

Although advocacy does not address the root causes of social inequality and, if practised indiscriminately can engender increased dependency on the part of the client, it is sometimes a very necessary prerequisite to stabilising a chaotic situation in order that the client can develop the skills of self-advocacy.

Community organisation The 1984 Home Office Statement of National Objectives and Priorities for the Probation Service [SNOP] (1984) states:

> ... the service should seek to ... encourage the involvement of the local community in the widest practicable approach to offending the offenders, taking account of the influence of family, schools and other social factors and of the potential contributions of other agencies ... develop the service to the wider public by contributing to initiatives concerned with the prevention of crime and the support of victims and playing a part in the activities of local and statutory organisations.

SNOP locates the community as, simultaneously, a consumer of the service's product and a resource to be utilised in its attempt to fulfill its aims and objectives. This suggests a strategy of **community organisation.** Community organisation is the branch of community work concerned with the coordination of existing resources and services in a neighbourhood or region in order to work collaboratively to achieve shared goals.

This approach is also commended by the Green Paper *Partnership in Dealing with Offenders in the Community* (Home Office [1990]) which foresees the probation service sharing its tasks with other voluntary and statutory agencies to a much greater extent than at present.

> the community-based approach of the Safer Cities Programme and of the drugs initiative could be developed to tackle crime more generally. This would involve setting up a local committee on which would be represented the local authority, the major statutory agencies [police, probation, social services etc.], the voluntary sector, community relations councils and local business. Such a committee might then analyse local crime patterns to identify particular 'trouble spots' and types of crime committed by, for instance, young adults; look at local sentencing patterns especially in relation to the target group; and then devise a strategy for reducing crime committed by people in that group.

As noted above, **community organisation** is one of the three major elements of **social crime prevention** strategies.

Coordination of resources [networking] Probation officers have traditionally sought to introduce those they supervise to 'a range of positive influences and experiences suited to their particular needs' and in this, 'to enlist the help of other agencies in the wider community' (*The Sentence of the Court: a Handbook for Courts on the Treatment of Offenders* Home Office 1986). This has entailed referral to and liaison with a variety of statutory and voluntary bodies offering educational, health and recreational service. The White Paper *Crime Justice and Protecting the Public* [1990] suggests that this will become an increasingly important role for the probation officer. It states that 'one to one work with offenders will not usually be enough to turn them away from crime'. The supervising officer should put together a programme for each offender which may involve many different services and voluntary organisations. In this scenario the probation officer moves from the position in which s/he is simply concerned to devise a solution with the offender to one in which s/he becomes the broker of solutions devised by a variety of agencies.

Face-to-face interventions

Community development Community development is the branch of community work concerned with developing social provision, under fives playgroups, womens' refuges, crash-pads for homeless young offenders etc. where a need has been demonstrated but no provision exists. As the service becomes more 'offence-focused' less and less attention is paid to this aspect of the probation officer's role.

In his book, *Act Natural* (1974) Bruce Hugman described the development of a 'detached probation project' in which officers lived in a 'red-light' district and attempted to develop, with people in trouble with the law in the area, relevant services. Social goals groupwork, referred to below, is a favoured method of intervention used by community development workers.

Family work Intervention with families acknowledges that the behaviour of an individual, criminal or otherwise, may be a product of, or maintained by, the family 'system' of which they are a part. Family therapists use the concept of 'identified patient' or 'client' whose 'deviant' or 'sick' behaviour 'acts out', or distracts attention from, the family's problem. Viewed in this way, offending is not simply the act of an individual but an outcome of the processes at work within the family. It follows from this that the target for intervention will be the family; the way it allocates roles; the way its members communicate; its generational and gender boundaries and its secrets. Ideas and techniques developed in family therapy are commonly utilised by probation officers engaged in civil work.

Few probation officers undertake *family therapy* but they often have an important role to play with the families of offenders. When an offender has been committed to custody there is often a problem of how a young, not very well-off, family will be able to maintain contact with a prisoner who may well be in a goal more than 100 miles from home. The probation officer engaged in *throughcare*, by offering emotional support, practical advice and by arranging transport, and/or applying for grants from charities, may support the family in its attempt to maintain contact. S/he may also act as an important channel of communication between client and family.

Group living Work with offenders in hostels or day-centres draws upon the same range of methods as community-based work. There is, however, an additional dimension which arises from shared daily living. Whether or not this experience is consciously utilised as a method of work, it will probably have an important impact on the outcome of that work.

Maxwell Jones (1968) was one of the first people to recognise this and it led him to develop the concept of the ***therapeutic*** *community*. He noted that the structure and regime of the shared living experience could, of itself, be either therapeutic or antitherapeutic. Jones believed that the factors which maximised the therapeutic potential of a group-living situation were:

>maximisation of communication;
>democratisation; and
>reciprocity.

In such a mileau the worker strives to create a community in which both the culture carried by the workers and the sub-culture of residents are subject to discussion, scrutiny and decision by all members of that community, staff and residents. There are obvious limitations on introducing the ***therapeutic community*** model, lock, stock and barrel into probation day centres or hostels because of the statutory nature of the relationship between residents and staff yet, as long as these limitations are acknowledged, the principles of ***communication, democratisation*** and ***reciprocity*** can serve as a solid foundation for such work.

Group work Group work is an increasingly popular method of working with adult offenders. The potential advantages of group work are that

1. Members may be able to gain support from others in a similar predicament.
2. Group pressure can be harnessed to bring about attitude change.
3. Members can learn from each others' ideas, attitudes and experiences.
4. Members' self esteem can be enhanced because they can act as helpers as well as the helped.
5. The group can be a safe setting in which members can try out new behaviours and attitudes.
6. Power may be dispersed more widely, and more democratically, in a group than in a one-to-one encounter with a worker.

The aims and theoretical underpinnings of groupwork are as diverse as in individual work but three broad categories of group can be identified

(i) *Remedial groups*: In a remedial group the primary objective is to bring about change in the members themselves. This may be attempted by means of an educational programme (about the effects of alcohol for example], psychodynamic group therapy, an offending workshop, social skills training or desensitisation programme.

[ii] *Reciprocal groups*: As their name implies, the objective of a reciprocal group is to encourage the growth of reciprocity, mutual support and mutual help, amongst people in a similar predicament. A prisoner's partners group or a support group for people who were once dependent upon drugs or alcohol would fall into this category. These are groups which are formed by workers. Reciprocal groups which arise spontaneously, adolescent peer groups for example, are referred to as *natural groups* to distinguish them from *formed groups*. Detached [street] workers work with such *natural* groups. Two of the best British examples of detached groupwork with offenders can be found in Hugman (1974) and Smith et al. (1972).

[ii] *Social goals groups*: A social goals group strives to bring about change in its external environment. The social goals group par excellence is the tenant's association. As we have noted, social goals groups are an integral part of social crime prevention, community action and community development initiatives.

Clarity about the type, purpose and duration of a group, leadership style and boundaries appear to be crucial to success in group work interventions.

Individual work [i] *Behavioural casework*: Behavioural work, based as it is on learning theory, aims to achieve specific behavioural change. It is not concerned to encourage reflection and introspection except insofar as this provides a clue to the triggers and reinforcers which have precipitated or maintained particular behaviour patterns. 'Desired' behaviour is identified and a system of rewards and punishments is structured in such a way that the desired behaviour may be learned.

Most behavioural work undertaken with offenders nowadays has abandoned 'strict' behavioural regimes in favour of a pragmatism which allows them to pick 'n' mix theories and method.

As McGuire and Priestley (1985) note:

> a constructive and effective response to the problem of offending behaviour would necessarily have many different ingredients.

They suggest that behavioural approaches should be broadened to encompass work on beliefs and values, self-image, social skills, self-control, risk-taking and decision-making.

Behavioural work with offenders, individually or in groups, commonly focuses on the way the offender understands the factors which precipitated their offending and alternative legitimate behavioural options available to them. Workers pursuing a correctional or offending curriculum will often encourage offenders to rehearse, by using role play or simulations, a wider 'repertoire of responses' to the 'criminogenic' circumstances they may encounter (Denman 1982, Thorpe et al. 1980).

[ii] *Client-centred counselling*: Client-centred therapy was pioneered and popularised by Carl Rogers (1967) who developed the concepts of the *real self* and the *false self*. The *real self* is the person we actually are. If, however, those around us are disapproving, rejecting and attempt to impose their view of who we ought to be, and how we ought to think and feel, we may be forced to conform to their expectations. This will require us to submerge our *real self* and take on a *false self* instead.

Too great an **incongruence** between the *real* and the *false* selves is a source of stress, anxiety and a sense of worthlessness. Client-centred counselling therefore attempts to help clients rediscover, or 'get back in touch with' the real feelings which have been submerged, or repressed.

This is not achieved by the worker doing anything 'to' the client. The worker's main task is to provide **unconditional positive regard** and a warm accepting atmosphere in which the client feels safe to explore their real feelings. The worker does not diagnose problems, set goals, give advice, or suggest solutions; all of this remains the responsibility, and under the control of, the client.

Because the method hinges on the quality of the relationship, the worker must have:

1. a capacity for empathy, i.e. understanding;
2. a capacity to communicate respect;
3. a facilitative genuineness;
4. a capacity for facilitative self-disclosure;
5. an ability to confront and use the *immediacy* of the relationship with the client as a means of furthering insight and understanding.

Although many probation officers employ elements of this approach in their work, its essential philosophy is not readily translatable into a setting in which the worker carries responsibility to enforce compliance with statutory requirements and where the client may be unwilling and unmotivated to change.

The significance of Roger's work theoretically is that it effectively brings together the **Psychodynamic** and **Social Reaction** perspectives.

[iii] *Control*: This is hardly a 'method of intervention' *per se* and yet the attempt to exercise control and surveillance features significantly in the repertoire of things probation officers do. Phrases like 'setting limits'. 'providing structure' or 'enabling her/him to come to terms with the consequences of their actions' are commonplace entries in probation officers records. Every probation officer has experienced situations in which the only feasible option is to try to ensure minimal compliance with the terms of the probation order or licence. Bottoms and McWilliams [1979] discuss the possibility that this type of surveillance and control may, for as long as it lasts, 'hold' clients and prevent them from re-offending.

[iv] *Psycho-social casework*: This approach does not offer a direct route to preventing offending. Rather it tries to enable people to attain a better adjustment, both to themselves and to their social environment so that the stress, depression or anxiety which may have contributed to their offending is minimised. Like **client-centred therapy** (see above) psycho-social work derives also its theoretical rationale from *psychodynamic* theory and places great emphasis on the relationship between worker and client. This is seen to be the medium through which ego-support: encouraging the 'healthy'.'coping' 'parts' of the client, is undertaken [Hollis 1964].

Alongside this, the worker tries to help the client understand the connections between unresolved conflicts in the past and present behaviour patterns. Proponents of this approach argue that this awareness (insight) may, of itself, be sufficient to release clients from these dysfunctional patterns of behaviour rooted in damaging early experiences and allow them to take control of, and organise, their lives on the basis of current realities.

Change of this sort is more likely to occur if intellectual understanding is accompanied by a *working through* at an emotional level, of past conflicts. This process occurs, characteristically, when a client develops a *transference relationship* with the worker in which strong feelings about figures from the past, usually parents, are projected onto the worker. Thus the feelings are re-experienced and being, therefore, 'present in the room', they can be more satisfactorily resolved.

It is important to distinguish here between **psychoanalysis**, **psychotherapy** and **psycho-social casework**. Probation officers and social workers do not undertake psychoanalysis or psychotherapy as part of their work with offenders. They may however engage in pyscho-social casework which is informed by concepts such as **unconscious motivation** and **transference** but focuses upon conscious material and current realities.

[v] . *Task-centred casework*: Task-centred work is, in effect, a fusion of **behavioural** and **client-centred** approaches. It focuses on the systematic attainment of limited, concrete goals within a mutually agreed time-span. The client carries responsibility for identifying the goals to be achieved and selecting the means whereby they will be achieved. This is seen to be a way of maximising the client's motivation and minimising their dependency on the worker.

In *Exploring the Task-centred Casework Method* Goldberg et al. [1975] state that:

> The underlying theory of this practice model is akin to crisis theory, namely that temporary breakdown in a person's problem-solving capacity triggers off corrective change forces. These forces, it is postulated, operate quickly to reduce problems to a tolerable level after which the intensity and the motivation for further change lessens. Setting limits in advance may increase and quicken these processes of change in two ways; by providing a deadline against which the client must work and by heightening his expectations that certain changes can occur within the time-limit.

Task-centred casework may be divided into five phases:

1. *Problem exploration*: problems are explored and ranked in order of importance.
2. *Agreement on target problem*: client and worker identify the problem to be worked on.
3. *Formulation of tasks*: the problem is broken down into a series of task and responsibility for the fulfilment of these tasks is clarified.
4. *Facilitation of task achievement*: the worker monitors and supports the client as they proceed through the previously agreed task towards the resolution of the problem.
5. *Termination*: client and worker review and evaluate the work done and, if necessary, formulate a contract for undertaking the next piece of work.

During the 1970s the Inner London Probation Service undertook an experiment in which probationers were worked with in accordance with the precepts of task-centred casework. This experiment was instrumental in prompting the introduction of the six month minimum probation order, prior to this the minimum period had been one year. (Folkard et al. 1976)

The major advantage of task-centred casework is that the client is fully, and usually willingly, involved in the process of change. Its limitation is that the way problems are identified and the time available to address them may mean that more complex and deep-rooted problems are not tackled. Beyond this, the statutory nature of the client–worker relationship will often mean that the probation officer will feel that s/he must place some limits on the client's freedom to select the goals they will pursue.

Postscript

But will it work?

Crime and justice are political hot potatoes. In the early 1980s the Home Secretary, Leon Britten, bemoaning what he saw as the sorry state of the relationship between probation officers and sentencers, called for a 'new partnership with the courts'. In so doing he gave expression to a belief, which was fairly widespread in the government of the day, that probation officers were colluding with the bad behaviour of their clients and, as such, helping to undermine the 'rule of law'. By 1990, however, the government was presenting probation officers to the courts, the public and their own back-benchers as hard-headed professionals who would confront offending behaviour wherever it raised its ugly head and 'protect the public' to boot (Home Office 1990, Davies and Wright 1989).

In 1989 the Home Office initiated a research programme aimed at identifying those components of an, as yet undefined, *intensive probation* which would 'work' [Mair 1989]. In spring 1991 participants at a national conference entitled 'what works: effective methods to reduce re-offending' were informed that

> The 'nothing works' doctrine is dead. A large and growing body of evidence shows that reoffending can be systematically reduced.

These were significant developments because it was not so long ago that many probation officers and most criminologists and penal reformers appeared to subscribe to the idea that

> It does not seem to matter what form of treatment in the correctional system is attempted, whether vocational training or academic education; whether counseling inmates

individually, in groups or not at all; whether therapy is administered by social workers or psychiatrists; whether the institutional context of the treatment is custodial or benign: whether the sentences are short or long; whether the person is placed on probation or released on parole; or whether the treatment takes place in the community or in institutions.
[Wilson 1975, p. 169]

This sombre assessment, based on Martinson's [1974] survey of 231 research studies, has been underscored by many subsequent investigations which have drawn similarly pessimistic conclusions [Hood 1967, Wilkins 1969, Sinclair 1971, Davies 1969, Dunlop 1975, Millham et al. 1975, Cornish and Clarke 1975, Folkard, Smith and Smith 1976, Bottoms and McWilliams 1979, Thorpe et al. 1980]. Indeed, it was on the basis of such evidence that in the mid-1970s, criminologists reluctantly announced 'the decline of the rehabilitative ideal'. Over the next decade and a half a broad political consensus emerged to support the view that the best we could hope for in our work with offenders was to minimise the negative impact of prosecution, imprisonment and social work intervention on their lives (Bottoms and McWilliams 1979, Thorpe et al. 1980, Morris et al. 1980).

That those who maintain that they have found a method which 'works' can produce no convincing evidence for this assertion, suggests that this renaissance of optimism is rooted in political rather than empirical considerations.

What we are in fact discovering is that the claims of the proponents of 'nothing works' have to be viewed as sceptically as those of the proponents of 'something works'. As Blagg and Smith (1989) note:

> ... the outcome research of the early 1970s was capable of being interpreted in other ways than 'nothing works'... This has recently led some writers, for example Ken Pease, who worked at the Home Office Research Unit in the 1970s to argue that the pessimistic conclusions drawn from this research were not necessarily justified.

The 'nothing works' doctrine, based as it was on a global analysis of reconviction rates, failed to pinpoint those individuals, projects and institutions whose endeavours did, in fact, 'work'. The problem with both the 'something' and 'nothing' works arguments is their determination to locate the method which works rather than to undertake the much harder job of discovering the complex interplay of time, place, relationships and methods which lead to effective interventions.

Effective work with offenders

The little we know about the things which actually reduce reoffending is that they require both initiative and commitment. They tend to be undertaken by thoughtful people who are offered the freedom to use their methods, or tools, in ways which seem sensible in the light of the predicament of the offender, available resources and new knowledge.

This begins to explain why research into the 'effectiveness' of 'methods of intervention' is a doomed endeavour. If a probation officer takes an ailing car to the garage s/he expects the engineer to use the tools which are necessary to remedy the fault. Before the engineer can do this however, s/he has to assess the fault and then, in the light of the make, model, age and condition of the car, select the right tools for the job(Pitts 1992).

If the probation officer arrived at the garage with a broken brake light s/he would be surprised and annoyed if the engineer set about the gear box with a hammer and chisel. If, moreover, the engineer said that s/he was doing this because the Ministry of Transport had issued a directive concerning the one and only solution to malfunctioning cars, s/he would probably phone the duty mental health social worker and vote for the opposition at the next election.

In reality, of course, methods are only effective if they are used in the right circumstances. The answer to the question, *'which is the most effective method?'* is the same as the answer to the question *'which is the most effective tool'* and it is *'it depends'*. Working out 'what' 'it' 'depends' on is what distinguishes professionals from technicians.

A professional is responsible for defining the problem and determining the response that will be made to that problem. A technician, by contrast, applies techniques devised by somebody else to problems defined by somebody else. Professionals and technicians must both develop skills and techniques but professionals carry on additional responsibility to exert judgement and discernment.

Effective rehabilitative ventures are reflexive not directive, they respond to a situation as it unfolds. Their language is an innovative dialogue not a prescriptive monologue. For these reasons, successful interventions can seldom be categorised, cloned and transplanted. To do so may be helpful to researchers, administrators and politicians because it tidies up a messy and idiosyncratic world, but, unfortunately, they do not seem to travel well.

If this is true, then in our choice of methods we are best advised to pursue a thoughtful and reflective diversity rather than a doctrinaire conformity. Crime is not a simple, undifferentiated monolith to be managed more effectively, its origins and manifestations are both complex and diverse. A service which is genuinely committed to reducing crime and protecting the victims of crime will reflect that complexity in the diversity of its practice.

References

Alinsky, S. 1970 *Rules for Radicals* New York: Vintage.
Bateson, G. 1975 *Steps to an Ecology of Mind* New York: Ballantine.
Beaumont, B. 1985 'Probation, working for social change' in Walker, H. and Beaumont, B. (eds) *Working With Offenders* Basingstoke: Macmillan.
Blagg, H. and Smith, D. 1989 *Crime, Penal Policy and Social Work* London: Longman.
Bottoms, A. et al. 1990 *Intermediate Treatment and Juvenile Justice. Implications and Findings from a Survey of Intermediate Treatment Policy and Practice Evaluation Project Final Report* London: HMSO.
Bottoms, A. and McWilliams, W. 1979 'A non-treatment paradigm for probation practice' *BJSW* **9** (2), 159–202.
Bright, J. and Petterson, G. 1984 *Safe Neighbourhoods* London: NACRO.
Cloward, R. and Ohlin L. 1960 *Delinquency and Opportunity* New York: Routledge & Kegan Paul.
Cornish, D. and Clarke, R. 1975 *Residential Treatment and Its Effects on Delinquency* London: HMSO.
Curtis, S. 1989 *Juvenile Delinquency: Prevention Through Intermediate Treatment* London: Batsford.
Davies, M. 1969 *Probationers in their Social Environment* Home Office Research Study No. 2, London: HMSO.
Davies, M. and Wright, A. 1989 *The Changing Face of Probation, Skills Knowledge and Qualities* Norwich, University of East Anglia: Social Work Monographs.
Denman, G. 1982 *Intensive Intermediate Treatment with Juvenile Offenders: A Handbook of Assessment and Groupwork Practice* Lancaster Centre for Youth Crime and Community.
DHSS 1983 *Further Development of Intermediate Treatment (IT)*, LAC (83) (3) 26 January.
Dunlop, A. 1975 *The Approved School Experience* London: HMSO.
Folkard, M., Smith D. and Smith, D. 1976 *IMPACT* Vol II London: HMSO.
Forrester, D., Chatterton, M. and Pease, K. 1988 *The Kirkholt Burglary Prevention Project, Rochdale* London: Home Office.
Forrester, D., Frenz, S., O'Conell, M. and Pease, K. 1990 *The Kirkholt Burglary Prevention Project Phase II* London: Home Office.
Goldberg, I. 1975 'Exploring the task-centred casework method' *Social Work Today*, **9**, No. 2.
Hollis, F. 1964 *Psychosocial Therapy* New York: Random House.
Home Office 1984 *Statement of National Objectives and Priorities for the Probation Service* London: HMSO.
Home Office 1986 *The Sentence of the Court: A Handbook for Courts on the Treatment of Offenders* London: HMSO.
Home Office 1990 *Crime, Justice and Protecting the Public* London: HMSO.
Home Office 1990 *Partnership in Dealing With Offenders in the Community* London: HMSO.
Hood, R. G. 1967 'Research on the effectiveness of punishments and treatments'

in Radzinowicz, L. and Wolfgang, M. [eds] [1971] *Crime and Justice* New York: Basic Books.
Hugman, B. 1974 *Act Natural* London: National Council of Voluntary Organisations
Jones, M. 1968 *The Therapeutic Community* Harmondsworth: Penguin.
King, M. 1988 *How to Make Social Crime Prevention Work: the French Experience* London: NACRO.
Mair, G. 1989 'Intensive Probation in England and Wales: origins and outlook', Paper presented to the British Criminology Conference, Bristol 17–20 July 1989, Unpublished.
Martinson, R. (1974) 'What works? – questions and answers about prison reform' *The Public Interest* Spring, pp. 22–54.
Mathiesen, T. 1974 *The Politics of Abolition* London: Martin Robertson.
Mc Guire, J. and Priestley, P. 1985 *Offending Behaviour* London: Batsford.
Millham, S., Bullock, R. and Cherrett, P. 1975 *After Grace, Teeth* London: Chaucer.
Mills, C. Wright 1959 *The Sociological Imagination* Harmondsworth: Penguin.
Morris, A., Giller, H., Szued, M. and Geech, H. 1980 *Justice for Children* London: Macmillan.
NACRO Youth Activities Unit 1988 *Golf Links Youth Project* London: NACRO.
Parker, H., Sumner, M. and Jarvis, G. 1989 *Unmasking the Magistrates* Milton Keynes: Open University Press.
Pincus, A. and Minahan, A. 1973 *Social Work Practice: Model and Method* Illinois: Peacock Press.
Pitts, J. 1988 *The Politics of Juvenile Crime* London: Sage.
Pitts, J. 1991 'Prevention is better than crime' *Social Work Today* May.
Pitts, J. 1992 'The end of an era' *Howard Journal* May.
Priestley, P., McGuire, J., Flegg, D. Hemsley, D., Welham, V. and Barnett, R. 1984 *Social Skills in Prison and Community* London; Routledge.
Rogers, C. 1967 *On Becoming a Person* London: Bantam.
Rutherford, A. 1986 *Growing Out of Crime* Harmondsworth: Penguin.
Satir, V. 1964 *Conjoint Family Therapy* Palo Alto: Science and Behaviour Books.
Shallice, A. and Gordon, P. 1990 *Black People, White Justice and the Criminal Justice System* London: Runnymede Trust.
Sinclair, I. 1971 *Hostels and Probationers* Home Office Research Study No. 6, London: HMSO.
Smith, C., Farrant, M. and Marchant, H. 1972 *The Wincroft Youth Project* London: Tavistock.
Thorpe, D., Smith. D., Green, C. and Paley, J. 1980 *Out of Care* London: Allen & Unwin.
Tipler, J. 1988 'Colour conscious justice' *Community Care (Supplement)* 30 March 1989.
Walker, H. and Beaumont, B. 1985 *Probation Work: Critical Theory and Socialist Practice* London: Macmillan.
Wilkins, L. T. 1969 *Evaluation of Penal Measures* New York: Random House.
Wilson, James Q. 1975 *Thinking about crime* New York: Basic Books.

14 The 'What kind of probation officer are you?' quiz

We don't have to tell you about the crucial part that self evaluation plays in the learning process and professional development. Now we have almost reached the end of our journey with you, we would like to provide you with the opportunity to reflect upon your travels and to contemplate the kind of probation officer you are or are going to be....

Select your most likely response to each of the following situations

1. Dave suggests that you meet in the pub in future as he is sure he will be able to relax and confide in you more in that setting.
   You say:

   (a) I can understand that you might find the pub more comfortable, as we would be avoiding the real issues, but I feel it would be more appropriate to continue meeting in my office?
   (b) Mine's a double gin and tonic?
   (c) Why don't we really make a night of it and go on to a club afterwards?
   (d) How dare you! Who do you take me for! I've never heard such an outrageous suggestion in my life! If you ever say that again I will have no alternative but to take you back to court?

2. Francis' friend who you know to be 16 years old arrives

to collect him in a gleaming red K reg Pontiac Firebird. Do you:

(a) Say 'Are you insured to drive this vehicle?'
(b) Ask whether you could take it for a spin down the motorway?
(c) Remark that it's very much like the car you have at home, although yours is a collectors item?
(d) Dial 999?

3. Her sister invites you to Claudette's coming home party. Do you:

(a) Thank her politely but explain that your professional boundaries do not allow you to socialise with clients?
(b) Say you'd love to go, but could she lend you something to wear?
(c) Offer to do the catering and have it at your place?
(d) Stutter, mumble and say you'll probably have to get written permission from the CPO?

4. The ACPO requests that your team makes a presentation to the probation committee about its work. Do you:

(a) Suggest that you set up a small working party and produce a paper?
(b) Volunteer to visit the last team that did it and pinch all their ideas?
(c) Offer to plan, organise and present the whole thing yourself, as everybody else works so hard and you feel you owe them so much?.
(d) Go off sick?

5. You are doing court duty and the magistrate questions an inappropriate recommendation in a PSR. Do you:

(a) Apologise and ask politely for the case to be put back so you can contact the author?
(b) Tippex out the bit they don't like?
(c) Rise and bow to the bench, before briefly commiserating with them about the falling standards in the probation service?
(d) Burst into tears and run from the courtroom?

6. The magistrates ask you to look after the four children of a defendant who are making a lot of noise in the back of the court. Do you:

(a) Explain to the court that this is not strictly speaking your

role, but if there is no alternative you are prepared to assist on this occasion?
(b) Give the kids a fiver and tell them to come back in an hour?
(c) Say that nothing would give you greater pleasure and that if the defendant goes to prison, you'd be happy to foster them?
(d) Dive under the bench and hope that the request was directed at somebody else?

7. You are preparing a PSR, when the client tells you they have committed several other offences for which they have not been charged. Do you:

(a) Advise them to confess all so that they are not constantly looking over their shoulder in future and can start with a clean slate?
(b) Congratulate them and tell them about a few offences you've got away with in your time?
(c) Tell them, with tears in your eyes, how moved you are that they have trusted you sufficiently to share such personally sensitive information?
(d) Dial 999?

8. You are visiting a client in prison, who asks you if you could deliver a letter for them. Do you:

(a) Explain that prison regulations clearly state that you are not allowed to receive anything from or give anything to someone serving a prison sentence?
(b) Slip it into your poachers jacket, and pass over the bottle of Scotch he paid you for last time?
(c) Tell the client that although you would do anything in the world for them you cannot break prison rules, for to do so would make it worse for everybody else?
(d) Press the panic button?

9. You are at a case conference and the chair asks you to comment on the quality of bonding between your client and their child. Do you:

(a) Answer fully and succinctly reading from your carefully compiled notes?
(b) Wink at the chair, saying that you have never actually seen parent and child tied together but bonding is one of your particular interests?
(c) Say you do not have a lot of specialist knowledge in this area but if the chair could spare some time, perhaps

What kind of probation officer are you 215

over dinner one evening, you'd be fascinated to learn more?
(d) Take out the complete works of Bowlby from your briefcase?

10. Your ACPO asks to see six case files prior to your annual appraisal. Do you:

(a) Ask her to select any six as they are all up to date?
(b) Borrow six from the colleague next door?
(c) Suggest that six would not reflect the true quality, depth, and breadth of your work, not to mention your commitment – offer her 15?
(d) Take all your case records home that night and stay up till 4 am rewriting them?

11. Your supervisor asks to alter a supervision session. Do you:

(a) Check, while you've both got your diaries out, that the next few are still mutually convenient?
(b) Say that there's no problem, you'd forgotten about it anyway, as your diary has been seized in a dawn raid.
(c) Ask if you could have your supervision session now, as they are so precious to you, such a source of support and guidance that you would feel lost without one for another week?
(d) Burst into tears and spend a sleepless night wondering whether your supervisor is trying to avoid you?

12. You are at a team meeting where the senior is attempting to allocate a record number of cases. Do you:

(a) Suggest that all the cases are weighted in terms of complexity as this would be the most equitable means of allocation?
(b) Take your fair share, and pay someone else to do them from the proceeds of fiddling your expenses?
(c) Offer to take them all as everyone is under so much pressure, and say it distresses you when no one volunteers as it leaves the senior in such a difficult position?
(d) Dial 999, burst into tears and run out of the office?

Mainly (a)s.... You're the kind of PO who brings a smile to the face of the Home Secretary. Don't forget, when you are promoted next week, that we taught you everything you know.
Mainly (b)s... You're the kind of PO who will have a PO of their

own very soon... don't forget, when you're facing your first disciplinary hearing, that it was nothing to do with us.

Mainly (c)s... You're the kind of PO who is going to slither your way up to the top if it kills you... where did we go wrong?

Mainly (d)s... You're the kind of PO who could do with a holiday... you seem a little stressed at the moment... nothing that a few years of psychotherapy can't cure however.

15 Postscript: The correctional crossword

NB. After each clue the figures in curved brackets ( ) indicate the number of letters in the answer: figures in square brackets [ ] indicate the chapter which would assist with the solution. Answers on p 220.

Across
1. What new officers should expect from seniors, and probationers from a probation officer. (11) [7, 11]
5. Court order for psychiatric treatment. (8) [4]
7. What Seymour hopes to be – in brief. (1.1) [1]
8. Representative of staff interests on the JNC. (1.1.1.1) [2]
9. Document ordering arrest. (7) [3]
11. Section on which initial assessments are recorded. (4.1) [10]
12. These should be made as soon as possible after an interview. (5) [6]
14. Discretionary means of diversion from prosecution. (7) [3]
16. Sort of damage that follows AB or GB (4)
18. Brief form of document replaced by the pre-sentence report. (1.1.1) [3]
19. A means of relating penalty to income. (4.4) [4]
20. Criterion for inclusion of material in a court report. (9) [6]

Down
2. Colloquial term for offending behaviour. (8)
3. The sort of cities sought after by a government crime prevention programme. (5) [13]
4. Barrister's apparel. (4) [3]
6. 1 across and 7 down in the community is a green one. (5) [2, 3, 7]
7. Means of deterrence. (10) [4]
10. Discharge with no strings attached. (8) [4]
11. Verbal positive reinforcement in a behavioural programme. (6) [12]
13. Sort of offences for which compensation cannot be ordered in criminal proceedings. (7) [4]
15. Maximum number of years for which a probation order can run. (5) [7]
17. Investigation into whether there are grounds to discontinue a prosecution. (1.1.1.1) [3]

Correctional crossword

Crossword solution

Index

advocacy 199
AIDS 4,128
Alinsky S. 193, 211
anti-sexism 24
Apex trust 134
appeal [against conviction] 56,57, [against sentence] 56, 57
arrest 48, 49, 57
assistant chief probation officers [ACPO] 37, 38, 39
assistant probation officer 25
Association of Black Probation Officers [ABPO] 14, 17, 42
Association of Community Workers 193
Atlee C. 194
attendance centre order 66

back to justice movement 175
bail 15, 76
Bail Act [1976] 76
bail hostel 15
Bateson G. 197, 210
Beaumont B. 191, 193, 210
Becker H. 180, 188
behavioural approach 28
behavioural casework 203
Belson W. A. 177, 188
bind-over 63
bio-genetic theories 176–177
black offenders 19, 83, 197
black prisoners 132
black women 3–4
Blagg and Smith 208, 210
Bonnemaison Report 195
Bottoms A. 197, 210
Bottoms A. et al 198, 210
Bottoms and McWilliams 205, 208, 210
Bowlby J. 179, 188,
Box S. 181, 188
Broadwater Farm 193

causal factors 85
caution [police] 49, 50
charge 49, 50, 51, 57
Chicago school 182
chief probation officer [CPO] 36, 38, 39
child abuse
    agency guidelines 25
    case conferences 26, 143
child protection register 26
emergency protection order 149
key worker 26, 140
liason with social services 133
predictive factors 23, 143–147
child protection 140–149
    guidelines for probation officers 142–143
    procedures for probation officers 141–142
    unborn child at risk 141
Children Act [1989] 65
Children and Young Persons Act [1969] 65
Cicourel A. V. 180, 188
classicism 175–176
Clarke J. 184, 189
classical conditioning 177
Cloward R. and Ohlin L. 183, 189, 195, 211
client-centred counselling 204
cognitive processes 178
combination order 67
community development 201
community organisation [method] 199
community service 16, 37
community service officers [CSOs] 37
community service order 66–67
compensation 61
compensation order 63–64
conflict theories 183–184
confrontation/confronting offending behaviour 9, 11, 13, 23, 130–131, 176
Cooper E. 105, 108, 122
Coulshead V. 86, 101
county courts 58
courtcraft 78–81
courts 47–59
court duty 74
court of appeal 58
court work 74–81
Crime Concern 195
Crime Justice and Protecting the Public 64, 71, 106, 122, 196, 200, 210
Criminal Justice Act 1988 61
Criminal Justice Act 1991 61, 67, 82, 83, 86, 102, 104, 123, 127, 128
criminal statistics 48, 59, 71
criminological theories 174–189

Index

Critcher C. 84, 101, 186, 189
control 205
Cornish and Clarke 208, 210
crown court 2, 55–58
crown prosecution service 15, 49, 50, 57, 86
curfew order 67
Curnock & Hardiker 86, 101
Curtis S. 198, 210

dangerous clients 128
Darwin J. 176
Davies M. 107, 122, 208, 210
Davies and Wright 207, 210
day centres 198
deferred sentence 70
deputy chief probation officers [DCPOs] 37, 38
Denman G. 178, 189, 204, 210
deferrence 61
discharge [absolute] 63, [conditional] 63
drop-in 128
Dunlop A. 208, 210
duty officer [court] 13
drug re-settlement project 2

European Court of Human Rights 59
endings 28, 118
Eysenck H. 176, 189

family proceedings court 53
family therapy 201
family work 201
feminist criminology 184–185
fine 64
first-year officer/new entrant 168
Folkard et al 207, 210, 208, 210
forms of address 79
Forrester et al 196, 211
Freud S. 179, 189

gay prisoners 132
Gallo & Roggerio 131, 138
gatekeeping 92, 198
Gelsthorpe L. & Morris A. 177, 185, 189
genograms 162–163
Gilroy P. et al 184,189
Glueck S. and E. 176
Goffman I. 180, 181, 189
Goldberg et al 206, 210
group living 201, 202
group work 202
guardianship order 70
Gunn 127, 138

Hall S. et al 184, 189
Hardiker & Willis 108, 122
'harm reduction' [drug regime] 4
Harris R. 42, 46
Heidenson F. 177, 185, 189
high court 58
HIV/AIDS 128

HMSO *Working Together under the Children Act* 140, 149
Home Office 35, 39
Home Office Circular [92/86] 82
homosexuality 18
Hood R. 208, 210
hospital order 70
House of Lords 59
Hugman B. 201, 211

ideological conflict 107
imprisonment 69
Information Systems Lancaster 198
intermediate treatment 176, [DHSS initiative (1983)] 197
intensive probation 207

Jones Maxwell 201, 211
justice model 176
justice principle 60
jury trial 54
justices of the peace [see also magistrates] 34

King M. 195, 211
Kirkholt Burglary Prevention Project 196

labelling theory [see also - social reaction theory] 180–181
Lea J. and Young J. 183, 184, 189
learning theory 177–178
left idealism 184
left realism 184
Leonard P. 40, 46
Lesbians and Gay Men in Probation [LAGIP] 42
levels of intervention 190–193
liason [by court duty officer] 75
licence supervision 123–126, [see also pre- and post release supervision]
local authorities 35
Lord Chief Justice 58
Lombroso C. 176

magistrates [see also justices of the peace] 34
magistrates [stipendiary] 34
magistrates court 49, 51, 52, 53, 57
Mair G. 207, 211
Mark P. 106, 107, 122
Martinson R. 208, 211
Master of the Rolls 58
Mathiesen T. 131, 138, 183, 189, 193, 211
Matza D. 181, 182, 183, 189
Maxwell Jones 201, 211
McGuire and Priestly 203, 211
mental health 127
Merton R. K. 40, 46, 183, 189
methods of intervention 193–207
Mills C. Wright 194, 211
Millham et al 208, 211
Mitterand F. 194

Index

money payment supervision order 64
Morris A. et al 176, 208, 211

National Association of Asian Probation Staff [NAAPS] 42
National Association of Probation Officers [NAPO] 41, 191, 194
NACRO (Briefing Paper) 4, 32, 83
NACRO (community projects) 134
NACRO 195, 211, 198
Neighbourhood Watch 195
networking 200
'nothing works' doctrine 208

oath [taking - in court] 80
operant conditioning 178

Park R. 182, 189
Parker H. et al 71, 198, 211
parole 7, 8
parole board 124
parole release plan 7
Partnership in Dealing with Offenders Green Paper 200
PBN blue 1: summary information sheet 152–153
PBN peach: record of court appearances and convictions 155, 158
PBN pink: Part B casework assessment 156
PBN white 1: Part A personal information sheet 153, 154–157
personal deterioration [in goal] 131
petty sessional division [PSD] 34
Pincus A. and Minahan A. 190
Pitts J. 128, 138, 195, 197, 209, 211
Platt A and Takagi P. 183, 189
post-sentence interview 6
practice theories 190–211
pre- and post-release supervision 123–138, 124, 135
    automatic conditional release 123–124, 125, 126, 127, 135
    breach of licence conditions 124–127
    deportees 124
    discretionary release 123–124, 125, 126, 127
    fine defaulters 124
    licensees 127–128
    life prisoners 124
    reports 135–137
    sentence plan 128
    sexual offenders 124
    short- and long-term offenders 123–124,
    supervision 128
    young offenders 124
pre-sentence reports [PSR] 54, 56, 57, 82–101
    preparation of 84–92
    purpose of 82–84
    referral form 16, (see also SPR 20, M1, FRB, Court Process Form)
pressure groups 193

previous offending 97 [form 609] 12, 15, 97
Priestly P. et al 107, 122, 178, 189
prisoners families 132–134
probation
    assistant [PSA] 14
    centre 104
    committees 34
    hostel 103
    inspectorate 35
    liaison committees 34
    officer 38, 39
    orders 5, 65, 102–122 [serving] 29, [conditions] 5, 103–104, [additional requirements] 103–104, [breach of] 105, 116, 117, [discharge] 105, [aims of] 105–108, [assessment and planning] 112–116
    service [organisation and structure of] 33–46
process recording 162
proportionality 60
protecting the public 61, 129
psychodynamic perspective/theory 13, 28, 106, 179, 185, 205
psycho-social casework 205–206

race, class and gender 110, 111
racial monitoring 191
racism 30, 92, 146
radical non-intervention 180
Raikes 83, 101
Raynor 84, 101, 87
recording groups and families 161
record-keeping 151–165
rehabilitation 62, 134
remand [in custody] 49, 51, 57 [on bail] 49
reparation 61–62
restriction order 70
risk of custody scales 198
risk of offending 96–97, 98, 129
Rogers C. 204, 211
rule 43 10, 132
Rutherford A. 177, 189, 198, 211

Safer Cities Programme 200
Sentence of the Court (The) 200, 210
schedule 11 day centre 21
Schur 180, 189
section 53 [Children and Young Persons Act 1933] 68
self-report studies 177
senior probation officers [SPOs] 37
sentencing 60–73
sentence plan 132
seriousness [of offence] 88, 89, 96–97
sexism 92, 146
sexual offences 8, 131, 185
Shallice A. and Gordon P. 197, 211
Sheldon W. 176
609 [form] 12, 15
Smith C. et al 203, 211

Smith D. 186, 189
SOS Racisme 194
social control theory 177, 181–182
social crime prevention 194–195
social disorganisation theory 177, 182–183
social reaction theory [see also labelling theory] 180–181, 205
social strain theory 183
specialist teams 37
Sinclair I. 208, 211
Stand down reports 77
Statement of National Priorities and Objectives [SNOP] 40, 60, 86, 103, 112, 122, 129, 199
summons 49, 51, 57
supervision 17–18, 29, [of juveniles - social services responsibilities] 65
Supervision and Punishment in the Community 33, 37, 40
supervision order 65–66
SUS [1834 Vagrancy Act] 193
suspended sentence 69
suspended sentence supervision order 69
systems approach [to intervention] [see also Pincus and Minahan] 190
systems management and intervention 196–199

targetting 77
tariff 20, 62, 77
task-centred casework 110, 206–207
Taylor I. et al 175, 177, 182, 183, 189
Taylor I. and Taylor L. 184, 189
temporary release schemes 135
therapeutic community 202
Thorpe D. et al 191, 204, 208, 211
throughcare 6, 9, 131, 201
time-management 170
Tipler J. 197, 211

voluntary associates [VAs] 37
vulnerable offenders 77
vulnerable prisoners units 132

warrant 31
Wilkins L. T. 208, 211
Wilson James Q. 174, 176, 184, 189, 208
working class 184

Young J. 180, 188
young adult offenders 128
young offender institution [YOI] 17, 37, 68, 197
youth courts 52

zone of transition 182